Se la felicità non è altro che un piatto di pasta, il vero amore è sapere che ce n'è abbastanza per due.

BIG MAMMA

PASTA

150 of the best Italian pasta recipes

WHITE LION PUBLISHING

BIG MAMMA

PASTA

150 of the best Italian pasta recipes

Photography by Lucile Casanova and Sam Gregg

Big Mamma is a team of enthusiasts from all over the globe, united by a common ambition: to introduce Italy, the real Italy, to people worldwide through its cuisine, incredible products and passionate producers, within restaurants of ultra-immersive design. All brought to life by a team of smiling faces and singing accents, driven by a single mission: to give you the best moment of your day.

PASTA is the number one staple food in Italy. It is also the first thing that brings the family together around the table, because it is around a pasta recipe that all generations get together to prepare, cook and share a meal. Within the team, it is also an ingredient that brings back countless memories and key moments in life. At Chef Manuel's, we make pappardelle al pesce on the terrace, making sure that Giulietta, the family poodle, doesn't stick her nose in the flour. At Chef Nino's, we cook pasta al forno con polpette with Iris (11) and Dafne (9), who already make meatballs like chefs under the watchful eye of their grandmother Silvia. At Chef Luigi's, pasta is prepared by a quartet with gnocchi alla sorrentina, which is baked in the oven after being carefully shaped. This is done with his brother Antonio, also a chef in Naples, and his parents Anna and Giovanni who whisper to their children whilst cooking that they would like to have them at home more often. As for Chef Flavia, her memories of pasta smell like honey. Because in her family, pasta is often associated with sweetness, preparing struffoli on the large marble table with Viviana, her mother, who passed on to her her love of baking, making Flavia the dessert queen of the team.

With all these memories in mind and more, we sat down together to concoct an anthology of our 150 favourite recipes, the best Italian cuisine has to offer in terms of pasta. Dry, fresh, but also shaped. Essential recipes ranging from gratins, cold salads, and even creative innovations, as well as sweet variations made from the same dough. This is your chance to create your very own unforgettable memories of cooking and sharing pasta with loved ones.

Tutti ai fornelli!

LAYING THE FOUNDATIONS

Since it is sometimes scary to dive in without having exact quantities, we thought it would be useful to share with you our love of both Q and B.

'QB', what on earth is that? Quanto basta – literally 'as much as required', meaning 'to taste'. True devotees of Italian cooking know that this provides scope to avoid following the rules down to the last detail. You don't have to guess quantities, but you are strongly encouraged to follow your instincts and trust your judgement. It's like riding a scooter in Naples or promising yourself ONE spritz on a terrace and ending up ordering a second – everything is decided on the spur of the moment.

Even so, here are some tips to make cooking your dinner that bit easier:

- Whatever your measuring cup may say, rest assured that, roughly speaking, 1g (gram) = 1ml (millilitre).
- When you come across a bunch or half a bunch of herbs, bear in mind that 1 bunch generally amounts to 100g (3½oz). And, when it comes to the choice of herbs and their quantities, you always have the last word. You decide when enough is enough.
- A teaspoonful of sugar or butter weighs around 5g (under a fifth of an ounce).
- A tablespoonful of oil or vinegar weighs around 15g (just over half an ounce).
- 250ml of milk, cream or water is always the equivalent of 1 glass (unless you only drink pints) or a US cup.

So, now you have the key to make the perfect dish, or almost . . . Because, really, the most important thing in cooking is to put your heart and soul into it. When you prepare a meal with plenty of love, everything will go smoothly.

QB*

QB* = QUANTO BASTA = AS MUCH AS NECESSARY

CHAPTER 1

ESSENTIAL PASTA DISHES

SPAGHETTI SCARPARIELLO

Easy as pie, quick as lightning

FOR 4 FRIENDS

- 400g (14oz) spaghetti (or spaghettoni, slightly thicker)
- 2 garlic cloves
- 500–600g (1lb 2oz–1lb 5oz) ripe cherry tomatoes (datterini or ciliegini – both melt beautifully in a hot pan and are perfect for quick sauces like this) or 500g (1lb 2oz) good quality peeled tomatoes (never mess around with tomatoes)
- 4 tbsp extra virgin olive oil
- 40g (1½oz) grated Pecorino Romano DOP
- 40g (1½oz) grated Parmigiano Reggiano DOP
- A few fresh basil leaves (plus extra ones for the finishing touch)
- Salt and black pepper QB

01 Heat the olive oil in a large frying pan. Add the roughly crushed garlic, cook gently over a low heat and remove when golden brown.

02 Cut the cherry tomatoes in half 'or crush the peeled tomatoes by hand, just like Italians do' and add them to the pan. Simmer over a medium heat for 15–20 minutes, until softened and the sauce has thickened slightly. Season with salt and pepper to taste and add a few basil leaves to enhance the flavour.

03 Cook the spaghetti in a large saucepan of salted boiling water until *al dente.* Before draining, reserve a ladleful of the cooking water – trust us, you'll want to keep it.

04 Add the spaghetti to the still-hot tomato sauce, stir vigorously and add a little of the cooking water to make the *sugo* creamy and shiny.

05 Remove from the heat and stir in the freshly grated Pecorino and Parmigiano. Mix quickly and serve immediately with extra grated cheese (for even more indulgence, if you like) and a few basil leaves for the finishing touch. *A tavola.*

\+ **On repeat in the kitchen:** The name *scarpariello* comes from *scarparo*, which means 'shoemaker'. In Naples, artisans used to whip up this quick and easy dish with whatever they had on hand. A simple and tasty recipe to enjoy while listening to 'Je so' pazzo' by Neapolitan maestro Pino Daniele!

FUSILLI ALLA GENOVESE

Our ultimate go-to ragù

For best results, let the sauce simmer gently for around three hours. It's a long time – we know. But when it comes to good food (and the people you're cooking for), time is never wasted. So put a podcast on and let it simmer. We promise, it's worth it.

FOR 4 FRIENDS

- 320g (11¼oz) fusilli
- 400g (14oz) beef, cut into pieces (here, you are spoilt for choice: shoulder, shank or chuck)
- 700g (1lb 9oz) golden onions
- 1 small carrot
- 1 stalk of celery
- 1 small glass of dry white wine (or two – you deserve a toast)
- 4–5 tbsp extra virgin olive oil
- Salt and freshly ground black pepper QB

01 In a large casserole dish (Dutch oven), heat the olive oil and brown the pieces of meat on all sides until they are nicely coloured.

02 Add the finely chopped onion, along with the diced carrot and celery. Season with salt and pepper, cover, and let simmer over a low heat for 3 hours. Time is the secret to this recipe's success. (You can't get perfectly caramelised onions and melt-in-your-mouth meat in just a few minutes!) If it starts to stick, don't hesitate to add a little water – the sauce should be rich, amber-coloured and slightly sticky. Halfway through cooking, pour in the first glass of white wine and let it evaporate slowly. The second is yours to enjoy.

03 Cook the fusilli *al dente* in a saucepan of salted boiling water. Drain, reserving a ladleful of the cooking water.

04 Once the meat is very tender, shred it in the still-hot casserole dish, then add the pasta. Add a little cooking water and mix well – this is where it all comes together.

05 Serve hot with a generous sprinkling of black pepper, on a plate worthy of the feast.

+ **On repeat in the kitchen:** despite its name, pasta 'alla genovese' is a dish from Naples (a little geographical deception, it happens). To get over this little confusion, listen to 'Gloria' by Umberto Tozzi at full blast, an Italian pop classic that gets the whole country dancing, from north to south. Turn up the volume and enjoy.

RISO AL SALTO

Crispy risotto rice

FOR 4 FRIENDS

For the risotto *alla milanese*

- 320g (11¼ oz) Carnaroli rice (avoid pre-cooked rice)
- 1 shallot or 1 small onion
- 1 small glass of dry white wine
- 1 litre (4 cups) hot meat or vegetable stock, as desired (see pages 316–317 for homemade recipes)
- A pinch of saffron stems, infused in a little hot water
- 40g (1½oz) butter
- 50g (1¾oz) grated Parmigiano Reggiano DOP
- Olive oil QB
- Salt and pepper QB

For sautéing

- A little butter and olive oil

For the Parmigiano *fonduta* (optional)

- 100g (3½oz) grated Parmigiano Reggiano DOP (aged 24 months)
- 120ml (½ cup) double cream
- White pepper QB

For the meat juices (optional)

- 200g (7oz) meat of your choice (or meat bone)
- 1 small carrot
- 1 shallot
- 1 garlic clove
- 1 tbsp tomato paste
- 200ml (generous ¾ cup) white wine
- 500ml (2 cups) meat stock (see recipe on page 316)
- 1 sprig of thyme
- 1 bay leaf
- 1 knob of butter

01 In a large saucepan, gently sauté the finely chopped shallot in a drizzle of olive oil. Add the rice and toast it for about 2 minutes, stirring constantly, until it turns translucent and pearly. Deglaze with the white wine and let it evaporate completely. Then begin adding the hot stock, one ladle at a time, stirring continuously. Halfway through cooking (around the 8th minute), add the saffron infusion: your risotto will then take on a beautiful sunny yellow colour.

02 After 16–18 minutes, remove from the heat and add the butter, 50g Parmigiano, salt and pepper – this is the sacred moment of *mantecatura*, when the magic happens and the risotto becomes creamy and shiny.

03 Spread the risotto in an even layer (about 3– 4 cm /1¼–1½ inches thick) in a pie or gratin dish. Refrigerate for at least 2 hours – don't skip this step, as chilling gives the risotto its structure. It's also an excellent way to use leftover risotto from the day before – often even better!

04 In Milan, this is sometimes served with a reduced meat *jus* and/or a small *fonduta* of Parmigiano. For the *fonduta*: heat the cream, stir in the 100g Parmigiano, season with pepper and blend in a food processor until smooth and shiny. Brown the pieces of meat in a little olive oil until they begin to catch on the bottom of the pan. Add the chopped shallot, carrot, garlic and tomato paste, and cook for 1–2 minutes until lightly caramelised. Deglaze with the white wine, scraping up all the flavourful bits from the base of the pan. Pour in the stock, add the herbs, and simmer gently for 15–20 minutes. Strain, then return the liquid to the pan and reduce for a further 5–10 minutes, until rich and concentrated. Remove from the heat and whisk in a knob of butter to give the *jus* a silky finish.

05 Time's up? Heat a mixture of butter and olive oil in a frying pan. Place the refrigerated rice patties in the pan, press down lightly, and cook over a medium heat for 6–8 minutes. Gently turn and cook the other side until crisp and golden. To be served with some Parmigiano *fonduta* spooned on top, if you like.

\+ **On repeat in the kitchen:** Because riso al salto is a Milanese speciality, play 'Milano' by Lucio Dalla, which captures the urban poetry of the city, a tender and realistic portrait of a vibrant metropolis full of contrasts.

GNOCCHI NERANO

Cheesy courgettes

FOR 4 FRIENDS

<u>For the gnocchi</u>

- 450g (1lb) potatoes (preferably floury yellow potatoes: they contain less water, which means you can use less flour. The result? Lighter, more delicious gnocchi)
- 150g (5½oz) type 00 flour
- Salt and pepper QB

<u>For the sauce</u>

- 4 or 5 medium courgettes
- 80–100g (2¾–3½oz) grated Provolone del Monaco (or, if unavailable, caciocavallo or another Italian cheese with a strong flavour)
- 1 garlic clove, squashed with the blade of a knife but kept whole
- 1 small bunch of fresh basil
- Olive oil (generous amount)
- Salt and freshly ground black pepper QB

01 Place the potatoes in a large saucepan of cold water and start cooking: they are cooked when a knife inserted in the middle comes out easily. Peel them while they are still hot (be careful not to burn yourself). In a salad bowl, mash them with a fork or potato masher, then add the flour, salt and pepper and mix roughly. Once the dough is smooth, knead it by hand on a floured work surface and then leave it to rest at room temperature. If the dough is still a little sticky, add a pinch of flour. The drier the potato flesh, the less flour you will need.

02 Meanwhile, cut the courgettes into very thin slices – a mandoline is your best friend here, but watch your fingers. Heat some olive oil in a pan and fry the courgettes until they turn a nice golden colour. Drain them on kitchen paper, salt them just enough, then set them aside with a few basil leaves torn over the top.

03 Meanwhile, shape your gnocchi using our guide on page 399.

04 Now prepare the Nerano sauce. In a large frying pan, gently sauté a lightly crushed garlic clove in a little olive oil. Add most of the fried courgettes, reserving a few for garnish – that '*oh, bellissimo*' finishing touch – and let them soften over low heat. Remove the garlic, then keep the pan warm – you'll finish the gnocchi in it.

05 Plunge the gnocchi into a large saucepan of salted boiling water and keep an eye on them. As soon as they rise to the surface, they're ready (spoiler alert, it happens very quickly). Using a slotted spoon, transfer them directly to the pan with the courgettes, reserving a little of the cooking water. Add a small ladleful of this starchy water and toss gently to bring everything together.

06 Remove from the heat, generously sprinkle with grated Provolone del Monaco and stir vigorously so the creamy, velvety sauce coats each gnocco. Season with pepper and sprinkle with chopped fresh basil.

07 Serve immediately, with a drizzle of extra-virgin olive oil, the reserved fried courgettes, and, if you like, an extra sprinkling of grated cheese. *Buon appetito.*

+ **On repeat in the kitchen:** typical of the village of Nerano, this recipe celebrates the Amalfi Coast like Paolo Sorrentino's film *Parthenope*. As a nod to its soundtrack, we listen to Richard Cocciante's 'Era già tutto previsto', a track filled with emotion, just like your dish.

GNOCCHI ON HEAVEN'S DOOR

Gnocchi gorgonzola e noci

FOR 4 FRIENDS

For the gnocchi

- 450g (1lb) potatoes (preferably yellow floury potatoes: they contain less water, which means you can use less flour. The result? Lighter, more delicious gnocchi)
- 150g (5½oz) type 00 flour
- Salt and pepper QB

For the sauce

- 60g (2oz) walnuts
- 150g (5½oz) Gorgonzola Dolce (the creamy kind)
- 100ml (scant ½ cup) double cream (or *panna da cucina*, its Italian equivalent)
- 30g (1oz) grated Parmigiano Reggiano DOP
- 20g (¾oz) butter
- Salt and freshly ground black pepper QB

01 Not sure what to cook on a lazy evening? You've come to the right place: these melt-in-the-mouth gnocchi are as easy as they are delicious. Go on, make your gnocchi: boil the whole potatoes, with their skins on, in a large saucepan of salted water. Once tender, peel them while they are still hot (be careful not to burn yourself) and mash them with a potato masher: do not use a blender, as this will turn your mixture into an elastic purée, which is not the desired result. Leave to cool, then add the flour and a pinch of salt. Knead with the palms of your hands until you obtain a smooth, even dough. If the dough is a little sticky, add a pinch of flour. The drier the potato flesh, the less flour you will need.

02 Meanwhile, roughly chop the walnuts (but keep a few aside for decoration) and take the Gorgonzola out of the fridge so that it is nice and creamy when you need it.

03 In a large frying pan, gently brown the butter with the cream. Add the Gorgonzola in pieces, melt over a low heat, stirring until the sauce is smooth and velvety. Season lightly with salt and generously with pepper.

04 After shaping some pretty gnocchi using our guide on page 399, plunge them into a pan of salted boiling water. As soon as they float to the surface (allow 2–3 minutes maximum), they are ready. Drain them gently with a slotted spoon and reserve a ladleful of the cooking water – your secret weapon for an ultra-creamy sauce.

05 Place the gnocchi in the pan with the Gorgonzola sauce. Mix gently to coat them well, adding a ladleful of cooking water to bind everything together if necessary. Add the chopped walnuts and half the Parmigiano.

06 Serve hot with a little grated Parmigiano on top (for that extra touch). A final twist of black pepper? *Certo.*

\+ **On repeat in the kitchen:** Flashback to the 1990s with a karaoke classic as comforting as these melt-in-the-mouth gnocchi: Ambra Angiolini's song 'T'appartengo', the nostalgic hit for an entire generation.

SPAGHETTI ALL'ASSASSINA

Criminally good pasta

FOR 4 FRIENDS

- 400g (14oz) spaghetti
- 400g (14oz) *passata di pomodoro* (see page 270 for how to make the best in the world, your own)
- 2 tbsp tomato paste
- 1 litre (4 cups) hot water
- 2–3 garlic cloves
- Red chilli pepper (fresh or flakes)
- 6 tbsp extra virgin olive oil
- Salt QB

01 Prepare your *sugo*. In a saucepan, mix together the *passata*, tomato paste, hot water and salt. Cook gently over a low heat and leave to simmer slowly. This sauce will be used to cook the spaghetti gradually, risotto-style.

02 Heat the olive oil in a large cast-iron or stainless-steel frying pan. Choose your weapon wisely: avoid non-stick, as the pasta needs a surface that allows it to caramelise. Don't have one? Time to get friendly with the neighbours. Then add the minced garlic and chilli pepper and fry everything together. When the garlic starts to brown, choose your side: remove it for a milder flavour, or leave it in for a bolder sauce.

03 Next, it's time for the butchery. Originally from Bari, this recipe with its ambiguous name comes from the particular cooking technique used for the pasta, which is 'assassinated' directly in the pan.

Be a *smooth criminal* by adding the spaghetti directly to your frying pan (without breaking it) and let it cook for 1–2 minutes over a high heat without stirring. A black crust should form on the surface of the pasta: this may seem surprising, but it is exactly the desired result.

04 Once the pasta has taken on some colour, reduce the heat to medium-low and add a ladleful of tomato sauce. Let the spaghetti absorb the liquid, then repeat the process – never covering the pan – until the pasta is fully cooked, about 15 minutes.

05 The spaghetti should be *al dente* on the inside and crispy on the outside, almost burnt, typical of *assassina*.

06 Serve in a deep plate and sit down to eat. The real crime is keeping your guests waiting.

\+ **On repeat in the kitchen:** A (nearly) perfect crime, filled with twists and turns, and a dramatic finale. *Spaghetti all'assassina* has all the makings of a good crime novel. So, of course, we hum 'Parla più piano', the Italian version of Coppola's *The Godfather*, the most famous gangster film ever made.

BUCATINI ALL'AMATRICIANA

The Italian good life

FOR 4 FRIENDS

- 400g (14oz) bucatini (spaghetti with a small hole in the middle)
- 150g (5½oz) *guanciale* (also known as cured pork cheek – if you don't have any to hand, you can use artisan pancetta or dried pork belly. In short, strike up a conversation with the butcher)
- 400g (14oz) peeled, chopped tomatoes, or even a *passata di pomodoro*, aka the tomato sauce of the century (if you have a little time, we'll show you how to make the best one, your own, on page 270)
- 1 glass of red wine
- 60g (2oz) grated Pecorino Romano DOP
- Salt and pepper QB

01 Before we begin, it's worth noting that this iconic Roman trattoria recipe (which takes its name from the town of Amatrice) is essentially a richer version of *gricia*. Same base, but with the addition of tomatoes. Now that you know everything, it's time to get your knives out. Start by cutting the *guanciale* into nice strips, then fry it in a pan over a medium heat. And don't even think about adding any fat to this pan. The meat will melt slowly and become crispy in 8–10 minutes, all on its own. Then deglaze with the red wine and add pepper while it simmers. When your strips are golden brown, remove them and keep them warm.

02 In the same pan, add your tomatoes (or your *passata* if you've been a *pomodoro* purist tonight) in the remaining oil from your *guanciale*. Simmer over a medium heat for at least an hour. And here, we're counting on you, because good cooking is all about love and patience: hang in there. Five minutes before the end of cooking, return the *guanciale* to the sauce and then gauge how long to leave it; it should remain long enough to flavour the sauce without losing its crunch.

03 Cook the bucatini *al dente* in a large saucepan of salted boiling water. Drain and reserve a ladleful of the cooking water to thicken the sauce.

04 Add the pasta to your *sugo* and toss everything together over a low heat, adding a little cooking water if necessary so that the bucatini is perfectly coated with the mixture.

05 Finally, remove from the heat, sprinkle with grated Pecorino, add a generous grinding of pepper, and that's it. There you have it, Rome on your plate.

\+ **On repeat in the kitchen:** 'Solo tu, questa mattina . . . questa sera . . . questa notte . . .' Like Matia Bazar, we sing it without shame: we only want her, our beautiful *Bucatini all'amatriciana*. It's not a dish, it's an obsession.

FUSILLONI ALLA NORMA

Aubergine is the drama

FOR 4 FRIENDS

- 400g (14oz) fusilloni, small propeller-shaped pasta
- 2 large, plump aubergines
- 700g (1½lb) peeled tomatoes (or 600ml *passata di pomodoro* – see page 270 for how to make the best in the world, your own)
- 2 garlic cloves
- 1 handful of fresh basil (torn by hand, like the Italians do)
- 150g (5½oz) *ricotta salata* – this will add salt and texture to the dish, so don't replace it with fresh ricotta (we're watching you)
- Extra virgin olive oil QB
- Oil for frying (sunflower or olive, whichever you like)
- Salt and freshly ground pepper QB

01 Wash the aubergines and cut them into cubes. Salt them and leave them to drain in a colander for at least 30 minutes. Pat dry and set aside for frying.

02 In hot oil, fry the aubergines until they are tender and golden brown. Here, there is no grill or oven; real Sicilian aubergines swim in oil like fish in the Mediterranean. Drain on kitchen paper and keep warm.

03 In a frying pan, sauté the crushed garlic cloves in a generous dash of olive oil. Add the tomatoes, simmer gently for 20 minutes, adding a little basil at the very end. Season with salt and pepper. It should smell like Italy right down the hallway.

04 Finally, cook the fusilloni *al dente* in a pan of salted boiling water, drain, then pour the pasta into the tomato sauce. Mix and serve hot!

05 To serve, place the fusilloni in a beautiful deep plate, topped with diced aubergine, a sprinkling of crumbled *ricotta salata* and basil leaves. Norma la Diva can now make her entrance.

\+ **On repeat in the kitchen:** It is said that this Sicilian dish was named in honour of Vincenzo Bellini, a native of Catania and composer of the opera 'Norma'. So, of course, play the aria 'Casta Diva' in Maria Callas' spellbinding version. It's time to tantalise your taste buds and your eardrums.

AVE BOLO

Spaghetti alla Bolognese e polvere d'alloro

For a truly amazing result, simmer this little gem of a bolognese sauce for at least 4 hours.

FOR 4 FRIENDS

<u>For the spaghetti</u>

- 320g (11¼oz) spaghetti

<u>For the bolognese sauce</u>

- 300g (10½oz) minced beef (or half beef, half ground pork, whichever you prefer)
- 1 small carrot
- 1 stalk of celery
- 1 small onion
- 2 tbsp extra virgin olive oil
- 100ml (scant ½ cup) dry red wine
- 40g (1½oz) tomato paste
- 300ml (1¼ cups) vegetable stock (see our recipe on page 317)
- Salt and black pepper QB

<u>For the finishing touch</u>

- 3 or 4 dried bay leaves
- 30g (1oz) grated Parmigiano Reggiano DOP (optional, but always welcome)
- A knob of butter (to make the pasta, your eyes and your tummy shine . . .)

01 Start by preparing a competition-worthy bolognese sauce: finely chop the onion, carrot and celery, *piccolo piccolo*. Sauté them over low heat in a generous drizzle of olive oil for about 10 minutes, until soft. Add the meat and brown it over medium heat. Deglaze with the red wine and let it reduce gently – your kitchen should smell like an Emilian nonna's house. Stir in the tomato paste, season, then pour in the stock and let it simmer over low heat for at least 4 hours. Good ragù takes time and patience – and we want only the best for you!

02 Once your *sugo* is ready, cook the spaghetti in a pan of salted boiling water, *al dente* of course. Drain but keep a ladleful of the cooking water (we can't stress this enough).

03 Next, prepare the bay leaf powder – the chef's little twist. Toast the bay leaves for a few seconds in a dry frying pan (or briefly in the microwave), then, once completely dry, grind or crush them into a fine powder.

04 In a large frying pan, mix the pasta with the hot bolognese sauce. Add a knob of butter, a little Parmigiano if you like and 1 spoonful of your cooking water until the sauce is smooth and creamy.

05 Give it one final toss, then serve the spaghetti on warm plates. Finish with a little grated Parmigiano and a pinch of ground bay leaf. And the award for best Bolognese goes to . . . we all know you deserve it!

+ **On repeat in the kitchen:** 'Ancora, ancora, ancora' . . . We can't get enough! Like *pasta alla bolognese*, this hit by Mina is a classic that spans generations. In 2023, Mark Ronson gave it a new twist, a bit like the bay leaves here.

LINGUINE ALLA BOTTARGA

She's a good egg

FOR 4 FRIENDS

<u>For the squid ink linguine (or tagliolini)</u>

- 250g (9oz) type 00 flour
- 100g (3½oz) *semola rimacinata* (remilled durum wheat semolina)
- 7 egg yolks
- 20g (¾oz) squid ink

<u>For the sauce</u>

- 60–80g (2–2¾oz) *bottarga*, salted cured mullet or tuna roe
- 1–2 garlic cloves
- 1 small red chilli pepper (fresh or in flakes, according to your preference)
- 5 tbsp extra virgin olive oil
- Zest of 1 organic or unwaxed lemon (and a little extra juice, for purists)
- Salt QB

01 Start by making your squid ink linguine or tagliolini. On a clean work surface, mound the flour and semolina, then make a well in the centre. Add the egg yolks and squid ink (apron highly recommended). Knead until you have a smooth dough. Cover with clingfilm and let it rest at room temperature for 30 minutes.

02 Heat the olive oil in a large frying pan. Add the finely chopped garlic and chilli, and let them gently sizzle over low heat until the garlic turns golden. Remove from the heat.

03 Roll out your dough with a rolling pin or pasta machine and cut your tagliolini (see our shaping guide on page 396).

04 Boil a large pot of salted water. Add the pasta and cook until *al dente* (9–10 minutes, no more). Keep a ladleful of the cooking water before draining, a chef's secret.

05 Add the linguine to the frying pan, pour in a little of the cooking water to bind everything together and mix gently over a low heat.

06 Remove from the heat, stir in the grated *bottarga* and melt it in, stirring gently. Be careful, *bottarga* should never be cooked, as it may become as bitter as an old ale, not the mood tonight. Zest in a little lemon and add a little juice if you like freshness.

07 Serve immediately and, to finish, add a little extra *bottarga*, a dash of olive oil, and voilà, it's ready. *Bravissimo*, you're as chic as your dish.

\+ **On repeat in the kitchen:** A staple of Italian karaoke, 'Sere nere' by Tiziano Ferro goes perfectly with the moody atmosphere of this squid ink linguine. Grab your ladle like a microphone and sing at the top of your lungs: 'Di sereeeee nereeeeee . . .'

VINO BIOLOGICO
ORGANIC WINE
VIN BIOLOGIQUE
CUSTOZA
di Origine Protetta
MONTRESOR

SAUSAGE PARTY
Cavatelli salsiccia e zafferano

FOR 4 FRIENDS

For the cavatelli
- 450g (1lb) *semola rimacinata* (remilled durum wheat semolina)
- 160ml (⅔ cup) lukewarm water

For the sauce
- 150g (5½oz) grated Pecorino Sardo cheese (medium-aged or mature, according to your preference)
- 150g (5½oz) sausages
- A pinch of saffron stems, infused in a little hot water
- A little grated Parmigiano Reggiano DOP for the finishing touch
- Freshly ground black pepper QB
- A few sprigs of fennel for a touch of green when plating up (optional, but it looks nice)

01 Start by preparing the cavatelli. Pour the semolina onto your work surface, make a small well and gradually pour the lukewarm water into the centre, mixing first with a fork then with your fingers when the dough begins to form. Knead for a good 10 minutes until the pasta is soft but not sticky. Cover with a tea towel or clingfilm and leave to rest at room temperature for 30 minutes.

02 For shaping, see page 397. Place your cavatelli on a tea towel or well-floured board as you make them, and leave to rest for a few minutes.

03 Prepare the pecorino cream: in a bowl, mix the grated Pecorino with your saffron infusion and whisk until you obtain a smooth, creamy texture with a beautiful sunset colour. Add a twist of pepper and it's ready.

04 Now for the sausage. Remove the casing and crumble the meat by hand – no need to be delicate here. Cook in a frying pan over medium heat until golden brown, then set aside.

05 Bring a large pot of salted water to the boil and add the cavatelli. Cook for 6–8 minutes: unlike gnocchi, these small pasta shapes do not necessarily rise to the surface. To check if they are ready, feel their texture. They should be tender but still firm, and the best way to test this is to taste one. Once cooked, reserve a ladleful of cooking water – your liquid gold – and drain.

06 Add the saffron Pecorino cream to the pan with the sausage meat, then the well-drained cavatelli and, if you like, a little of the cooking water to bind everything together.

07 Serve immediately, finished with grated Parmigiano and chopped fennel leaves.

\+ **On repeat in the kitchen:** This rustic and ultra-comforting dish is perfect for large gatherings and Sundays with the family. So, naturally, we put on Carmen Consoli's 'Una domenica al mare' and imagine a lazy Sunday afternoon.

PRAWN TO BE WILD

Spaghettoni gamberi e zucchine

FOR 4 FRIENDS

- 320g (11¼oz) spaghettoni (note: the size matters here, it matters. Thicker than spaghetti, spaghettoni absorbs the sauce better)
- 300–350g (10½–12oz) raw, peeled red prawns or king prawns. This is the star of the dish, so choose a variety that you really like
- 2 medium, firm courgettes
- 2 garlic cloves
- 4 tbsp extra virgin olive oil
- 60ml (¼ cup) dry white wine
- Zest of ½ organic or unwaxed lemon
- A few basil leaves
- A pinch of red chilli pepper or peperoncino for those who like a little tingle on their taste buds
- Salt and freshly ground black pepper QB

01 Start by preparing your ingredients. Rinse the raw prawns, then pat them dry with kitchen paper. Wash and slice the courgettes into thin rounds (a mandoline is ideal), and finely chop the garlic. Feeling like a chef? That's a good sign.

02 Heat a generous drizzle of olive oil in a frying pan. Fry about 10 courgette slices until golden and crisp (2–3 minutes per side). This little step makes all the difference. Drain on kitchen paper and set aside.

03 In a large frying pan, heat the olive oil, add the minced garlic (and chilli, if you're feeling adventurous) and fry until lightly browned. Add the rest of your courgettes, season lightly with salt and fry for 5–7 minutes over a medium heat, until tender but still firm. Deglaze with the dry white wine and let it evaporate completely over high heat – feel free to pour yourself a glass while you're at it.

04 Next, cook the spaghettoni in a large saucepan of salted boiling water until *al dente*. Remember to keep a ladleful of the cooking water before draining.

05 Blend the courgette mixture until you have a creamy green sauce. If necessary, add a little of the pasta cooking water to achieve a smooth, shiny result.

06 Remove from the heat, pour the drained pasta into the pan with the courgette pesto, then stir gently for 1–2 minutes so that the flavours blend perfectly. Then stir in the lemon zest, basil, a twist of pepper and a drizzle of olive oil.

07 Serve immediately – or cold, if you prefer – topped with the fried courgette slices and the prawns. *Parmigiano* with seafood is not allowed, don't even try that!

\+ **On repeat in the kitchen:** Winner of Festivalbar 1992, an institution in Italy at the time, 'Mare Mare' is one of Luca Carboni's biggest hits. A sunny hit that sings of the irresistible call of the sea . . . just like this recipe, which makes you want to cast off at the first bite.

FREGOLA NERA AL RAGÙ DI SEPPIE

The recipe that will cause quite a stir

FOR 4 FRIENDS

For the pasta

- 320g (11¼oz) *fregola nera*, small wheat pasta pearls from Sardinia, coloured with squid ink. If you can't find any, another small pasta will work just as well. The key idea, as you've probably guessed, is that it should be black for dramatic effect.

For the *ragù di seppie*

- 500g (1lb 2oz) fresh cleaned cuttlefish (with tentacles and ink sacs, otherwise you will need a sachet of ready-to-use ink)
- 2–3 tbsp extra virgin olive oil
- 1 small shallot or ½ onion
- 1 small garlic clove
- ½ glass of dry white wine
- 1 tbsp tomato paste (optional)
- Red chilli pepper (dried or fresh, whichever you prefer)
- Fresh flat-leaf parsley
- Sea salt and black pepper QB

For the mussels

- 250g (9oz) fresh mussels
- 1 garlic clove
- 1 sprig of parsley
- 1 tbsp extra virgin olive oil

For the finishing touch

- Sautéed pieces of cuttlefish
- Zest of 1 lime, preferably organic or unwaxed (optional)
- Fresh flat-leaf parsley
- Fresh chervil
- A few fresh basil leaves
- A few sun-dried tomatoes
- A few mussels (without their shells)

01 Let's start with the cuttlefish. This isn't the quickest step, but I promise it's nothing you can't handle. Rinse it under cold running water to remove any small grains of sand. Then gently pull out the 'feather' (also known as the cuttlebone), the stiff, translucent blade inside the body. Cut the body open lengthways and lay it flat. Remove the innards, setting aside the ink sac if it's intact (handle with care – preferably not over your white T-shirt). Peel away the thin grey skin, then give it a final rinse and slice the cuttlefish into thin strips.

02 In a large saucepan, heat 1 tablespoon of olive oil with the crushed garlic clove and the sprig of parsley. Add the mussels, cover and leave them to open over a high heat for 4–5 minutes. As soon as they are all open, remove them with a slotted spoon, set aside and shell them for a beautiful presentation.

03 Now for the *ragù*: in a frying pan, sauté the shallot and garlic in a generous drizzle of olive oil. Add the sliced cuttlefish (keep some small pieces to fry for the finishing touch). Leave to sweat gently. Once it's released its juice, deglaze with the white wine and allow to evaporate. Add a little tomato paste, if you like, and – if available – the ink sac diluted in a little hot water. Otherwise, use prepared squid ink. Simmer over low heat for about 35 minutes, until the sauce thickens. Season with salt and pepper, and add a little chilli and chopped parsley just before removing from the heat.

04 Cook the *fregola nera* in a large saucepan of salted boiling water. Drain, reserving a ladleful of the cooking water. Pour the pasta into the pan and stir gently to coat it with the *ragù*. Add a little of the cooking water to bind it together and the magic happens. Meanwhile, in a separate frying pan, quickly sear the reserved pieces of cuttlefish in a little olive oil over a high heat until lightly golden and just cooked through.

05 Serve in deep plates. A little fresh parsley, chervil, a few basil leaves, small sun-dried tomatoes, lime zest, pieces of seared cuttlefish and a few shelled mussels. Every bite is a real gourmet treat.

+ **On repeat in the kitchen:** This black dish does not exude sadness, quite the opposite, like the song 'Amore disperato' (Desperate Love), in which singer Nada plays on the contrast between pain and desire.

SPAGHETTINI AL PESTO DI PISTACCHIO

Pistachio lovers only

FOR 4 FRIENDS

- 320g (11¼oz) spaghettini (or capellini no. 1 or 2, the idea is to use thin, long pasta)
- 40g (1½oz) butter
- Juice of ½ organic or unwaxed lemon
- 40g (1½oz) grated Parmigiano Reggiano DOP
- Salt and freshly ground black pepper QB

For the pistachio cream
(note: this must be prepared the day before, *ragazzi*)

- 80g (2¾oz) unsalted, shelled pistachios
- A drizzle of extra virgin olive oil
- A pinch of salt

For the finishing touch

- 30g (1oz) pistachios
- Lemon zest for garnishing

01 The day before, soak the pistachios for the cream (shelled, of course) in cold water for 12 hours. The next day, blend them with a drizzle of olive oil and a dash of cold water until you obtain a smooth, creamy paste. Season lightly with salt and set aside.

02 Meanwhile, toast the remaining 30g (1oz) of pistachios in a hot frying pan without adding any oil. Crush them coarsely – ASMR moment.

03 Cook the spaghettini (without ever, ever breaking them) in a large saucepan of salted boiling water until *al dente*. Before draining, carefully reserve a ladleful of the cooking water (what our chefs call 'liquid gold').

04 In a frying pan, gently melt the butter with the lemon juice. Add the spaghettini and toss gently, gradually incorporating some of the reserved cooking water, until each strand is coated in a glossy sauce.

05 Add the grated Parmigiano and black pepper, then mix to obtain a rich and creamy texture. Now we're talking.

06 Remove from the heat and add the pistachio cream to the pan, but be careful not to stir too vigorously so as not to split the buttery sauce. '*Chi va piano, va sano*', as they say in Italy.

07 To serve, twirl the spaghettini into deep plates and finish with the crushed pistachios and a little lemon zest. *A tavola.*

+ **On repeat in the kitchen:** When serving, play 'Splendido Splendente' by Donatella Rettore, an extravagant disco whirlwind for this vibrant and energetic dish.

CORZETTI CON BURRO

A recipe to butter you up

FOR 4 FRIENDS

For the corzetti
- 180g (6½oz) type 00 flour
- 180g (6½oz) *semola rimacinata* (remilled durum wheat semolina)
- 7 egg yolks

For the sauce
- 100g (3½oz) good quality unsalted butter
- A few hazelnuts
- 80g (2¾oz) grated Parmigiano Reggiano DOP (optional)
- Salt and freshly ground black pepper QB

01 Let's start with this typical pasta from Liguria, shaped like a Genoese coin: the corzetto. On a work surface, pour the flour and semolina into a small mound, make a well in the centre and add the egg yolks. Knead until you obtain a smooth dough. Cover with clingfilm and leave to rest for 30 minutes at room temperature.

02 Prepare the sauce. In a large frying pan, melt the butter over a low heat with a few crushed hazelnuts, then season. Let it infuse for a few minutes, until the butter turns a light golden brown – the colour of hazelnuts – but without burning.

03 Take your ball of dough, roll it out thinly with a rolling pin or pasta machine, and shape the corzetti following our instructions on page 390.

04 Bring a large pot of salted water to the boil, add your corzetti and cook for 3–5 minutes, until *al dente*, of course. Before draining, keep a ladleful of the cooking water, your secret weapon.

05 Add the drained 'coins' to the pan with a little cooking water to bind everything together. Stir gently to coat them in the fragrant butter.

06 They say money can't buy happiness – we think these corzetti might prove them wrong.

\+ **On repeat in the kitchen:** Play Edoardo Bennato's 'Il Gatto e la Volpe'. His satire on the perils of wealth and the joy in simple pleasures. A philosophy that fits perfectly with the classic nature of these corzetti.

RISOTTO ALLA SORRENTINA

With smoked provola cheese

FOR 4 FRIENDS

For the risotto

- 320g (11¼oz) Carnaroli rice (avoid pre-cooked 'risotto rice' in sachets)
- ½ onion
- 600g (1lb 5oz) *passata di pomodoro* (see page 270 for how to make a delicious homemade version)
- 1 litre (4 cups) vegetable stock (see our recipe on page 317)
- 40g (1½oz) butter
- 60g (2oz) grated Parmigiano Reggiano DOP
- 2 tbsp olive oil
- Salt and freshly ground pepper QB

For the provola cream

- 150g (5½oz) smoked provola (smoked mozzarella) (as it is smoked, it has already lost a lot of water, which prevents your preparation becoming soggy)
- 80ml (⅓ cup) double cream

For the finishing touch

- A few basil leaves
- A little reduced tomato sauce – set aside a little of your *passata di pomodoro* and reduce it for a few minutes, stirring regularly so that the liquid evaporates as much as possible (optional)
- A drizzle of olive oil

01 Start by preparing the provola cream, the star of the show. Cut the cheese into small pieces. Blend it with the cream until you obtain a smooth texture that is neither too runny nor too thick. Heat slowly in a bain-marie or microwave (but not too much), as the sauce must remain smooth and creamy. Set aside at room temperature.

02 Meanwhile, get started on the risotto. In a large saucepan, gently fry the onion over a medium heat with a generous drizzle of olive oil. Add the rice and toast it for 2–3 minutes, stirring continuously (really, don't take your eyes off it, no one likes burnt rice). When the grains turn pearly, add a ladleful of hot stock and stir. Reduce to medium-low heat and, as the liquid is absorbed, add a ladleful of passata, then continue alternating with the stock, one ladle at a time, stirring continuously. Be at your risotto's disposal because it needs your full attention! Cook for 15–18 minutes, ensuring it remains creamy and never dry or sticking.

03 Once the rice is cooked, remove from the heat, add the butter, the Parmigiano and stir vigorously. The risotto will become creamy, which is what we want. Taste, season with salt and pepper.

04 Serve the risotto in a deep plate and pour a generous spoonful of provola cream on top (without mixing). Add a little fresh basil, a dash of olive oil and, if desired, a drizzle of well-reduced tomato sauce. It's ready.

+ **On repeat in the kitchen:** With his velvety voice and Americanised Neapolitan accent, Dean Martin transports you to the Amalfi Coast with 'Come Back to Sorrento'. A soundtrack that melts hearts like *provola* in the sun.

ORECCHIETTE CIME DI RAPA

Broccoli-rave party

FOR 4 FRIENDS

<u>For the orecchiette</u>

- 450g (1lb) *semola rimacinata* (remilled durum wheat semolina)
- 160ml (⅔ cup) lukewarm water

<u>For the sauce</u>

- 500g (1lb 2oz) *cime di rapa* (broccoli rabe or broccolini)
- 2 anchovy fillets in oil
- 1 small red chilli pepper (fresh or dried)
- 1 garlic clove (optional, but she loves to crash a party)
- 4 tbsp extra virgin olive oil
- Breadcrumbs
- Salt QB

01 Start with the pasta. On a floured work surface, pour the semolina into a small mound, make a well in the centre and pour in the lukewarm water as you knead. You should end up with a very soft dough. Cover and leave to rest for 30 minutes at room temperature.

02 Meanwhile, wash the *cime di rapa* in cold water and keep only the florets (the stalks are sometimes tough).

03 Get your dough and go to page 397 to shape your 'little ears'.

04 Bring a large pot of salted water to the boil, add the *cime di rapa* first then, after 2 minutes, the orecchiette. Cook until the pasta is *al dente* (about 8–10 minutes, depending on the thickness of the orecchiette). Reserve a ladleful of the cooking water – your liquid gold – then drain.

05 In a large frying pan, heat a generous drizzle of olive oil. Add the anchovies, chilli and garlic (if using), and cook gently until the anchovies melt into the oil. Remove the garlic.

06 Add the pasta and *cime di rapa* to the pan and stir continuously over a medium heat for 1–2 minutes. Pour in the ladleful of reserved cooking water to create an emulsion: the sauce should delicately coat the pasta. This is called *mantecatura*.

07 Serve immediately, piping hot, with a drizzle of olive oil. For an indulgent finishing touch in front of your guests, add some breadcrumbs. No applause, no second helping.

\+ **On repeat in the kitchen:** Typical of Puglia, orecchiette pays homage to this southern region where Domenico Modugno and his hit song 'Nel blu, dipinto di blu' were born. 'Volaaaaaare, oh, oh . . .' Yes, you have the right to sing, no matter what the rest of the household says.

HABEMUS PASTA

THE SACRED FOUNDATION OF DAILY LIFE IN ITALY

Whilst each region has its own way of cooking and enjoying pasta, all Italians agree on one thing: it is the basis of any good Italian meal. And that goes for everyday meals too.

Sometimes made from durum wheat, particularly in southern Italy (Puglia, Sicily, Calabria), sometimes from ancient grains, as is more often the case in the centre and north of the country (such as spelt or farro in Tuscany or in Umbria), this precious yellow commodity is not only appetising, it is also nutritionally important. So, if you sometimes feel guilty about feeding your kids pasta too often, silence that little voice in your head and keep going, because it's good for the heart and good for the body.

The Italian diet – the very foundation of the Mediterranean diet – is based on a pyramid structure in which complex carbohydrates are the foundation. And in this category, *pasta* has played a central role since at least the thirteenth century (the period when the first written references of the production and consumption of dry pasta in Sicily, particularly in Trabia, near Palermo, appear – at least according to history).

Since then, every family has eaten a pasta dish every day, and no matter where you are in Italy, it is common to gather around the table as soon as it is ready. The tricks of the trade are passed down from one generation to the next, the gestures of making the dough and shaping it are repeated, before sitting down to enjoy the meal.

In Emilia-Romagna, for example, particularly in Bologna, the *sfogline* roll out the dough by hand into thin sheets before shaping it into tagliatelle, tortellini, lasagne and other culinary gems. In Bari, orecchiette are shaped by hand on wooden boards. In Campania, it is more common to cook short pasta such as penne, rigatoni, ziti, or fusilli (those little nuggets that sauces coat so well).

And while there are countless shapes of pasta and ways of making it, the same is true for dishes. *Bucatini all'amatriciana* in Lazio, *Orecchiette cime di rapa* in Puglia, or *Maccheroncini al ragù* in the Marche . . . So many recipes and stories that reveal Italian culture and its culinary heritage which bring everyone together around the table, regardless of age or heritage.

Imperia
Restaurant

THE PATHOLOGY OF PASTA

Don't break your pasta! Don't throw away pasta water! There are big and small myths surrounding Italy's finest export, now its time to dispel them. Read these few lines and become THE person everyone calls to find out whether throwing sticky pasta at the fridge is really the best way to tell if it's cooked, or whether it's really taboo to cut spaghetti with a knife. In short, in a word: il maestro.

POURING OIL INTO THE COOKING WATER WILL PREVENT PASTA FROM STICKING

FALSE: For those who were more likely to be at the back of the class during physics lessons, oil and water do not mix. The oil will simply float to the surface of the water, without adding any real value. The real solution? Plenty of water, patience, and a little stir with a spoon from time to time.

YOU HAVE TO DISCARD THE WATER USED TO COOK PASTA

TRUE ... BUT ALSO FALSE: Of course, you should empty the pan to drain the pasta, BUT not without saving 1 or 2 ladles. This liquid gold, full of starch, will help you to thicken the pasta sauce.

THE LONGER PASTA IS COOKED, THE EASIER IT IS TO DIGEST

FALSE: Contrary to popular belief until the last century, overcooked pasta has a higher glycaemic index. The (only) right way to eat it is *al dente*, i.e. firm to the bite.

PASTA MAKES YOU FAT

FALSE: It is actually one of your best allies in a balanced diet. These carbohydrates are just as important nutritionally as proteins and fats. The underlying problem is the proportion of them in your meal and the time at which you eat them.

YOU EAT SPAGHETTI WITH A SPOON AND A FORK

FALSE: The only correct answer to this equation is a fork. Unless you are 5 years old.

IT IS NORMAL TO BREAK SPAGHETTI BEFORE COOKING

FALSE: And who is the person with the wrong-sized pan who dared to spread this myth?
Pasta needs to be cooked whole and will soften on its own whilst cooking. Relax, it'll be fine.

MORE SALT = FASTER COOKING

FALSE: Salt has no impact on how pasta cooks. If you've ever seen a *capo* add a pinch or two to the steaming pot, it's to create a tasty little salt bath *full of love* for these gems, not to save time.

FRESH PASTA IS ALWAYS BETTER THAN DRIED PASTA

FALSE: These are two different products, each with their own virtues in the kitchen. Fresh pasta is better suited to delicate sauces, while dried pasta is ideal for rich sauces or recipes that require long cooking times. So, to each their own, and let's not judge.

YOU NEED A SMALL AMOUNT OF WATER TO COOK PASTA

FALSE: You need at least 1 litre (4 cups) of water for every 100g (3½oz) of pasta. So make sure you keep a large saucepan handy in your cupboards. If you cook pasta at least once a day (and we hope you do!), you'll use it 365 times a year, or 1,825 times in 5 years. Let's face it, it's worth it.

THE PERFECT COOKING TIME FOR PASTA IS INDICATED ON THE PACKET

FALSE: The times indicated on the packet are for guidance. The only real benchmark is you and your taste. To check that your pasta is perfectly *al dente*, i.e. neither too soft nor too crunchy, you need to bite into it. Because the type of pan you use, the power of your hob or the level of limescale in your water are all factors that will affect the cooking, and no packet can take that into account better than you.

ORECCHIETTE ALLA CARLOFORTINA

You've got great taste

FOR 4 FRIENDS

For the orecchiette

- 450g (1lb) *semola rimacinata* (remilled durum wheat semolina)
- 160ml (⅔ cup) lukewarm water

For the sauce

- 300g (10½oz) fresh tuna
- 3 tbsp pesto *alla genovese* (see recipe on page 289)
- 2 tbsp extra virgin olive oil
- A few fresh basil leaves (optional, but we love them)
- Salt and freshly ground black pepper QB

For the sun-dried tomatoes

- 200g (7oz) ripe cherry tomatoes (go for Datterini tomatoes, which are date-shaped, for their sweet and delicate flavour)
- 2 tbsp olive oil
- A pinch of fine salt
- A pinch of sugar
- A few leaves of thyme or oregano (optional)

01 Start with the pasta. On a floured work surface, pour the semolina into a small mound, make a well in the centre and pour in the lukewarm water as you knead. You should end up with a very soft dough. Cover and leave to rest for 30 minutes at room temperature.

02 Meanwhile, cut the tomatoes in half and place them on a baking tray lined with greaseproof paper, flesh side up. Drizzle with olive oil, season with a pinch of salt and a little sugar, and scatter over a few thyme or oregano leaves. Bake for 1–2 hours at 100°C fan/120°C/250°F/GM ¼ (or your oven's lowest setting), until the tomatoes are gently dried but still soft.

03 As soon as you get home from the fishmonger (or the supermarket, or the sea, if you prefer), dice your fresh tuna.

04 Now it's time to shape the orecchiette: go to page 397 to learn how to make these 'little ears', typical of Puglia.

05 Cook the orecchiette in a large saucepan of salted boiling water (usually 8–10 minutes). Drain and immediately rinse under cold water.

06 In a large bowl, mix the pesto, orecchiette and oven-roasted cherry tomatoes, keeping a few aside for the finishing touch.

07 Time to plate up. Serve the orecchiette in a large serving dish or directly onto individual plates and top with the tuna, fresh basil leaves if you like, a few cherry tomatoes on top and a final drizzle of olive oil. An ideal salad for hot summer days.

\+ **On repeat in the kitchen:** Fabrizio de André's 'Il pescatore', a monumental Italian song which takes us to the only inhabited town on the island of San Pietro, nestled in the south of Sardinia and renowned for its tuna fishing. With the sea stretching as far as the eye can see, nets strewn across the ground and colourful little houses, welcome to Carloforte.

OLIVE ME TENDER
Calamarata alla puttanesca

FOR 4 FRIENDS

- 400g (14oz) calamarata (these typical pasta shapes from Campania are so named because they resemble small squid rings)
- 4 anchovy fillets in oil, drained
- 2 garlic cloves
- 400g (14oz) tinned peeled chopped tomatoes
- 80g (2¾oz) pitted black olives (Gaeta or *Taggiasca* variety, harvested when fully ripe, they are super tasty)
- 2 tbsp desalted capers
- 4 tbsp extra virgin olive oil
- Red chilli pepper (fresh or flakes, according to taste)
- Fresh flat-leaf parsley (optional as a finishing touch, but it's nice)
- Salt QB
- 1 tbsp extra virgin olive oil

01 Heat a generous drizzle of olive oil in a large frying pan over low heat. Add the minced garlic, anchovy fillets and chilli, if using. Gently melt the anchovies, crushing them with a wooden spoon – they will infuse the oil and fill your kitchen with a wonderful aroma . . . close your eyes and you're in Sorrento.

02 Add the chopped tomatoes and simmer over a medium heat for 25–30 minutes until the sauce thickens slightly. Patience is the secret to a successful *sugo*.

03 Next, add the black olives and rinsed capers, stir and cook for another 5 minutes over a low heat until everything is well combined. Taste and adjust if needed – usually no extra salt is required, as the anchovies and capers provide plenty of seasoning, but a twist of black pepper is always welcome, you are the chef!

04 While the sauce continues to simmer over a low heat, cook the calamarata *al dente* in a large pot of salted boiling water. Drain, reserving a ladleful of the cooking water.

05 Pour the pasta into the sauce, stir gently and add a little of your hot water to coat each little ring.

06 Serve immediately and sprinkle with chopped flat-leaf parsley. And one last rule: no Parmigiano or Pecorino here, or your Italian in-laws might kick you out! When you have Italy in your heart or in your blood, you don't put cheese on fish dishes.

+ **On repeat in the kitchen:** This dish is a manifesto, a fist banged on the table. Puttanesca does not pull its punches. Its name evokes audacity and sultry nights, as does the pioneer Renato Zero with his song 'Mi vendo'.

SPAGHETTI POMODORO E RICOTTA AL FORNO

The oven takes centre stage

FOR 4 FRIENDS

For the spaghetti with tomato sauce

- 320g (11¼oz) spaghetti
- 800g (1lb 12oz) tinned whole peeled tomatoes (whatever you do, keep their juice)
- 1 garlic clove (unpeeled)
- 2–3 tbsp extra virgin olive oil
- 1 tsp dried oregano
- A few fresh basil leaves (optional)
- Salt and freshly ground black pepper QB

For the baked ricotta

- 200g (7oz) firm ricotta (sheep's or cow's milk, whichever you prefer)
- A drizzle of olive oil
- A little salt

01 Start by preparing the tomato sauce. Place the peeled tomatoes, along with all their juices, in an ovenproof dish – keeping the juices ensures a rich, deeply flavoured sauce. Add the lightly crushed unpeeled garlic clove, oregano, olive oil and a little salt and pepper. Mix gently without crushing the tomatoes. And now, be patient: bake at 120°C fan/140°C/275°F/GM 1 for 2–3 hours. It may seem like a long time, but it's what gives the sauce its wonderful flavour. For a truly traditional Neapolitan touch, leave it overnight in a low wood-fired oven – if you're lucky enough to have one!

02 Once the sauce is cooked, squeeze the garlic from the clove and blend the mixture until smooth and shiny. Adjust the seasoning if necessary.

03 Next, prepare the cheese. Place the whole ricotta in a small oiled dish and lightly salt the surface. Bake at 160°C fan/180°C/350°F/GM 4 for 30–40 minutes until it forms a golden crust while remaining soft in the centre. Leave to cool, then crumble coarsely, taking care not to burn yourself.

04 Meanwhile, cook the spaghetti *al dente* (without breaking them: never, never) in a large saucepan of salted boiling water. Drain and immediately toss with the tomato sauce while still hot, so the pasta is evenly coated. Add a drizzle of olive oil, if you like.

05 Arrange the spaghetti on a plate, sprinkle generously with crumbled baked ricotta, add a little oregano or a few fresh basil leaves for decoration, and *buon appetito.*

\+ **On repeat in the kitchen:** A sauce simmering gently in the oven for hours to the sound of 'Almeno tu nell'universo', lulled, like you, by the sweet and melancholic voice of Mia Martini.

TAJARIN AL RAGÙ DI CONIGLIO

A love letter from Piedmont

FOR 4 FRIENDS

For the tajarin

- 180g (6½oz) type 00 flour
- 180g (6½oz) *semola rimacinata* (remilled durum wheat semolina)
- 7 egg yolks

For the rabbit *ragù*

- 500g (1lb 2oz) boneless rabbit, cut into small pieces (or roughly chopped with a knife). For a more rustic version, you can mix rabbit meat with pork. And if you want to stick even closer to the tradition of this recipe from the Piedmont hills, marinate the meat the day before with white wine, rosemary and 1 garlic clove
- 1 small onion
- 1 small carrot
- 1 stalk of celery
- 2 garlic cloves
- 1 sprig of rosemary
- 1 bay leaf
- 150ml (⅔ cup) dry white wine
- 300ml (1¼ cups) chicken or vegetable stock (see pages 316–317 for recipes)
- 3 tbsp extra virgin olive oil
- Salt and pepper QB
- Pecorino or Parmigiano Reggiano (optional)

01 On a clean work surface, pour the flour and semolina into a small mound, make a well in the centre and add the egg yolks. Knead until you obtain a smooth dough. Cover with clingfilm and leave to rest for 30 minutes at room temperature.

02 In a large frying pan, heat the oil with the whole garlic, rosemary and bay leaf. Allow to infuse gently, then add the finely chopped onion, carrot and celery. Fry this little lot for 5 minutes over a low heat.

03 Next, add the rabbit. Quickly sear the pieces on each side in the frying pan and deglaze with the white wine. Allow the liquid to evaporate.

04 Pour in the stock, season with salt and pepper, cover halfway and simmer gently for at least 1½ hours. The meat should be falling apart and the sauce should be reduced but still juicy.

05 Meanwhile, take your dough, roll it out very thinly with a rolling pin or pasta machine and turn to page 389 to learn how to shape these Piedmontese gems.

06 Cook the tajarin in a large saucepan of salted boiling water for 3–4 minutes. Drain, reserving a ladleful of the cooking water. Then pour the pasta directly into the pan with the hot *ragù*. Over a low heat, stir until the *pasta* is well coated. If the sauce isn't silky enough, pull out your trump card: your delicate starch-filled liquid.

07 Serve hot, with a sprinkling of pecorino or Parmigiano if you feel like it (although in Piedmont, they prefer it without) and you'll feel like you're in the Langhe hills.

\+ **On repeat in the kitchen:** 'Montagne Verdi', sung by the vibrant voice of Marcella Bella, blends nostalgia and nature against a backdrop of bucolic landscapes and childhood memories in the green mountains. Instant round trip to Piedmont.

TAGLIATELLE PAGLIA E FIENO ALLA PARMIGIANA

Make hay whilst the sun shines

FOR 4 FRIENDS

For the 'straw' tagliatelle

- 180g (6½oz) plain flour
- 180g (6½oz) *semola rimacinata* (remilled durum wheat semolina)
- 7 egg yolks

For the spinach 'hay' tagliatelle

- 350g (12oz) fresh spinach
- 180g (6½oz) type 00 flour
- 180g (6½oz) *semola rimacinata* (remilled durum wheat semolina)
- 3–4 egg yolks
- 1–2 tbsp water

For the sauce

- 1.2 litres (5 cups) vegetable stock (see our recipe on page 317) or simply hot salted water if you're in a pinch
- 80g (2¾oz) butter (unsalted, the Parmigiano Reggiano will do the work)
- 80g (2¾oz) freshly grated Parmigiano Reggiano DOP (the more mature it is, the more flavourful it will be)
- Zest of 1 organic or unwaxed lemon
- Freshly ground black pepper QB
- Salt

01 Start with the pasta. Put the flour and semolina on a clean work surface, make a small well in the centre and break the eggs into it. Mix with a fork, gradually bringing the flour from the edges towards the centre. Separate the dough into 2 separate balls. For the 'hay' dough, blanch the spinach, drain it well, then blend it with a little water to obtain a smooth green purée. Incorporate this into one portion of the dough. Knead both doughs by hand for about 10 minutes, until smooth and elastic – one yellow, the other green. Cover with cling film and let them rest at room temperature for 30 minutes.

02 Once ready, roll out your dough with a rolling pin or pasta machine, then go to page 395 for cutting instructions.

03 In a large dry saucepan, add both types of uncooked tagliatelle and lightly toast them over a gentle heat for 1 minute. Then add the stock or hot water, ladle by ladle, stirring as you would for a risotto. Keep a close eye on your dish: watch it, stir it, pamper it. Continue cooking for about 10–12 minutes until *al dente*. The mixture should be creamy and never dry.

04 Remove from the heat and stir in the cold diced butter and grated Parmigiano. Mix vigorously – this is where everything comes together and turns silky and glossy.

05 Finish with a twist of black pepper and adjust the seasoning if needed. Serve immediately, with a drizzle of extra-virgin olive oil and, if you like, a little extra Parmigiano or a touch of lemon zest. A dish to fall in love with.

+ **On repeat in the kitchen:** A colourful dish that celebrates the joy of being together, accompanied by the sunny notes of Raffaella Carrà's 'Pedro'.

CREAM OF THE CROP

Sedanini integrali panna, salsiccia, funghi

FOR 4 FRIENDS

- 400g (14oz) *sedanini integrali*
- 300g (10½oz) *salsiccia* (fresh sausage with fennel – typical of southern Italy – or plain)
- 300g (10½oz) mushrooms (button mushrooms, oyster mushrooms, chanterelles or porcini mushrooms, depending on the season)
- 200ml (generous ¾ cup) double cream
- 1 small shallot or ½ sweet onion, chopped (optional, but recommended)
- 2 tbsp extra virgin olive oil
- 1 small glass of dry white wine (it's tradition)
- A little thyme
- 30g (1oz) grated Parmigiano Reggiano DOP (optional, but you're not going to say no, are you?)
- Salt and freshly ground black pepper QB

01 Prepare your ingredients: gently clean the mushrooms with a damp cloth then slice; remove the skin of the sausages and crumble their flesh – no need to be delicate here, we're going for a rustic look.

02 Pour a generous dash of olive oil into a large frying pan, fry the shallot (or onion) and leave it to soften gently for 1–2 minutes. Add the salsiccia meat, stir and cook over a medium-high heat until golden brown and fragrant. Deglaze with the white wine: a little for the pan, a little for you. Cheers.

03 Let the mushrooms join the party (in the pan, obvs), season lightly with salt and pepper, then simmer until they have released all their liquid. Allow 8–10 minutes.

04 Lower the heat and pour in the cream. Stir gently for 3–4 minutes, do not let it boil, or it may split! Taste and adjust the seasoning: the sauce should be mild, but full of flavour.

05 Meanwhile, cook the *sedanini* in a large saucepan of salted water. Always *al dente*. Drain, reserving a ladleful of the cooking water.

06 Add the pasta to the pan, stir over a low heat, adding a little of your liquid gold if necessary to achieve a silky sauce. This is the *mantecatura*, the moment when everything comes together. Finish with a little thyme and Parmigiano, unless you're one of those who dared to say no to it.

07 Serve piping hot and enjoy under a blanket or in front of a good Italian film (we've put together a shortlist for you on pages 232–233). Comfort food just the way we like it.

+ **On repeat in the kitchen:** Want to warm up your winter evenings? Put on Ornella Vanoni's 'Ti voglio', a sweet retro tune that whispers of intense yet gentle love, just like this rustic and indulgent dish.

SHOW US YOUR MUSSELS

Calamarata cozze e pecorino

FOR 4 FRIENDS

For the mussels

- 1kg (2lb 4oz) fresh mussels
- 1 garlic clove
- 1 sprig of fresh parsley
- 1 tbsp extra virgin olive oil

For the pasta

- 2 tbsp extra virgin olive oil
- 1 garlic clove
- 1 small red chilli pepper (fresh or dried, depending on your preference)
- 100ml (scant ½ cup) dry white wine
- 120g (4¼oz) Datterini tomatoes
- 1 tbsp smooth tomato passata (or *passata di pomodoro*, see page 270 for instructions on how to make your own)
- 400g (14oz) calamarata (small hoops typical of Campania, named because they resemble small squid rings)

01 Start by washing the mussels thoroughly under cold running water. Remove any small filaments, scrub the shells, and discard any that remain stubbornly open.

02 In a large saucepan, heat 1 tablespoon of olive oil with the crushed garlic clove and sprig of parsley. Add the mussels, cover and let them open over a high heat for 4–5 minutes. Once they are all open, remove them with a slotted spoon. Strain their cooking liquid and set aside. Without burning yourself, shell the mussels – except for a few that we'll keep in their shells for presentation and wow factor. Yes, together, we're going to make art.

03 In a large frying pan, sauté another crushed garlic clove and a small chilli pepper in 2 tablespoons of olive oil. Add the tomatoes, cut in half lengthwise. Fry them for 3–4 minutes, just until they start to soften. Deglaze with the white wine and let it evaporate, then add a ladleful of the strained mussel liquid and 1 tablespoon of tomato sauce. Simmer for 2–3 minutes, then return the mussels to the pan and stir gently. Can you smell it? That's the Mediterranean.

04 Meanwhile, stay on track and cook your calamarata in a large saucepan of salted boiling water. *Al dente*, as ever. Drain them, keeping a ladleful of the cooking water aside to adjust the sauce later.

05 Add the pasta to the pan with the mussel sauce. Stir over a high heat to coat well: it will sizzle a little in the pan. Adjust the texture with a little cooking water if necessary.

06 Serve immediately, with a few mussels in their shells on top, adding an arty touch that will enhance your creation.

+ **On repeat in the kitchen:** Invite the streets of Naples to the table, with the aroma of fish, roar of scooters and sea in the background, by playing 'Tu t'e scurdat'e me' by rapper Liberato.

A GREAT VINTAGE
Linguine limone ombrina

FOR 4 FRIENDS

For the linguine
- 320g (11¼oz) linguine

For the sauce
- Zest of 2 organic or unwaxed lemons
- Juice of 1 organic or unwaxed lemon
- 60g (2oz) unsalted butter
- 40g (1½oz) Parmigiano Reggiano DOP – freshly grated, that's the golden rule
- Fine salt and freshly ground black pepper QB

For the meagre (stone bass) tartare
- 200g (7oz) very fresh meagre (stone bass) fillet, skinless and boneless – ask your fishmonger if needed! (Meagre, with its noble and delicate flesh, is perfect here. If not available, sea bass or wild sea bream will do the job very well.)
- 1 tsp lemon juice, for a touch of acidity
- 1 tbsp extra virgin olive oil
- Fine salt and white or black pepper (use your judgement) QB

For the finishing touch
- Zest of 1 organic or unwaxed lemon (optional)
- 2 tbsp extra virgin olive oil

01 Prepare the tartare. Carefully dice the meagre fillet into small, even cubes. Add a little olive oil, a dash of lemon juice, a pinch of salt and a few turns of the pepper mill. Mix, cover and refrigerate.

02 Next, cook the linguine – *al dente*, obviously – in a large saucepan of salted boiling water. Before draining, save a ladleful of the cooking water: your secret weapon.

03 In a large frying pan, gently melt the butter with the lemon zest. Then add the lemon juice, reserved cooking water and Parmigiano into the pan. Season with salt and pepper. Leave to infuse and stir very gently until you obtain a smooth, velvety cream.

04 Add the pasta. Mix gently so that it is completely coated in the silky sauce.

05 Serve immediately, while everything is still piping hot. For a stunning presentation: roll the linguine with a fork in the hollow of a ladle to form a pretty nest. Place it delicately in the centre of a plate (preferably a slightly deep one) and, once this masterpiece is complete, add 1 spoonful of fresh meagre tartare on top, a drizzle of raw olive oil and, if desired, a little lemon zest. What a beauty! That's what your guests should say when they see their plates (reconsider your list of close friends if this isn't the case).

+ **On repeat in the kitchen:** 'I search for summer all year long, and suddenly, here it is . . .' Thus begins Adriano Celentano's 'Azzurro' and this is exactly what this dish offers: a bright slice of sunshine that touches the body and the heart.

FAMIGLIA CIUFO

Nino, Iris & Dafne

MINTURNO

LUMACHE RIGATE E FASÒ

The only time you can use bacon

Does combining legumes with pasta seem surprising to you? And yet, it is a staple of cucina povera, designed to fill the stomachs of field workers – the kind of dish that warms the body and the heart. Today, it has left the countryside to find its way into everyday cooking.

FOR 4 FRIENDS

- 320g (11¼oz) lumache rigate (or ditali rigati or conchiglie . . . as long as it catches the sauce well, we trust you)
- 1 small carrot
- 1 stalk of celery
- 1 small onion
- 50g (1¾oz) bacon (or, if unavailable, pancetta or good old smoked lardons (bacon bits))
- 100ml (scant ½ cup) *passata di pomodoro* (we explain how to make your own delicious version on page 270) or 1 tbsp tomato paste
- 250g (9oz) cooked borlotti beans (fresh, dried after soaking, or from a jar, it doesn't matter, as long as they are good quality)
- 2 tbsp extra virgin olive oil
- 1 bay leaf or a little sage (optional, but it adds a lovely scent of the French countryside)
- Salt and freshly ground black pepper QB
- Grated Parmigiano Reggiano DOP (optional, but if you're feeling indulgent . . .)

01 Prepare your 'soffritto': finely chop the carrot, celery and onion. Sweat them gently in a drizzle of olive oil, then let the bacon join in. Leave everything to melt slowly.

02 Add the *passata di pomodoro* or tomato paste diluted with a little hot water and simmer for 5–10 minutes.

03 Add the cooked borlotti beans (with a little of their cooking water, if possible, but hot water will do just fine if you've already washed everything down the sink). Then add a bay leaf or a little sage, to your liking, and simmer for another 15–20 minutes.

04 Meanwhile, cook your lumache rigate in a large saucepan of salted boiling water. As ever, *al dente*. Keep a ladleful of the cooking water before draining. We can't stress this enough: treasure this liquid like gold.

05 Add the pasta to the sauce, stir over a low heat, season and add a little cooking water if necessary to bind everything together.

06 Serve piping hot, with a drizzle of olive oil, a sprinkling of grated *Parmigiano* and, why not, a pinch of sage for the finishing touch? Rustic, generous, and easy to make – comfort food at its best!

+ **On repeat in the kitchen:** If you're going to be getting cosy, you might as well spend an evening 100% comforted while listening to Pupo's 'Su di noi'. A unifying hit that has become a true generational anthem, inviting us to believe that anything is possible and to rise 'above the clouds'. SU DI NOI NEMMENO UNA NUUUUUUVOLA.

RIGATONI CON I BROCCOLI ARRIMINATI
A cute Sicilian dish

FOR 4 FRIENDS

For the rigatoni
- 320g (11¼oz) rigatoni
- Approximately 4 tbsp breadcrumbs
- 1 tbsp olive oil for browning the breadcrumbs

For the broccoli sauce
- 1 large broccoli (or a romanesco, Sicilian green cauliflower, if you are lucky enough to find one, approximately 600–700g/1lb 5oz–1½lb)
- 1 onion
- 3–4 anchovy fillets in oil
- 30g (1oz) sultanas, soaked in warm water
- 30g (1oz) roasted pine nuts
- A pinch of saffron stems, infused in a little hot water
- 4 tbsp extra virgin olive oil

01 Start by cutting your broccoli – or romanesco – into nice florets. Place the florets in a large saucepan of salted boiling water and cook for about 10–12 minutes, until they are tender.

02 Drain using a slotted spoon and reserve the cooking water. Full of flavour, it will be used to cook the pasta. Yes, in Palermo, nothing is wasted. Mash the broccoli with a fork to make a rustic, textured purée.

03 In a large frying pan, gently fry the chopped onion in a generous drizzle of olive oil. Add the anchovies and let them melt into the oil. Once dissolved, add the sultanas, pine nuts and mashed broccoli, and stir well – this step is key. In Sicily, they call it *arriminare*: everything should move and mingle in the pan. Add the saffron infusion and simmer over low heat for 10–15 minutes.

04 Meanwhile, cook the rigatoni in the boiling broccoli water until *al dente*. Drain, reserving a ladleful of the precious liquid, then add to the pan with the sauce. Sauté the pan like a maestro for 1–2 minutes, adding a little cooking water if necessary, until the pasta is coated with the sauce. This is the final embrace (or *mantecatura*).

05 In the meantime, toast the breadcrumbs in a small pan with 1 tablespoon of olive oil until golden and crisp.

06 Serve immediately, generously topped with the toasted breadcrumbs and finished with a drizzle of olive oil. *Benvenuti a Palermo!*

+ **On repeat in the kitchen:** As your Broccoli *arriminati* – 'stirred' in Sicilian dialect – twirls around happily in the pan, make them to the rhythm of Franco Battiato's 'Voglio vederti danzare' and in the *cucina*, it's twirl, twirl, twirl. A little group dance is also allowed for the adults.

PASTA MISTA PATATE

Cheese is life

FOR 4 FRIENDS

- 320g (11¼oz) *pasta mista*, a delightful mix of pasta shapes that originated in the kitchens of southern Italy as a way to reduce waste. If you don't have any leftover pasta to use up, a mix of short pasta will do just fine
- 600g (1lb 5oz) potatoes (with a floury texture, such as Monalisa)
- 150g (5½oz) smoked provola (smoked mozzarella) (needed to give it that wood-fired flavour)
- 1 small carrot (optional, but why not add a touch of colour?)
- 1 stalk of celery (also optional, but we like it)
- ½ onion or 1 shallot
- 4 tbsp extra virgin olive oil
- 40g (1½oz) grated Parmigiano Reggiano DOP or Pecorino Romano DOP
- 1–1.2 litres (4¼–5 cups) vegetable stock (see our homemade recipe on page 317)
- Salt and pepper QB

01 Prepare the vegetables. Start by peeling and cutting the potatoes into small cubes of about 1–1.5cm (½–¾in) – no bigger, otherwise they take too long to cook. Finely chop the onion, carrot and celery.

02 Heat the olive oil in a large saucepan (or casserole/Dutch oven). Add the onion (and the other vegetables, if using) and cook gently for 3–4 minutes, until soft and translucent but not browned. Add the potatoes, season lightly with salt, and cook for 5 minutes, stirring to coat them well in the oil.

03 Cover with hot vegetable stock, then simmer the sauce over a medium-low heat for about 10 minutes. The potatoes should be tender but, be careful, we don't want baby food either.

04 Pour the uncooked pasta directly into the saucepan (or casserole dish/Dutch oven) – no pre-cooking here, we do it Neapolitan-style, as for a risotto. Add the hot stock gradually, stirring often as it evaporates. The starch from the potatoes and pasta will work their magic, bringing everything together into a creamy sauce. After 8–10 minutes, you should have a creamy, almost sticky texture, *azzeccata* as they say in Naples.

05 When it is really really creamy, remove from the heat. Immediately add the diced provola and grated cheese. Stir vigorously: you want everything to melt, stretch and become deliciously indulgent.

06 Serve piping hot, with a drizzle of extra virgin olive oil for shine and a twist of pepper. *Buon appetito.*

\+ **On repeat in the kitchen:** Like this dish, Pino Daniele's song 'Napule è' is warm and inviting, popular and a little melancholic. It speaks of a simplicity that touches the heart and that very Neapolitan way of turning nothing into something that lasts an eternity.

BIGOLI IN SALSA
Anchovy XCX

FOR 4 FRIENDS

For the bigoli
- 450g (1lb) *semola rimacinata* (remilled durum wheat semolina)
- 160ml (⅔ cup) lukewarm water

For the sauce
- 6 onions
- 6–8 anchovy fillets in oil
- Extra virgin olive oil
- Salt (just a little, the anchovies already do the work)
- Freshly ground black pepper QB

01 We start with bigoli, a typical pasta from Venice with a rough surface, ideal for holding sauces. On a clean work surface, place the semolina in a small mound, make a well in the centre and pour in the lukewarm water little by little. Knead until you obtain a soft, smooth and elastic dough. Cover with clingfilm and leave to rest for 30 minutes at room temperature.

02 Finely chop your onions (and get your tissues ready). Pour a generous dash of olive oil into a large frying pan and fry the onions over a low heat for 20–30 minutes. They should melt slowly and become translucent, almost caramelised. Add a little water during cooking, if necessary, to prevent them from caramelising too much.

03 When your onions are ready, add the anchovy fillets. Stir gently for a few seconds. Add a little black pepper, but no salt is needed as the anchovies have a big personality already. Keep the sauce warm.

04 Take your dough and shape the bigoli according to our guide on page 398, under *Pici* or *bigoli*.

05 Then cook these little gems in a saucepan of lightly salted boiling water until *al dente*, 8–10 minutes depending on the thickness of your pasta. Drain them, keeping a ladleful of the cooking water.

06 Pour the bigoli into the frying pan, add a little of your hot water to bind everything together and stir until the pasta is well coated with sauce. After that, the only thing left to do is eat.

+ **On repeat in the kitchen:** Because this is a typical recipe from the City of the Doges, we set the mood with 'J'adore Venise', first sung by Ivano Fossati, then passionately covered by Loredana Bertè. The 80s in all their glory.

SERVIZI SMS: INFORMAZIONI

PESTO PRESTO

Busiate col pesto alla Trapanese

FOR 4 FRIENDS

For the busiate

- 450g (1lb) *semola rimacinata* (remilled durum wheat semolina)
- 160ml (⅔ cup) lukewarm water

For the pesto

- 6 ripe tomatoes (beefsteak or San Marzano type)
- 80g (2¾oz) blanched almonds (without skins)
- 1 garlic clove
- 1 bunch of fresh basil
- 60g (2oz) grated Pecorino Siciliano (or Parmigiano Reggiano DOP, but shhh)
- 80ml (⅓ cup) extra virgin olive oil
- Salt and pepper QB

For the sun-dried tomatoes

- 200g (7oz) tomatoes (Datterini or cherry)
- 2 tbsp extra virgin olive oil
- A pinch of fine salt
- A pinch of sugar
- A few leaves of thyme or oregano (optional)

01 Start by preheating the oven to 100°C fan/120°C/250°F/GM ¼. Cut the Datterini tomatoes in half, place them on a baking tray lined with greaseproof paper, flesh side up. Drizzle with olive oil, add a pinch of salt, a little sugar and sprinkle with a few leaves of thyme or oregano. Bake for 1–2 hours; the tomatoes should dry gently while remaining soft.

02 Then prepare the busiate, a typical pasta from the province of Trapani, Sicily, which has a spiral shape, as if wrapped around a *busà* (a rush stem). Pour the semolina onto your work surface, make a small well and pour the lukewarm water into the centre little by little, mixing first with a fork and then with your fingers when the dough begins to form. Knead for a good 10 minutes until the pasta is soft but not sticky. Cover with a tea towel or clingfilm and leave to rest at room temperature for 30 minutes.

03 Let's get started with the *pesto alla trapanese*, the Sicilian version of Genoese pesto, with tomatoes, and almonds instead of pine nuts. First, plunge your tomatoes into boiling water for 1 minute, peel them gently, then cut them into pieces. Crush the garlic with a pinch of salt, in a mortar if you're a purist; others can use a blender. Then add the almonds – our chef Alberto lightly grills/dry-fries them without oil to give them a slightly toasted flavour (reserve some for serving). Next, add the tomatoes, fresh basil (reserve 4 whole leaves for serving) and a twist of pepper. Blend gently: you want a textured sauce, not a smoothie. Finally, stir in the Pecorino and a drizzle of olive oil. Taste. Close your eyes. You're in Trapani.

04 Take your dough and shape your busiate using our guide on page 398.

05 Then cook the pasta in a large saucepan of salted boiling water. *Al dente*. Be sure to keep a small ladleful of cooking water before draining.

06 Pour the pasta into a large bowl or frying pan, off the heat. Add the pesto, sun-dried tomatoes and a little cooking water to bind everything together. Mix to coat each spiral.

07 Serve immediately, with a sprinkling of Pecorino, crushed almonds, a few sun-dried tomatoes and a basil leaf on top, your 'cherry' on the pasta.

+ **On repeat in the kitchen:** This sunny vegetarian dish gets straight to the point, just like Levante's 'Lo stretto necessario'. A recipe and a song that celebrate Sicily and its treasures with simplicity.

FETTUCCINE ALLA PAPALINA

Holy Fettuccine

In the 1930s, Pope Pius XII – a gourmet before the Lord – demanded a lighter and more refined version of the famous carbonara. The result: pecorino cheese gave way to Parmigiano Reggiano, and onions and peas joined the feast. Introducing Papalina, a pasta blessed by the taste buds.

FOR 4 FRIENDS

For the fettuccine
- 180g (6½oz) type 00 flour
- 180g (6½oz) *semola rimacinata* (remilled durum wheat semolina)
- 7 egg yolks

For the sauce
- 100g (3½oz) *guanciale*, but you can use cured ham (ideally Parma ham, not too mature) or lardons/bacon bits
- 1 small onion
- A few fresh peas
- 40g (1½oz) unsalted butter
- 30g (1oz) grated Parmigiano Reggiano DOP
- 2 egg yolks
- Salt and pepper QB

01 Start by preparing the fettuccine dough. On a clean work surface, pour the flour and semolina into a small mound, make a well in the centre and add the 7 egg yolks. Knead lovingly until you obtain a soft, smooth and elastic dough. Cover with clingfilm and leave to rest for 30 minutes at room temperature.

02 Gently melt a little butter in a frying pan. Fry the finely chopped onion over a low heat until it sweats and turns slightly golden. Add the *guanciale*, cut into strips, and the fresh peas and sauté quickly.

03 In a bowl, beat the 2 egg yolks with the grated Parmigiano. Salt sparingly (the *guanciale* does that job) and season generously with pepper.

04 Roll out your dough thinly with a rolling pin or a pasta machine, then cut your fettuccine following the guide on page 390.

05 Cook the fettuccine *al dente* for about 4 minutes in a large saucepan of salted boiling water. Drain them but carefully reserve a little of the cooking water. This is your magic elixir.

06 Add the pasta to the pan with the *guanciale*, peas and onions, and stir everything together.

07 Remove from the heat and stir in the egg and cheese mixture. Stir to obtain a smooth, creamy sauce and, if necessary, add 1 or 2 spoonfuls of cooking water to perfect the texture.

08 Final blessing: serve immediately with a sprinkling of Parmigiano and a twist of pepper. Amen.

+ **On repeat in the kitchen:** When you think 'Vatican' you think 'Rome', so let's get carried away by Matia Bazar's 'Vacanze romane', a melancholic ode to the Eternal City, combining lyrical flourishes and electro beats.

PORCINI STAR

Fettuccine ai funghi porcini

FOR 4 FRIENDS

<u>For the fettuccine</u>

- 180g (6½oz) type 00 flour
- 180g (6½oz) *semola rimacinata* (remilled durum wheat semolina)
- 7 egg yolks

<u>For the sauce</u>

- 350–400g (12–14oz) fresh porcini mushrooms (or 80g/2¾oz dried porcini mushrooms)
- 2 garlic cloves
- 4 tbsp extra virgin olive oil
- 60g (2oz) butter
- Fresh parsley
- Salt and freshly ground pepper QB
- Grated Parmigiano Reggiano DOP (optional, but why not?)

01 Start with the fettuccine. On a clean work surface, pour the flour and semolina into a small mound, make a well in the centre and add the egg yolks. Knead until you obtain a smooth dough. Cover with clingfilm and leave to rest for 30 minutes at room temperature.

02 Next, prepare the porcini mushrooms. If they're fresh, treat them like the treasures they are. Clean them gently with a soft brush, scrape the stems with a small knife if needed, and finish with a slightly damp cloth. Avoid rinsing them under water – mushrooms absorb moisture like sponges, which dulls their texture and flavour. If using dried porcini, soak them in warm water for about 30 minutes, then drain, reserving the soaking liquid for the sauce. Once cleaned or rehydrated, cut the mushrooms into pieces.

03 Roll out the fettuccine dough thinly with a rolling pin or pasta machine, then turn to page 394 for cutting instructions.

04 Heat the olive oil and butter in a large frying pan over a low heat. Add the whole garlic cloves, lightly crushed, and let them brown gently to flavour the oil before removing them.

05 Add the porcini mushrooms to the pan. Fry them over a medium heat for about 8–10 minutes, until they are golden brown, tender and fragrant. Season with salt and pepper, add a small ladleful of mushroom water or a little hot water if necessary to obtain a smooth sauce.

06 Bring a large saucepan of salted water to the boil. Add the fettuccine and cook until *al dente*, about 4 minutes. Drain quickly, reserving a little of the cooking water.

07 Add the fettuccine to the pan with the mushrooms. Mix gently to coat the pasta with the sauce and, if necessary, add 1 or 2 spoonfuls of cooking water to bind.

08 Serve in a deep plate, sprinkle generously with chopped fresh parsley, a dusting of Parmigiano for the greedy ones and it's ready. *Buon appetito.*

+ **On repeat in the kitchen:** Ah, the porcini mushroom . . . king of the forest floor, the undisputed star of autumn. With its firm flesh and its nutty aroma, it enhances everything it touches. We savour it with our eyes closed while Anna Oxa sings 'Un'emozione da poco' and a wave of woody thrills envelops us.

VA VA VONGOLE

Lorighittas al pomodoro e vongole

FOR 4 FRIENDS

<u>For the lorighittas, a type of pasta typical of the village of Morgongiori in Sardinia</u>

- 450g (1lb) *semola rimacinata* (remilled durum wheat semolina)
- 160ml (⅔ cup) lukewarm water

<u>For the vongole sauce</u>

- 500g (1lb 2oz) *vongole* (clams)
- 250g (9oz) fresh tomatoes, ideally Datterini or cherry
- 2 shallots
- 1 small fresh red chilli pepper (optional)
- ½ glass of dry white wine
- 2 tbsp extra virgin olive oil
- Fresh flat-leaf parsley
- Salt and pepper QB

01 Start with the pasta. Place the semolina on your work surface, make a small well and pour in the lukewarm water. Mix with a fork at first, then with your fingers when the dough begins to form. Knead for a good 10 minutes until it is smooth but not sticky. Cover with a cloth and leave to rest for 30 minutes at room temperature.

02 Next, prepare the clams. Rinse them quickly in cold water, then place them in a large bowl of cold, well-salted water (about 35g/1oz of salt per 1 litre/4¼ cups of water) and leave them to drain for 1–2 hours, changing the water once or twice (and re-salting them each time). This step ensures that the clams do not have any small grains that crunch when you bite into them, so it is essential. Once this is done, drain them and discard any that are broken or remain open.

03 In a large frying pan, pour in a generous dash of olive oil and fry a chopped shallot, the small chilli pepper and the clams. Cover and leave the clams to open over a high heat for 3–5 minutes, shaking the pan from time to time like a maestro. Deglaze with the dry white wine: it adds zest and smells like summer. Once the clams have opened, strain their juice and set aside the shellfish (you can remove every other shell for the final presentation).

04 Meanwhile, prepare your tomato sauce: gently fry a shallot in a frying pan in olive oil, add the halved cherry tomatoes and simmer for 15–20 minutes over a low heat until the *sugo* is smooth. Then blend a little if you like smooth sauces.

05 Take your dough and shape your lorighittas using our guide on page 398. Cook them in a large pot of salted water a little longer than most pasta. Taste to check that they are *al dente* – that's the rule – then drain them, keeping a little of the cooking water.

06 Mix the pasta with the tomatoes and your liquid gold, then add the clams and their strained juice and stir again.

07 Serve in a large deep plate or a sharing dish. Finish with a drizzle of raw olive oil, a twist of pepper and a few parsley leaves. A one-way ticket to the Amalfi coast.

+ **On repeat in the kitchen:** Giuni Russo's song 'Un'estate al mare', the hit of the summer par excellence: it smells of warm sand, holiday romances and late nights. A sunny classic, just like this iconic dish.

FAMIGLIA CIUFO

Nino, Iris, Dafne & Silvia

MINTURNO

PAPPARDELLE AL RAGÙ DI CINGHIALE

A ragù for the ages

For a truly delicious result, marinate the meat for 12–24 hours . . .
It takes a long time, but patience is the secret to success, isn't it?

FOR 4 FRIENDS

For the pappardelle

- 180g (6½oz) type 00 flour
- 180g (6½oz) *semola rimacinata* (remilled durum wheat semolina)
- 7 egg yolks

For the marinade

- 600g (1lb 5oz) wild boar meat (boneless shoulder or leg)
- 1 carrot
- 1 stalk of celery
- 1 onion
- 2 garlic cloves
- 2 bay leaves
- 1 sprig of rosemary
- 4 black peppercorns
- 2 cloves
- ½ bottle of full-bodied red wine (from Tuscany to stay on theme, such as Chianti or Montepulciano)

For the *ragù*

- 2 tbsp extra virgin olive oil
- 1 carrot
- 1 stalk of celery
- 1 onion
- 2 tbsp tomato paste
- 400g (14oz) tomato pulp
- Salt and black pepper QB
- A dash of red wine (optional)

For the finishing touch

- Grated Pecorino Toscano DOP (optional)

01 On a clean work surface, pour the flour and semolina into a small mound, make a well in the centre and add the egg yolks. Knead until you obtain a smooth dough. Cover with clingfilm and leave to rest for 30 minutes at room temperature.

02 Place the chopped meat in a bowl with all the marinade ingredients, then pour over a generous amount of red wine. Cover and refrigerate overnight (at least 12 hours, or up to 24 for deeper flavour). Game rewards patience. Once marinated, drain the meat and discard the herbs. Pour a generous dash of olive oil into a hot casserole dish (Dutch oven), sear the meat over a high heat to brown it, then set the wild boar aside.

03 In the same pan, add the finely chopped carrot, celery and onion, and cook gently over low heat for 8–10 minutes until softened. Return the meat to the pan, add the tomato paste and a small glass of red wine, and let the alcohol evaporate. Stir in the tomato pulp, season, and partially cover. Simmer over low heat for 2–2½ hours, until the meat is meltingly tender. Stir occasionally and add a little water if needed to prevent the *ragù* from sticking.

04 Get the dough and roll it out thinly with a rolling pin or pasta machine. Cut your pappardelle (see page 390). Cook them *al dente* in a large saucepan of salted boiling water. Drain them, keeping a ladleful of this precious cooking water.

05 Add the pasta to the *ragù*, along with a little of the cooking water, and toss to coat.

06 Serve with a drizzle of olive oil, grated Tuscan Pecorino and a few leaves of thyme or rosemary. *La festa comincia!*

+ **On repeat in the kitchen:** Toscana-Fanboy for life! That's what you'll be humming after listening to 'Toscana Fanboys' by Peter Fox feat. Adriano Celentano. A catchy chorus for an iconic Tuscan dish: rustic, intense, irresistible.

PICI ALL'AGLIONE

Garlic, garlic and more garlic

FOR 4 FRIENDS

For the pici

- 500g (1lb 2oz) *semola rimacinata* (remilled durum wheat semolina)
- 250ml (1 cup) lukewarm water

For the *aglione* sauce

- 6–8 cloves of *aglione della Val di Chiana* (if unavailable, regular garlic will do, but be sure to remove the germ)
- 500g (1lb 2oz) tinned peeled tomatoes (or *passata di pomodoro*, see page 270 for instructions on how to make your own)
- 4 tbsp extra virgin olive oil
- 1 dried red chilli, crumbled by hand for extra heat (optional)
- Salt QB

01 Let's start with a Tuscan classic from the hills of Siena and Val di Chiana: pici, a thick, hand-rolled pasta typical of southern Tuscany. On a floured work surface, pour the semolina into a small mound, pour the lukewarm water into the centre, add salt and knead until you obtain a smooth, elastic dough. Cover with a clean cloth (a tea towel works perfectly) and let it rest at room temperature for 30 minutes.

02 Peel the *aglione*, a very mild and delicate garlic (be careful – once you've tasted it, you won't be able to do without it), then finely chop it or crush it with the flat of a knife. Gently fry it in a large frying pan in a generous drizzle of olive oil for 2–3 minutes. It should not brown, just simmer gently.

03 Add your peeled tomatoes (crushed by hand for a rustic touch, or use a *passata di pomodoro* if you're in a hurry). Season lightly with salt and add a little chilli pepper for spice lovers. Cover and simmer over a low heat for 25–30 minutes, stirring regularly.

04 Retrieve your dough and turn to page 398 under the heading *Pici* or *bigoli* to shape your wonderful creations.

05 Bring a large pot of salted water to the boil and add your pasta. Cook for 5–7 minutes depending on its thickness. Drain it, keeping a little water aside (we can't say it enough: always keep this trick up your sleeve).

06 Then pour your pici into the sauce, add a drizzle of olive oil, a small ladleful of cooking water if necessary, and mix gently to coat everything well.

07 Serve immediately. No cheese here – purists would call it sacrilege – but a few fresh basil leaves are always welcome. *Basta.*

\+ **On repeat in the kitchen:** Fulminacci's 'Aglio e Olio' is the perfect song to accompany this recipe. It's catchy, warm chorus goes perfectly with the aroma of garlic filling the kitchen. Quite simply, a perfect match.

QUADRUCCI IN BRODO

A broth to heal your soul

For truly perfect results, your broth must simmer for at least 2 hours. It takes a long time, but it's really worth it.

FOR 4 FRIENDS

For the quadrucci

- 180g (6½oz) type 00 flour
- 180g (6½oz) *semola rimacinata* (remilled durum wheat semolina)
- 7 egg yolks

For the homemade chicken stock

- 1 free-range chicken leg (with bones and skin, use everything)
- 1 carrot
- 1 stalk of celery
- 1 small garlic clove (optional)
- 1 small bouquet garni (flat-leaf parsley, thyme and bay leaf)
- ½ onion, peeled and studded with a clove
- 1.2 litres (5 cups) cold water
- Fine salt and black pepper QB

01 Here is the type of winter dish we love for warming both body and soul. We start with quadrucci, small square-shaped pasta typical of the Abruzzo region. On a clean work surface, pour the flour and semolina into a small mound, make a well in the centre and add the egg yolks. Knead until you obtain a smooth dough. Cover with clingfilm and leave to rest for 30 minutes at room temperature.

02 Now let's make the stock. In a large saucepan, place your chicken leg, chopped carrot and celery, the onion, the garlic, salt and pepper. Cover with about 1.2 litres of cold water, add the bouquet garni and bring to the boil.

03 At this point, a slightly suspicious foam will form on the surface. This is normal. Remove it with a skimmer and repeat until the broth is as clear as possible. Leave to simmer, covered, for at least 2 hours, checking occasionally. Taste, adjust the salt, and strain through a sieve. Remove the chicken, which you can save for your Caesar salad the next day: nothing goes to waste.

04 Roll out your dough thinly with a rolling pin or using a pasta machine, then cut your quadrucci using our guide on page 390.

05 When the broth is ready, bring it back to a gentle boil, then carefully add your quadrucci: they are cooked as soon as they rise to the surface.

06 Serve piping hot in a deep plate or a bowl for even more comfort.

+ **On repeat in the kitchen:** These quadrucci *al brodo* are a remedy for colds and the blues, a shot of nostalgia straight from childhood. To accompany this trip down memory lane, play 'Bambino' by Dalida: sweetness, warmth, filled with memories.

IN COD WE TRUST

Scialatielli al sugo di baccalà e olive

FOR 4 FRIENDS

<u>For the scialatielli</u>

- 450g (1lb) *semola rimacinata* (remilled durum wheat semolina)
- 160ml (⅔ cup) lukewarm water

<u>For the sauce</u>

- 400g (14oz) desalted cod
- 300–350ml (1¼–1½ cups) *passata di pomodoro* (we explain how to make your own on page 270)
- 1 small shallot
- 1 garlic clove (optional)
- 80g (2¾oz) pitted black olives, such as Gaeta olives, the black pearl of Italian olives
- 1 tbsp desalted capers
- ½ glass dry white wine
- 2–3 tbsp extra virgin olive oil
- A little fresh flat-leaf parsley
- Salt and pepper QB

01 We start with scialatielli, a short, thick pasta from the Amalfi Coast. Pour the semolina onto your work surface, make a small well and gradually pour the lukewarm water into the centre, mixing first with a fork, then with your fingers when the dough begins to form. Knead for a good 10 minutes until the pasta is soft but not sticky. Cover with a tea towel or clingfilm and leave to rest for 30 minutes at room temperature.

02 Now make the sauce. In a frying pan, sauté the finely chopped shallot (and garlic, if used) in a generous drizzle of olive oil. When they start to brown, add the pieces of desalted cod. Sauté them quickly on each side, just to brown them a little. Deglaze with the white wine (and pour a small glass for the chef . . . but check the label first, as not all cooking wines are good for drinking), allow the alcohol to evaporate, then pour in the tomato *passata*. Cover and simmer over a low heat for 15–20 minutes. When cooked, add the black olives and capers, a pinch of salt – the cod has already done that job – a good grinding of pepper, and *basta*.

03 Get your dough and turn to page 398 to learn how to cut your scialatielli, whose name comes from the combination of two words in the Neapolitan dialect: *scialare* (to feast) and *tiella* (frying pan). A good omen for your dinner tonight.

04 Cook the pasta in a saucepan of salted boiling water for 5–6 minutes, depending on its thickness. Tasting it is the best way to check you haven't messed up. Drain the pasta, keeping a little of the cooking water.

05 Mix the scialatielli into the sauce and adjust the texture with your precious liquid if necessary: the sauce should be silky smooth. A drizzle of extra virgin olive oil, some chopped parsley . . . and it's ready.

06 Serve on warm plates and add a dash of chilli oil for the daring. You're now in Naples.

\+ **On repeat in the kitchen:** In the late 1960s, Nino Ferrer settled in Italy (his native country) and recorded a deliciously offbeat Italian version of his hit 'Les cornichons', renamed 'Il baccalà'. Pa la la la la, it's swinging in the *cucina*.

SWEET LIKE PEPPER

Foglie con peperone crusco e mollica

FOR 4 FRIENDS

For the foglie

- 450g (1lb) *semola rimacinata* (remilled durum wheat semolina)
- 160ml (⅔ cup) lukewarm water

For the sauce

- 4–5 *cruschi* peppers, the crispy pride of Basilicata. If you don't have any on hand, you can substitute dried sweet red peppers, rehydrated then fried.
- 4 tbsp extra virgin olive oil
- Salt and freshly ground black pepper QB

For the *mollica*

- 100g (3½oz) stale bread (or panko, or a lighter texture)
- 3 tbsp extra virgin olive oil
- 1 garlic clove (optional, but adds flavour)
- 1 tbsp fresh parsley
- 1 tbsp fresh basil (or oregano, or thyme, whichever you prefer)
- Grated zest of ½ organic or unwaxed lemon (optional, for freshness)
- Salt and freshly ground black pepper QB

01 Start with the foglie, a type of pasta typical of southern Italy, shaped like an elongated, slightly curved leaf. Pour the semolina onto your work surface, make a small well in the centre and gradually pour the lukewarm water into it, mixing first with a fork and then with your fingers when the dough begins to form. Knead for a good 10 minutes until the pasta is soft but not sticky. Cover with a tea towel or clingfilm and leave to rest for 30 minutes at room temperature.

02 Meanwhile, prepare the peppers. Fry the whole dried *cruschi* briefly in hot olive oil (160–170°C/320–338°F). They will puff up and turn crisp almost instantly – watch carefully, as they burn easily. Drain them on kitchen paper, then crumble them with love.

03 Prepare the *mollica*. To do this, blend the stale bread to obtain crumbs (skip this if using panko). In a non-stick frying pan, heat the oil with the crushed garlic clove and simmer for 1–2 minutes to release the flavour, then remove the garlic. Add the breadcrumbs and fry over a medium heat, stirring regularly, until they become golden brown and crispy. Remove from the heat and add the chopped herbs, lemon zest (if using), a little salt and pepper and mix well.

04 Get your dough and go to page 397 to shape your foglie.

05 In a large saucepan of salted boiling water, cook your foglie until *al dente* then drain them, keeping a ladleful of the cooking water – liquid gold, as chefs say.

06 Heat a generous drizzle of olive oil in a frying pan, add the foglie, the crumbled *cruschi* peppers and most of the golden breadcrumbs, then pour in a little of the cooking water to bind everything together. Mix gently to coat each 'leaf' of dough.

07 Place your foglie on warm plates and sprinkle with a final dusting of crispy breadcrumbs. You should feel all fired up from the very first bite.

+ **On repeat in the kitchen:** When you think 'sunshine ingredients', you say 'bright song': let's play Lucio Battisti's 'La canzone del sole'. A timeless classic that, for over 50 years, has brought together every generation around a chorus sung at the top of their voices.

WE NO SPECK AMERICANO

Chicche verdi alla panna, speck e erba cipollina

FOR 4 FRIENDS

For the chicche verdi, mini gnocchetti

- 390g (13¾oz) potatoes
- 130g (4¾oz) plain flour
- 200g (7oz) fresh spinach
- Salt and pepper QB

For the sauce

- 150ml (scant ⅔ cup) extra-thick double cream or Italian *panna da cucina*, which is even smoother and creamier than crème fraîche
- 150g (5½oz) speck, cut into thin strips
- 1 small bunch of fresh chives
- 30g (1oz) butter
- 1 tbsp extra virgin olive oil
- Pepper QB

01 Prepare the chicche verdi dough. Cook the potatoes whole (with their skins on) in a large saucepan of salted water. Drain then peel them while they are still hot (be careful not to burn yourself) and mash them with a potato masher. Wash the spinach, blanch for a few minutes in boiling water, drain well and blend for 10 minutes. Add this green juice to your mash. In a large bowl, mix the potatoes with the flour, a little salt and a little pepper, then knead by hand until you obtain a soft green dough that is slightly sticky but holds together well. If it is too sticky, add a little more flour. Then shape your chicche using our guide on page 399. Set your little balls aside on a floured tea towel.

02 Now for the sauce. In a large frying pan, gently melt the butter with a generous drizzle of olive oil. Add the speck and let it brown gently, just enough to make it crispy and fragrant. Then pour in the cream (or *panna*) and stir over a low heat: the sauce should be smooth and shiny. Season lightly with salt and pepper (go easy, as the speck already adds flavour) then set aside.

03 Meanwhile, bring a large saucepan of salted water to the boil. Add the chicche and cook until they rise to the surface, a little clue which tells you when they are ready. Drain them thoroughly.

04 Add the small balls to the frying pan and sauté gently to coat each piece of pasta with the speck-flavoured cream. Then remove from the heat, stir in the chopped chives for freshness and a touch of vim. Don't skimp, it's this little green twist that makes all the difference.

05 Serve on warm plates, sprinkle with a few extra chives (you can never have too much) and finish with a twist of pepper. And there you have it: rustic and creamy, the dream.

+ **On repeat in the kitchen:** This dish, straight from the valleys of Trentino and South Tyrol, smells of fresh air and snow-capped peaks. So, to recreate that hiking atmosphere at home, we put on Vasco Rossi's 'Un senso', an introspective ballad that's perfect for letting your thoughts wander while dinner simmers.

PASSATELLI IN BRODO DI CARNE

A broth for the meat-lovers

For best results, we strongly recommend simmering your delicious broth for at least 3 hours. It takes a long time, but it's (very) good.

FOR 4 FRIENDS

For the passatelli

- 200g (7oz) fine breadcrumbs (homemade if possible)
- 200g (7oz) grated Parmigiano Reggiano DOP (aged at least 24 months)
- 4 eggs
- Zest of 1 organic or unwaxed lemon, finely chopped
- 4g (scant 1 tsp) salt

For the homemade brodo di carne (meat broth)

- 1 chicken or a piece of lean beef (such as shank or rib)
- 1 marrowbone (optional, but highly recommended for the sake of tradition)
- 1 carrot
- 1 stalk of celery
- 1 onion
- 1 bay leaf
- 2 cloves (stuck into the onion)
- A little coarse salt
- Salt QB

01 Need a comforting dish to warm you up on a rainy Sunday? Look no further: *passatelli in brodo*, a classic from Emilia-Romagna, is here to take care of you. Start by preparing the pasta. In a bowl, mix the breadcrumbs, Parmigiano, salt, lemon zest and add the eggs. Knead lovingly until you obtain a soft, smooth and elastic dough. Cover with clingfilm and leave to rest for 30 minutes at room temperature.

02 Now for the broth: in a big pot put your meat (chicken or lean beef), a carrot, a stalk of celery and a whole onion studded with 2 cloves, a marrowbone, a bay leaf and a handful of coarse salt. Cover with about 3 litres of cold water and bring to the boil.

03 As it heats, a light foam will rise to the surface – this is perfectly normal. Skim it off carefully; the clearer the broth, the better the result. Then leave to simmer, covered, for at least 3 hours, checking on it from time to time. Taste, adjust the salt, and strain.

04 Meanwhile, get your dough and shape your passatelli like a *maestro* using our guide on page 399.

05 When the broth is ready, bring it back to a gentle boil. Gently dip your passatelli into it: they are cooked as soon as they rise to the surface (2–3 minutes max).

06 Serve piping hot in a deep plate. Then all that's left to do is grab a blanket and put on a film worthy of your masterpiece (we've put together a short list on pages 232–233).

+ **On repeat in the kitchen:** 'Acqua e sale' by the duo Mina e Celentano, of course. A timeless classic, as delightful as ever, which sticks in your head and comforts you.

HOT TO GO
Busiate alla 'nduja

FOR 4 FRIENDS

For the busiate
- 450g (1lb) *semola rimacinata* (remilled durum wheat semolina)
- 160ml (⅔ cup) lukewarm water

For the sauce
- 150g (5½oz) 'nduja, the spicy, spreadable Calabrian sausage
- 2 tbsp extra virgin olive oil
- 2 garlic cloves, squashed with the blade of a knife but kept whole
- 400g (14oz) tomato pulp (or peeled San Marzano tomatoes)
- Grated ricotta *salata* or Pecorino Romano DOP (optional, for serving)

01 Start with the busiate, a traditional pasta from the province of Trapani in Sicily, shaped into spirals as if wound around a *busà* (a thin reed stem). Pour the semolina onto your work surface, make a small well in the centre and gradually pour the lukewarm water into it, mixing first with a fork and then with your fingers when the dough begins to form. Knead for a good 10 minutes until the pasta is soft but not sticky. Cover with a tea towel or clingfilm and leave to rest for 30 minutes at room temperature.

02 In a large frying pan, heat a generous dash of olive oil and fry the whole crushed garlic cloves over a low heat until they are golden brown (but not burnt). Then remove them and set aside.

03 Next, the 'nduja. Add the 'nduja to the pan and let it melt gently over medium heat, stirring until it blends into the oil.

04 Add the tomato pulp, stir and cover the pan halfway. Simmer over a low heat for 15–20 minutes until the sauce thickens and the flavours come together. Is it a little spicy? You're on the right track.

05 While the sauce is simmering, take your dough and shape your busiate pasta using our guide on page 398.

06 Then cook the busiate in a large saucepan of salted boiling water until *al dente* (8–10 minutes, depending on the pasta). Drain, carefully reserving a ladleful of the cooking water.

07 Add the pasta to the hot spicy sauce and mix in a little cooking water if necessary to bind everything together.

08 Serve with a sprinkling of ricotta *salata* or grated Pecorino, if you like, and a final drizzle of olive oil. And there you have it, something to spice up your dinner tonight!

\+ **On repeat in the kitchen:** Italy's number one hit, 'Urlando contro il cielo' by Ligabue is the cry from the heart that perfectly suits these super-spicy noodles. Take a bite, open the windows and shout: 'URLANDO CONTRO IL CIELO OH OH OH OH!'

FAZZOLETTI DI ZUCCA ALLA MANTOVANA
Gourd vibes only

This recipe is a classic dish from the city of Mantua, traditionally eaten on Christmas Eve during the magro (lean) dinner.

FOR 4 FRIENDS

For the fazzoletti
- 200g (7oz) type 00 flour
- 150g (5½oz) *semola rimacinata* (remilled durum wheat semolina)
- 8 egg yolks

For the filling
- 600g (1lb 5oz) Mantovana squash (pumpkin or butternut) (slightly sweet in flavour, ideal for this sweet and savoury dish)
- 100g (3½oz) Parmigiano Reggiano DOP (aged 30 months)
- 80g (2¾oz) finely crumbled dry *amaretti* biscuits (this is one of the signature ingredients of the recipe: don't skip it, find a way to get hold of some, life is full of possibilities)
- 1–2 tbsp pear or melon *mostarda di frutta senapata* (this is a condiment made from candied fruit with mustard essential oil that you can find in any good *alimentari* and which adds a sweet and spicy contrast essential to the recipe. Down with the Dijon mustard)
- Nutmeg
- Salt and pepper QB

For the sauce
- 100g (3½oz) unsalted butter
- Fresh sage leaves
- Grated Parmigiano Reggiano DOP, for serving

01 Start by preparing the squash. Cut it into quarters, remove the seeds, then bake it in the oven at 180°C fan/200°C/400°F/GM 6 for 40–50 minutes. Remove the flesh, mash it with a fork or potato masher, then leave it to rest overnight in the fridge in a fine sieve over a bowl to remove excess water.

02 The next day (or straight away, if patience isn't your strong suit), prepare the filling. Combine the well-drained squash with the crushed *amaretti*, grated Parmigiano, and finely chopped *mostarda* – well done if you've tracked some down. Add a pinch of freshly grated nutmeg, season with salt and pepper, then taste and adjust.

03 For your dough: on a clean work surface, pour the flour and semolina into a small mound, make a well in the centre and add the eggs. Knead until you obtain a smooth dough. Cover with clingfilm and leave to rest for 30 minutes at room temperature. Once ready, roll out with a rolling pin or pasta machine and shape each fazzoletto mantovano using our instructions on page 394. Set aside on a floured work surface while you make your sauce.

04 In a large frying pan, melt the butter with a few sage leaves until they are lightly browned.

05 Cook the fazzoletti for 3–4 minutes in salted boiling water. Drain and immediately toss in the sage butter, mixing gently.

06 Serve hot, sprinkled with Parmigiano. There you have it, a festive classic that has graced Italian tables for centuries! Merry Christmas!

\+ **On repeat in the kitchen:** 'Bianco Natale' is one of Italy's best-known Christmas classics. Adapted from Irving Berlin's 'White Christmas', it has been covered by numerous artists (we recommend Irene Grandi's version). A warm and gentle classic, just like these *fazzoletti di zucca.*

TAGLIOLINI AL TARTUFO

Here comes truffle

FOR 4 FRIENDS

For the tagliolini

- 180g (6½oz) type 00 flour
- 180g (6½oz) *semola rimacinata* (remilled durum wheat semolina)
- 7 egg yolks

For the sauce

- 80g (2¾oz) high-quality unsalted butter, such as *Burro di malga* (mountain butter) or cultured butter, which has a flavour reminiscent of crème fraîche
- 30–40g (1–1½oz) black truffle, such as melanosporum, or white truffle, such as Alba truffle
- Fine salt QB

01 On a clean work surface, pour the flour and semolina into a small mound, make a well in the centre and add the egg yolks. Knead until you obtain a smooth dough. Cover with clingfilm and leave to rest for 30 minutes at room temperature.

02 Finely grate half of the truffle using a Microplane grater or a mandoline (be careful with your fingers, they're not part of the recipe). Then melt the butter gently in a large frying pan, without browning it. Add the grated truffle and leave it to infuse over a very low heat for 2–3 minutes, just long enough for the magic to happen.

03 Meanwhile, once your dough has rested, roll it out very thinly with a rolling pin or pasta machine and turn to page 396 to learn how to shape these gems.

04 Cook the tagliolini in a large saucepan of salted boiling water for 3–4 minutes. Drain them quickly, keeping a little of the cooking water – your secret for a creamy sauce.

05 Pour the pasta into the pan with the truffle butter and mix gently to coat well. Taste and add salt if necessary, as some farmhouse butters already have a strong flavour.

06 Serve immediately and add the finishing touch at the table, in front of your guests, by shaving the rest of the truffle on top generously. No cheese, no pepper, no frills: *just the truffle.*

\+ **On repeat in the kitchen:** 'Mi sei scoppiato dentro al cuore', sings Mina in her unforgettable voice, 'You burst into my heart'. Well, get ready to experience the same thing from the very first bite of these taglioni. An explosion of flavours, love at first taste.

COUSCOUS DI PESCE

Welcome to Sicily

FOR 4 FRIENDS

<u>For the fish stock</u>

- 800g (1lb 12oz) rock fish (scorpion fish, gurnard, red mullet, etc.) and/or shellfish. Feel free to ask your fishmonger for advice.
- 200g (7oz) prawns or langoustines
- 1 stalk of celery
- 1 carrot
- 1 onion
- 2 garlic cloves
- 2 ripe tomatoes or 200g (7oz) tomato pulp
- 1 bunch of parsley
- A few saffron stems or 1–2 tsp of turmeric
- Extra virgin olive oil
- Salt and pepper QB

<u>For the couscous</u>

- 2 glasses of medium couscous (approximately 300g/10½oz)
- 500ml (2 cups) of hot salted water
- 1 organic or unwaxed lemon (optional)
- A few pinches of cinnamon and black pepper
- A dash of chilli powder or harissa (optional)
- 2 tbsp olive oil

01 An iconic Sicilian dish, Trapani couscous reflects the rich blend of Arabic, Italian and Mediterranean influences found along the coast. Let's start with the heart of the recipe: the fish stock. In a large saucepan, sauté the chopped onion, garlic, carrot and celery in olive oil. Add the tomatoes, then the fish (gutted and cleaned) and the shellfish, if using. Cover with water, add the parsley, a pinch of salt, pepper and saffron or turmeric, and simmer gently for 30–40 minutes. While it simmers, take a moment to enjoy the process, perhaps even put together a playlist for the occasion (your next commute to work will sound different!). Then strain the broth through a fine sieve and set aside the cooked fish and seafood. Carefully remove any bones or skin.

02 Place the couscous in a large bowl, drizzle with olive oil and mix well. Then gradually pour in the hot salted water, stirring with a fork or your fingertips – the aim is to avoid clumps, as no one likes lumpy couscous. Cover and leave to swell for about 10 minutes, then stir again. Break up the grains with your fingers to obtain a light and fluffy couscous. Season with cinnamon, pepper and, for those who like a bit of spice, add a pinch of chilli or a dash of harissa.

03 In a large serving dish or in individual bowls, arrange the hot couscous, pour over the broth, then add the pieces of fish and a few prawns or langoustines. Drizzle with olive oil and sprinkle with parsley and a little lemon juice for even more freshness, and it's ready. Welcome to Sicilia.

\+ **On repeat in the kitchen:** Summery, fresh and vibrant like your recipe, the song 'Musica leggerissima' by Colapesce & Dimartino takes you straight to sunny Trapani. The melody will stay in your head all day long – you have been warned!

PACCHERI AL RAGÙ NAPOLETANO

Napoli has our hearts

FOR 4 FRIENDS

<u>For the pasta</u>

- 400g (14oz) paccheri (or ziti, those laaaaarge pasta shapes that resemble straws, cut by hand according to Neapolitan tradition)
- Parmigiano Reggiano DOP or grated pecorino, QB

<u>For the meat</u>

- 300g (10½oz) beef brisket or shank
- 300g (10½oz) pork ribs or fresh sausages
- 1 onion
- 1 glass of red wine
- 1 litre (4¼ cups) *passata di pomodoro* (we tell you how to make the best one, your own, on page 270) or blended peeled tomatoes
- 2 tbsp tomato paste
- A few fresh basil leaves
- Chilli pepper, if you like it spicy – we do!
- 2 tbsp extra virgin olive oil
- Salt and pepper QB

01 In a large saucepan, gently fry the chopped onion in a generous dash of olive oil, then add the whole pieces of meat, season lightly with salt and brown on all sides. Deglaze with the red wine and allow to evaporate.

02 Add the *passata*, tomato paste and a little water if necessary (the sauce should cover all the meat). Season with pepper, add the basil and a little chilli for those who like it hot. Simmer, covered, over a very low heat for at least 3 hours, stirring occasionally with a wooden spoon (if you don't have one, find one; wooden is best).

03 Then cook the paccheri *al dente* in a large saucepan of salted boiling water, drain and mix with the *ragù* and a few pinches of Parmigiano or pecorino, depending on your preference.

04 Two options for serving afterwards: serve the paccheri with the *ragù* and the meat, or serve the pasta and sauce as a *primo* and the meat as a *secondo*. Two dishes in one, Neapolitan style. Either way, you're in for a treat.

+ **On repeat in the kitchen:** To imagine you are eating this in Naples, accompany this recipe with one of the most famous Neapolitan songs: 'Caruso' by Lucio Dalla. The title of this recipe is a nod to this world-famous refrain, which means 'I love you very much', our declaration of love to *ragù*.

TONNARELLI ALLA CARBONARA
When in Rome

FOR 4 FRIENDS

For the tonnarelli
- 180g (6½oz) type 00 flour
- 180g (6½oz) *semola rimacinata* (remilled durum wheat semolina)
- 7 egg yolks

For the carbonara
- 150g (5½oz) *guanciale* (aka cured pork cheek, and this is non-negotiable: anyone who replaces this with bacon should call their dish something else)
- 4 egg yolks + 1 whole egg
- 100g (3½oz) grated Pecorino Romano DOP
- Freshly ground black pepper QB

01 On a clean work surface, pour the flour and semolina into a small mound, make a well in the centre and add the egg yolks. Knead until you obtain a smooth dough. Cover with clingfilm and leave to rest for 30 minutes at room temperature.

02 Meanwhile, cut the *guanciale* into thick strips or cubes and fry gently in a cold frying pan without adding any fat. It will release its fat and become ultra-crispy. Remove from the heat but keep the *guanciale* and melted fat in the pan.

03 Get your dough, roll it out thinly with a rolling pin or pasta machine, if you have one in your cupboards, and turn to page 398 for cutting instructions.

04 Cook your tonnarelli in a large saucepan of salted boiling water, *al dente* of course (3–4 minutes). Keep a ladleful of the cooking water.

05 Beat the egg yolks and whole egg in a bowl. Add the grated Pecorino and a generous amount of black pepper – don't skimp – and mix to obtain a thick cream.

06 Off the heat, pour the tonnarelli into the pan with the *guanciale* and its fat, mix, then stir in the egg and Pecorino cream. Add a little cooking water to obtain a creamy sauce and bind the pasta. This is where the magic of the recipe happens and you officially become someone who makes Italian-style carbo (unless you've added bacon, as we mentioned earlier).

07 Serve immediately with a sprinkling of grated Pecorino and freshly ground black pepper on top for even more colour. Your *Vacanza Romana* starts now.

\+ **On repeat in the kitchen:** *Lasciatemi cantaaaaaaare con la chitarra in mano . . .* the first notes of Toto Cutugno's 'L'italiano' sets the mood. An ode to Italianness that's perfect for this dish as it celebrates, among other things, spaghetti cooked *al dente.*

KISS MY ASPARAGUS

Risotto agli asparagi

FOR 4 FRIENDS

For the rice

- 320g (1 1/4oz) Carnaroli or Arborio rice, the only ones worth using (best to avoid ready-cooked rice)
- 1 bunch of green asparagus (about 500g/1lb 2oz)
- 1 shallot
- 1.2 litres (5 cups) vegetable stock (see homemade recipe on page 317)
- 1 glass of dry white wine
- 40g (1½oz) butter
- 40g (1½oz) grated Parmigiano Reggiano DOP (to bind the risotto)
- 3 tbsp extra virgin olive oil
- Salt and freshly ground black pepper QB

For the Parmigiano *fonduta*

- 80g (2¾oz) grated Parmigiano Reggiano DOP
- 80ml (⅓ cup) double cream

For the green sauce

- 1 bunch of fresh flat-leaf parsley
- 10 fresh mint leaves
- 2 tbsp extra virgin olive oil

01 Start by washing and trimming the asparagus by bending the fibrous end until the asparagus breaks off naturally, then peel the stalks with a vegetable peeler. Next, remove the tips and cut the stalks into small pieces.

02 Blanch the tips quickly by immersing them in a pan of salted boiling water for 2 minutes, then cool them under ice-cold running water, a little trick that helps them retain their bright green colour. Set aside.

03 In a saucepan, gently heat the cream, add the grated Parmigiano and whisk until you obtain a smooth sauce. Keep the heat very, very low (feel free to turn the heat off and on again to prevent the cream from boiling).

04 For the green sauce, boil the herbs for 15 seconds, then rinse them under cold water. Blend with the olive oil and strain if necessary. Your sauce should be shiny and silky smooth.

05 In a large saucepan, sauté the finely chopped shallot in a generous drizzle of olive oil, then add the asparagus stalks and let them soften gently. Remove half of the stalks and blend them until smooth.

06 Add the rice to the pan with the remaining stalks and cook for 2 minutes, until it becomes slightly translucent. Deglaze with the white wine. Allow to evaporate, then add 1 or 2 ladles of hot stock. Continue cooking for a good 20 minutes, adding ladles of hot stock regularly. The secret? Add stock as soon as the last ladle evaporates and stir continuously to prevent sticking. We trust you to never take your eyes off your precious creation. Once the risotto is creamy, remove from the heat and stir in the butter, asparagus cream and grated Parmigiano. Season with salt and pepper.

07 Spoon the risotto onto plates, place the asparagus tips on top and add a drizzle of hot Parmigiano *fonduta* as a finishing touch. An ideal vegetarian recipe to celebrate the arrival of spring.

+ **On repeat in the kitchen:** With its fresh chorus, play 'nord, sud, ovest, est' by the band 883. An anthem for an entire generation, perfect for this nostalgic risotto.

OUR REGIONS HAVE TALENT

You knew that the Colosseum is in Rome and La Scala is in Milan (which is already quite impressive), but did you know that it is in Emilia-Romagna that sfogline make tagliatelle, or that it is in Tuscany that you can eat the best pici? Now is the time to discover where your favourite pasta comes from and become what we call 'a connoisseur'.

LOMBARDIA

Iconic pasta dishes:
Casoncelli alla bergamasca, ravioli with a sweet and savoury filling

The signature sauce:
Butter, pancetta and sage

VALLE D'AOSTA

Iconic pasta:
Chnéffléne, small gnocchi similar to spätzle

The signature sauce:
Butter, cream and fontina cheese, to warm you up on winter evenings

PIEMONTE

Iconic pasta:
Tajarin, very thin and enriched with egg yolks

The signature sauce:
Melted butter with white truffles from Alba

LIGURIA

Iconic pasta:
Trofie, twists

The signature sauce:
Pesto alla genovese, a classic sauce made with basil, pine nuts, olive oil, Pecorino and Parmigiano Reggiano DOP

TRENTINO-ALTO ADIGE

Iconic pasta dishes:
Spätzle with spinach

The signature sauce:
Cream, ham and onion

FRIULI-VENEZIA GIULIA

Iconic pasta dishes:
Cjarsons, sweet and savoury stuffed ravioli

The signature sauce:
Melted butter and grated smoked ricotta

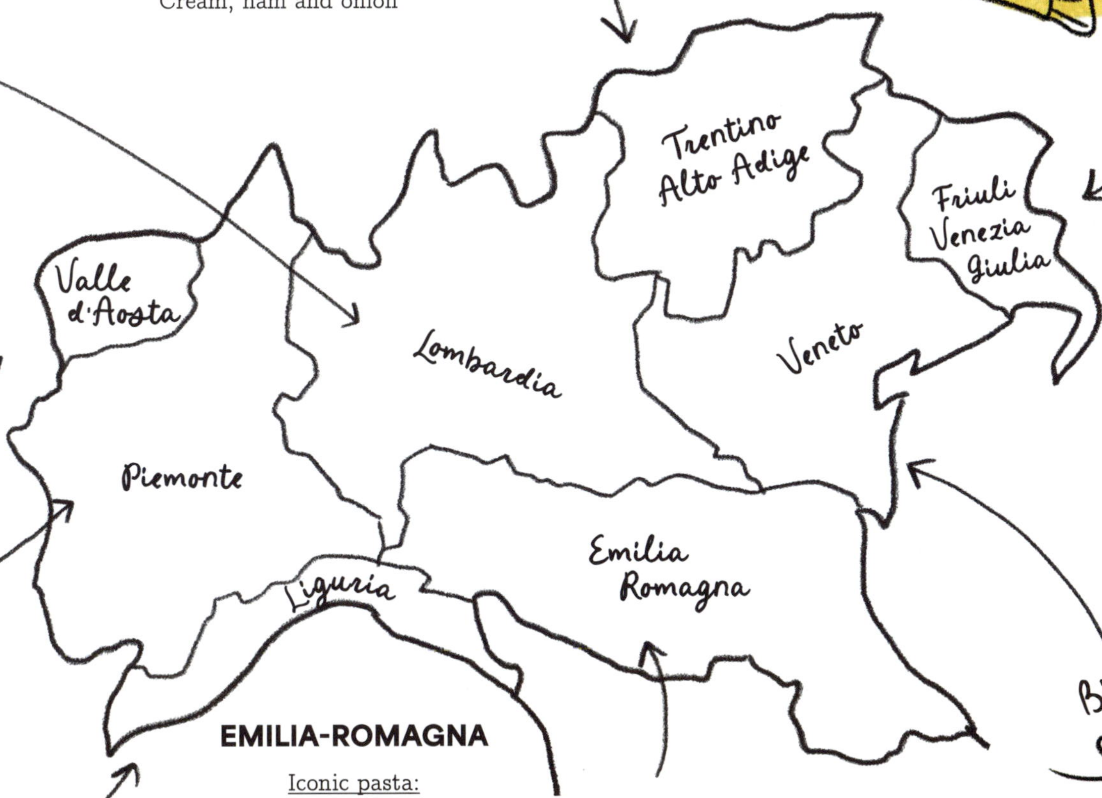

EMILIA-ROMAGNA

Iconic pasta:
Tagliatelle

The signature sauce:
Bolognese *ragù*

VENETO

Iconic pasta:
Bigoli, very long and very rough to catch the sauce

The signature sauce:
À l'anatra (with duck) or *sarde in saor* (sweet and sour sardines)

NORTHERN ITALY

CENTRAL ITALY

TOSCANA

<u>Iconic pasta:</u>
Pici, thick spaghetti rolled by hand

<u>The signature sauce:</u>
'Aglione' (with tomato and garlic)

UMBRIA

<u>Iconic pasta:</u>
Strangozzi, a variety of long rectangular pasta

<u>The signature sauce:</u>
With black truffles from Norcia

ABRUZZO

<u>Iconic pasta:</u>
Spaghetti alla chitarra, named after the utensil used to make it

<u>The signature sauce:</u>
Lamb *ragù* or 'pallottine', with mini meatballs

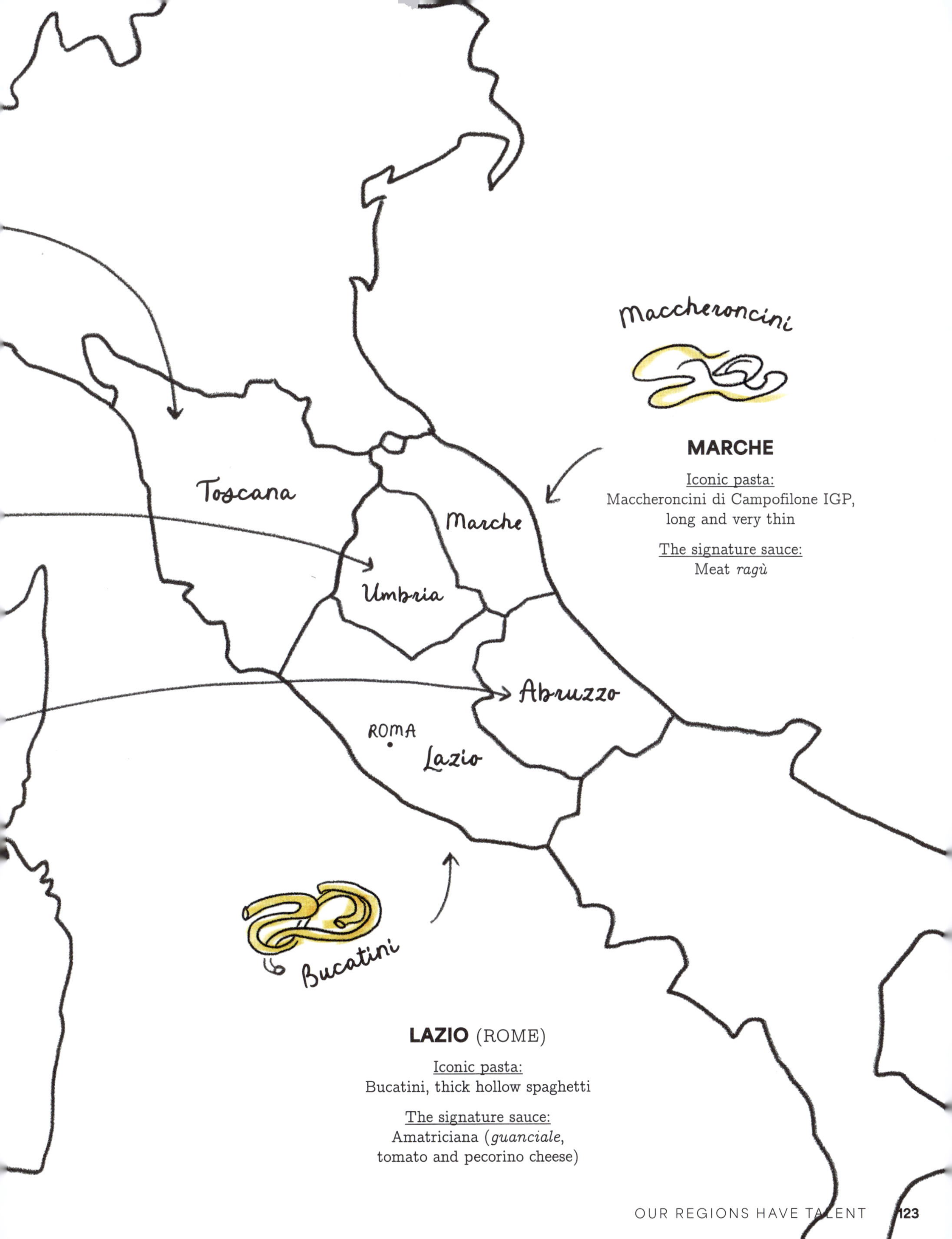

MARCHE

Iconic pasta:
Maccheroncini di Campofilone IGP, long and very thin

The signature sauce:
Meat *ragù*

LAZIO (ROME)

Iconic pasta:
Bucatini, thick hollow spaghetti

The signature sauce:
Amatriciana (*guanciale*, tomato and pecorino cheese)

SOUTHERN ITALY

SARDEGNA

Iconic pasta:
Malloreddus, also known as 'gnocchetti sardi'

The signature sauce:
With sausage and saffron

CAMPANIA

Iconic pasta:
Ziti, long and hollow

The signature sauce:
Baked with tomato sauce, ricotta and meatballs

SICILIA

Iconic pasta:
Busiate, a twisted shape, ideal for holding sauce

The signature sauce:
Pesto alla trapanese made with almonds, tomatoes and basil

MOLISE

Iconic pasta:
Cavatelli, small pasta shapes with a hollow centre

The signature sauce:
Tomato and sausage sauce

PUGLIA

Iconic pasta:
Orecchiette, shaped like little ears

The signature sauce:
Cime di rapa (broccoli rabe), garlic, anchovies and chilli pepper

BASILICATA

Iconic pasta:
Strascinati, slightly longer and wider than orecchiette

The signature sauce:
Breadcrumbs, *cruschi* peppers (dry and crunchy) and olive oil

CALABRIA

Iconic pasta:
Fileja, tube-shaped, shaped around a small stick

The signature sauce:
'Nduja (spicy spreadable sausage) and tomato

MAMMA I'M A SICILIAN-AIRE

Spaghetti con le sarde alla Siciliana

FOR 4 FRIENDS

- 400g (14oz) spaghetti
- 400g (14oz) fresh sardine fillets
- 1 small fresh fennel bulb + 1 tbsp fennel seeds
- 40g (1½oz) sultanas
- 40g (1½oz) pine nuts
- 6 anchovy fillets in oil
- 1 medium onion
- A pinch of saffron stems, infused in a little hot water
- 80g (2¾oz) crispy breadcrumbs (dry bread crumbled and lightly toasted in a pan with a drizzle of olive oil)
- 6 tbsp extra virgin olive oil
- Salt and freshly ground black pepper QB

01 Wash the sardine fillets and remove all the bones, then cut them into 2–3cm (¾–1¼in)pieces and set aside in the fridge.

02 Soak the sultanas in a small bowl of warm water for 15 minutes. Meanwhile, lightly toast the pine nuts in a dry frying pan. Remove them from the heat as soon as they turn a nice golden colour.

03 In a large frying pan, gently fry the finely chopped onion with the anchovy fillets in olive oil until they melt, just like your guests will when they see such beauty. Add the fennel seeds and finely chopped bulb and stir gently for 4–5 minutes.

04 Add the sardine pieces and cook for a few minutes. Finally, add the saffron and the infused water and season with salt and pepper. All aboard for Palermo.

05 Bring a large saucepan of salted water to the boil and cook the spaghetti until *al dente*. Reserve a ladleful of the cooking water, then drain.

06 Pour the pasta into the frying pan with the sardines and fennel. Add the drained sultanas, the pine nuts and a little cooking water if necessary to bind everything together. Mix thoroughly to coat the spaghetti well. Serve immediately and sprinkle generously with the toasted breadcrumbs. This typical Sicilian dish is traditionally enjoyed between May and September, when the markets are overflowing with fresh sardines, but feel free to enjoy it all year round if your fishmonger allows you this little treat.

+ **On repeat in the kitchen:** Umberto Tozzi's popular hit 'Tu' resonates like a declaration of love. Just like this recipe, which, after the first bite, may well become a whole new reason to live.

JUST GIROLLE WITH IT

Gnudi di ricotta ai finferli

FOR 4 FRIENDS

For the gnudi

- 400g (14oz) well-drained ricotta
- 80g (2¾oz) grated Parmigiano Reggiano DOP
- 1 whole egg + 1 organic or free-range egg yolk
- 80–100g (3–3½oz) type 00 flour (depending on the moisture content of the ricotta)
- A pinch of grated nutmeg (optional)
- Salt and freshly ground black pepper QB

For the sauce

- 300g (10½oz) cleaned *finferli* (small girolles mushrooms)
- 60g (2oz) unsalted butter
- 2 tbsp extra virgin olive oil
- 1 garlic clove, squashed with the blade of a knife but kept whole
- 2–3 tbsp fresh flat-leaf parsley
- Chives (optional)
- Salt and freshly ground black pepper QB

01 Start by preparing the *gnudi* – small ricotta dumplings from the provinces of Grosseto and Siena in Tuscany. In a bowl, mix the drained ricotta with the Parmigiano, whole egg, egg yolk, a pinch of salt, pepper, and nutmeg. Gradually add the flour until you achieve a soft but not overly wet dough. Shape into small balls about the size of a walnut. Place them on a floured tray then place in the fridge for 20 minutes. The perfect break you needed to practise your Rubik's Cube skills.

02 Next, bring a large pot of salted water to the boil and immerse the *gnudi* in it for a few minutes. Tip: they are cooked as soon as they float to the surface. Drain them gently with a slotted spoon.

03 In a large frying pan, melt 30g (1oz) of butter with the olive oil and crushed garlic clove. Add the cleaned *finferli*, season lightly with salt and sauté quickly. Remove the garlic and set the mushrooms aside.

04 In the same frying pan, add the rest of the butter and fry the gnudi so that they are well coated, then add the sautéed mushrooms. Sprinkle generously with finely chopped fresh parsley and chives (if you want even more green) and a twist of pepper.

05 Serve these little *gnudi* wonders immediately. Did you know that their name comes from the Tuscan term *nudi*, which means 'naked' (as you might have guessed)? A subtle way of pointing out that, unlike their ravioli counterparts, they are not covered in an outer layer of dough. A little fun fact, perfect as an icebreaker at the table, even with the mother-in-law!

\+ **On repeat in the kitchen:** No words or frills are needed for this simple dish: the soundtrack from Federico Fellini's 'Amarcord' is enough. A light, almost childlike melody by Nino Rota that has become an iconic tune in Italy.

IT'S MINT TO BE

Trofie al pesto di carciofi, menta e mandorle

FOR 4 FRIENDS

For the trofie

- 180g (6½oz) type 00 flour
- 180g (6½oz) *semola rimacinata* (remilled durum wheat semolina)
- 7 egg yolks

For the artichoke pesto

- 4 artichoke hearts (cooked then stored in water with a dash of lemon juice – a trick to prevent them from turning brown too quickly, plus it adds a welcome touch of freshness)
- 30g (1oz) fresh mint leaves
- 40g (1½oz) blanched almonds
- 50g (1¾oz) grated Parmigiano Reggiano DOP
- 80ml (⅓ cup) extra virgin olive oil
- 1 small garlic clove
- Salt and freshly ground pepper QB

For plating

- 150g (5½oz) smoked stracciatella (or smoked burrata)
- Lightly toasted flaked almonds
- Zest of 1 organic or unwaxed lemon (optional)

01 Let's start with the pasta. Put your flour and semolina on your work surface and form a small well. Place the egg yolks in the middle and mix them in with a fork until you obtain a smooth dough. Knead by hand for 10–12 minutes, the dough should become soft and elastic.

02 Next, chop the artichoke hearts into pieces, keeping a few aside for the final decoration. Blend the rest in a food processor with the mint leaves, blanched almonds, Parmigiano and garlic, gradually adding the olive oil until you obtain a creamy but slightly grainy texture. Taste (no better way to check, right?) and adjust the seasoning with salt and pepper if necessary, then set aside at room temperature.

03 Get your dough and go to page 397 to shape your trofie, small, thin, twisted pasta shapes.

04 Put the pasta in a large saucepan of salted boiling water and cook for 3–4 minutes. Drain, reserving a little of the cooking water.

05 In the hot saucepan, gently mix the trofie with the artichoke pesto, adding a little of your precious cooking water as needed to bind the sauce to the pasta.

06 Time to plate up: arrange your pasta in the centre of the plate, generously spoon the smoked stracciatella over it, add a few pieces of artichoke and sprinkle with toasted flaked almonds. For a final touch of freshness, zest a lemon over the top. Finish with a drizzle of extra virgin olive oil and serve immediately. *Buonissimo.*

\+ **On repeat in the kitchen:** This simple, healthy recipe will be your secret weapon in relationships. Why not take the opportunity to declare your love by playing the song 'Non avere paura' by Tommaso Paradiso?

FUSILLI SEASON

Fusilli con crema di castagne e guanciale croccante

FOR 4 FRIENDS

- 320g (11¼oz) fusilli (or other short pasta)
- 200g (7oz) cooked chestnuts
- 100g (3½oz) *guanciale* (or pancetta), thickly sliced
- 1 small onion (or shallot)
- 1 sprig of rosemary
- 200ml (generous ¾ cup) milk or single cream (depending on how indulgent you feel)
- 2 tbsp extra virgin olive oil
- Grated Pecorino Romano DOP
- Salt and black pepper QB

01 Let's start with the chestnut cream, the star ingredient in this 100% comforting recipe. Finely chop the onion and gently fry it in a pan with a little olive oil and the sprig of rosemary. When it starts to become translucent, add the chestnuts and brown them lightly to bring out their nutty flavour. Pour in the milk (or cream, if you've opted for a richer version) and simmer for 10 minutes. Remove the rosemary, then blend everything together until you have a smooth, fragrant sauce with an earthy flavour. Season with salt and pepper and set aside.

02 Cut the *guanciale* into small cubes and fry them over a medium heat in a hot pan, without adding any fat (do yourself a favour). Once they are super-crispy, place them on kitchen paper and move on to cooking the pasta.

03 Place the fusilli in a large saucepan of salted boiling water and cook until *al dente*, then drain, remembering to keep a ladleful of the cooking water, the secret to a perfectly smooth sauce.

04 Mix the fusilli with the chestnut cream and add a little of your cooking water to achieve a smooth, creamy consistency.

05 Serve in warm soup bowls, dressed with your crispy *guanciale*, a twist of pepper, a pinch of rosemary and, most importantly, a generous sprinkling of grated Pecorino cheese. A delicious, crunchy autumn dish, ideal for enjoying on a rainy day or any other time because it is simply wonderful.

\+ **On repeat in the kitchen:** Is it raining outside? Play 'Se piovesse il tuo nome' ('If it rained your name') by Elisa and Calcutta. A song that evokes missing someone dear but in a beautiful way.

LA GAZZETTA DELLO SPORT
CAMPIONATO MONDIALE PER CLUB

CAPELLINI ALLA GENOVESE DI CIPOLLOTTO

The ultimate spring fling

FOR 4 FRIENDS

- 300–320g (10½–11¼oz) capellini
- 300g (10½oz) cipollotti (spring onions or red Tropea onions. If you find them at the greengrocers, they could have been staring at you all along without you knowing it)
- 2 garlic cloves
- 2 bay leaves (or thyme, which also works)
- ½ tsp fresh chilli or dried chilli flakes
- 100g (3½oz) cherry tomatoes (ideally Pachino)
- 200ml (generous ¾ cup) vegetable stock (see page 317 for the recipe)
- 6 tbsp extra virgin olive oil
- 20g (¾oz) Parmigiano Reggiano DOP (preferably aged around 30 months)
- A few leaves of fresh basil
- Salt and pepper QB

01 In a large frying pan, gently heat 3 tablespoons of olive oil with the chopped garlic and bay leaves. Add the finely chopped spring onions and leave them to sweat over a low heat for about 15 minutes. Gradually add the hot stock; the onions should become tender and shiny, but never brown. Remove from the heat, add the chilli and season to taste. The bay leaves can be left in or removed, depending on your preference. Then leave everything to rest.

02 Meanwhile, cook your pasta in a large saucepan of salted boiling water – *al dente, ovviamente.* Then drain it, keeping a ladleful of cooking water, it will act as a magical binding agent.

03 Add the capellini to the frying pan with the spring onions, pour in a generous drizzle of olive oil and a little cooking water for the *mantecatura* and sauté for a good minute over a high heat. Finally, add the seeded and diced tomatoes, Parmigiano and fresh basil. Mix, taste and adjust seasoning.

04 To serve, grab a fork and a ladle. Stick the fork into the pasta and gently turn it in the ladle, as if you were winding a thread. In a few quick turns, you'll have a nice, tight nest, ready to be placed in the centre of the plate. Finish with another generous drizzle of olive oil – because there's never too much oil in an Italian recipe – a few basil leaves and *buon appetito, capo.*

+ **On repeat in the kitchen:** Simple, quick and tasty, this recipe is your secret weapon for a perfect evening with friends. And when the plates are empty, prolong the pleasure by putting the world to rights to the sound of Vasco Rossi's 'Vivere'.

STRACCIATELLA VERSACE

Spaghettoni con colatura di alici, limone e stracciatella

FOR 4 FRIENDS

- 320g (11¼oz) spaghettoni (or spaghetti no. 7 or 8, because whatever anyone tells you, size does matter)
- 1½–2 tbsp *colatura di alici* (a sauce with fermented anchovy extract, you'll find it)
- 200g (7oz) stracciatella di burrata
- 2 garlic cloves
- 50g (1¾oz) coarse breadcrumbs (made from stale bread from the day before, or even the day before that)
- Grated zest of 1 organic or unwaxed lemon
- Fresh parsley (optional)
- 3–4 tbsp extra virgin olive oil
- Black pepper QB

01 Start by toasting the breadcrumbs in a frying pan with a drizzle of olive oil until golden brown and crispy. Remove from the pan and set aside.

02 In another frying pan, heat a generous drizzle of olive oil with the whole or crushed garlic cloves and leave to infuse (without burning) before removing the garlic. Remove the cloves before serving . . . or not! It all depends on how much your guests love you.

03 Then cook the spaghettoni in a large saucepan of very lightly salted water (the anchovy *colatura* will do the salting very nicely, and it's important to monitor your blood pressure). Drain them, keeping a little of the cooking water.

04 Off the heat, mix the pasta in the flavoured oil, add the *colatura di alici* and a little cooking water to bind everything together. Add the grated lemon zest, a little pepper and chopped parsley, if you like.

05 Serve hot with a sprinkle of breadcrumbs for crunch and a generous spoonful of stracciatella on top. Finish with a drizzle of olive oil for extra creaminess, richness, and flavour – yummy!

+ **On repeat in the kitchen:** A recipe as simple as pie, the perfect opportunity to play the melancholic pop ballad 'Semplicemente' by the duo Zero Assoluto, a big hit in the noughties.

FAMIGLIA VENTURO

Luigi, Anna & Giovanni

GIUGLIANO

CRESPELLE ALLA VALDOSTANA

Hansel and Crêpel

FOR 4 FRIENDS

For the crêpes

- 250g (9oz) plain flour
- 3 organic or free-range eggs
- 500ml (2 cups) whole milk
- 30g (1oz) melted butter (and a little extra for cooking the pancakes)
- A pinch of salt

For the filling

- 200g (7oz) ham from the Aosta Valley (raw or cooked, according to your preference)
- 200g (7oz) Fontina cheese from the Aosta Valley (a semi-hard cheese typical of the region; ask your cheesemonger)
- 300–400ml (1¼–1⅔ cups) thick double cream
- 1 small garlic clove
- Grated nutmeg (optional)
- Freshly ground black pepper QB

01 Sift the flour into a large bowl with a pinch of salt. Make a well in the centre and crack in the eggs. Whisk, gradually adding the milk little by little – because we're aiming for a smooth batter, not a lumpy soup. Add the melted butter, mix well, and leave the batter to rest in the fridge for at least 30 minutes.

02 Once the batter has rested, melt a knob of butter in a non-stick crêpe pan (or a regular frying pan). Over a medium heat, pour in a ladleful of batter, spread it quickly to make a thin crêpe, and cook for about 1 minute on each side until lightly browned. Then stack your golden crêpes, covering them to keep them warm and soft.

03 For the filling, cut the Fontina cheese into thin slices, cut the ham into small pieces or strips and set aside.

04 Then, in a saucepan, gently heat the cream with the crushed garlic, a twist of the pepper mill, a pinch of grated nutmeg, and after 2–3 minutes of simmering, remove the garlic. Spread a thin layer of garlic cream on each crespelle, top with a few pieces of ham and slices of Fontina cheese. If you have any crêpes left over, save them for afternoon tea – there's always someone who'll be happy to enjoy them!

05 Before diving in – stay strong and resist eating them just yet – place everything in the oven. Butter a gratin dish, arrange the filled crêpes side by side, pour over the remaining cream, and dot with small knobs of butter.

06 Bake in a preheated oven for 15–20 minutes at 180°C fan/200°C/400°F/GM 6 until the Fontina melts and browns. You can enjoy them hot on their own or with a salad for a touch of greenery.

+ **On repeat in the kitchen:** What if this was the real cure for the cold? Let's tuck into 'Ma che freddo fa' by Nada whilst savouring these cheesy crêpes in the warm, after a day of skiing, hiking up a hill or riding the underground.

SCIALATIELLI AL CARTOCCIO

The queen of the sea

FOR 4 FRIENDS

For the scialatielli

- 450g (1lb) *semola rimacinata* (remilled durum wheat semolina)
- 160ml (⅔ cup) lukewarm water

For the papillote

- 300g (10½oz) mussels
- 250g (9oz) squid, cleaned and cut into rings
- 200g (7oz) raw peeled prawns
- 3 garlic cloves
- 250g (9oz) cherry tomatoes or tomato pulp
- 100ml (scant ½ cup) dry white wine
- Extra virgin olive oil
- Fresh chopped parsley
- Salt and pepper QB
- Greaseproof paper or aluminium foil for cooking *en cartoccio* (en papillote)

01 Start with the scialatielli, a short, thick pasta from the Amalfi coast. Pour the semolina onto your work surface, make a small well in it and gradually pour the lukewarm water into the centre, mixing first with a fork, then with your fingers when the dough begins to form. Knead for a good 10 minutes until the dough is soft but not sticky. Cover with a tea towel or clingfilm and leave to rest at room temperature for 30 minutes.

02 Meanwhile, prepare the seafood. Open the mussels over a high heat in a large saucepan with a little olive oil and 2 garlic cloves. As soon as the mussels open, remove them from the heat. Discard any that do not open. Set aside the mussels with their juice. Sauté the squid and prawns for 2–3 minutes in a hot frying pan with a generous dash of olive oil and the last garlic clove. Deglaze with the white wine and remove the seafood from the pan.

03 In the same pan, add the remaining juice from the mussels, add a drizzle of oil and the halved cherry tomatoes or tomato pulp. Simmer for 10 minutes to allow the flavours to develop. Adjust the seasoning and add the chopped parsley. Remove from the heat, stir in the seafood and mussels and mix gently.

04 Take your dough and turn to page 398 to learn how to shape your scialatielli. It is said that their name comes from the combination of two words in the Neapolitan dialect: *scialare*, to enjoy, and *tiella*, pan. A good omen for your dinner tonight.

05 Cook the scialatielli in a saucepan of salted boiling water. Drain and mix with the seafood sauce.

06 Cut 4 large sheets of greaseproof paper or aluminium foil, place a portion of pasta and shellfish in the centre of each one, then fold into a parcel and bake in a preheated oven for 7–8 minutes at 200°C fan/220°C/425°F/GM 7.

07 Serve your closed parcels to all your guests and unwrap your little packages around the table. No hiding gifts in the *scialatielli*.

+ **On repeat in the kitchen:** Play Rocco Granata's 1960s global hit 'Marina'. This song is the quintessence of Italian passion: fiery, joyful and devilishly catchy. A bit like your dish.

DIVINE WINES

Discover everything you need to know about Italian wine before visiting your wine merchant. Find the bottle that will transform your meal into a moment of delight with the perfect food and wine pairing. Enjoy your tasting.

CHIANTI

RED

Region: Tuscany
Grape variety: Mainly Sangiovese
Its superpower: Its acidity and tannins counterbalance rich dishes.
What should you drink it with?
It pairs perfectly with pasta dishes featuring savoury sauces such as *ragù* or pappardelle with wild boar. Chianti enhances meat dishes or rich tomato sauces, not to mention mushrooms, truffles and semi-mature cheeses.

PINOT GRIGIO DELLE VENEZIE

WHITE

Region: Veneto
Grape variety: Pinot Grigio
Its superpower: Fresh and light, it pairs well with many dishes thanks to its lively acidity and fruity notes.
What should you drink it with?
Dishes made with fresh vegetables, such as courgettes, or light salads and sauces, flavoured with extra virgin olive oil and aromatic herbs.

NERO D'AVOLA

RED

Region: Sicily
Grape variety: Nero d'Avola
Its superpower: Its supple tannins can tame spicy dishes.
What should you drink it with?
Fiery dishes: 'nduja, arrabbiata or Norma, to counterbalance the salted ricotta.

PRIMITIVO

RED

Region: Puglia
Grape variety: Primitivo
Its superpower: It pairs beautifully with rich, flavourful dishes, thanks to its full-bodied structure and fruity aromas.
What should you drink it with?
Typical Apulian recipes, such as orecchiette, but also with *pasta al forno* or with red meat sauces.

GRECO DI TUFO

WHITE

Region: Campania
Grape variety: Greco
Its superpower: Its freshness and mineral notes give it character and liveliness on the palate.
What should you drink it with?
It pairs very well with dishes based on fish or shellfish.

BAROLO

RED

Region: Piedmont
Grape variety: Nebbiolo
Its superpower: Powerful tannins, marked acidity, but with delicate notes of flowers and red fruits that enhance the powerful aromas.
What should you drink it with?
Barolo and truffle pasta is a classic pairing.

MONTEPULCIANO D'ABRUZZO

RED

Region: Abruzzo
Grape variety: Mainly Montepulciano
Its superpower: Aromas of red and black fruits punctuated with herbaceous notes, with a beautiful roundness and supple tannins that reveal the aromas.
What should you drink it with?
Ideal for taming the bold flavours of garlic, capers and olives (think *penne alla puttanesca*). Its beautiful length on the palate also stands up to the salty intensity of anchovies.

VERMENTINO

WHITE

Regions: Sardinia, Liguria, Tuscany
Grape variety: Vermentino
Its superpower: Fresh, lively and light, it reveals citrus notes and a minerality that evokes the Mediterranean terroir and the sea.
What should you drink it with?
All aromatic sauces, such as pesto, or a fresh fish dish.

LAMBRUSCO

RED SPARKLING

Region: Emilia-Romagna
Grape variety: Lambrusco
Its superpower: Sparkling, dry Lambrusco (and not sweet, which is important) rebalances the palate when faced with rich dishes.
What should you drink it with?
Hearty dishes and flavourful sauces (mushrooms, *ragù*, pesto) or baked pasta. It also pairs beautifully with local pasta dishes such as tagliatelle and tortellini.

PROSECCO DI VALDOBBIADENE

SPARKLING WHITE

Region: Veneto
Grape variety: Glera
Its superpower: Its delicate and dry taste perfectly balances salty foods.
What should you drink it with?
Pasta with shellfish such as oysters, prawns, lobster and other seafood.

IT'S A MATCH

As a little bonus, here are our 10 favourite pairings, to be enjoyed without moderation.

Risotto alla Milanese con midollo page 236

+

Valtellina superiore

To accompany your **Risotto alla Milanese con midollo**, opt for a **valtellina superiore** to discover the best that Lombardy has to offer. Nebbiolo (known locally as Chiavennasca) displays notes of red fruit, rose and earth, which echo the saffron, while its acidity cuts through the richness of the marrow and butter.

Gnocchi gorgonzola e noci page 24

+

Corvina Veronese

With **Gnocchi gorgonzola e noci**, let yourself be seduced by the velvety smoothness of **corvina veronese**. The star grape variety of Amarone, it also shines on its own: round, fruity and smooth. Its silky texture envelops the gorgonzola, whilst its subtle bitterness echoes the walnuts.

Calamarata con pesce spada, melanzane e menta page 338

+

Falanghina del Beneventano

For **Calamarata con pesce spada, melanzane e menta**, we open a **falanghina del Beneventano**. It's a favourite of ours: its notes of citrus, stone fruit and white flowers work wonders. As for the generous flesh of the swordfish, it is perfectly balanced by the mineral and aromatic freshness of the Falanghina.

Fregola nera al ragù di seppie page 40

+

Vermentino

With the **Fregola nera al *ragù* di seppie**, we'd go straight for a **vermentino**. Crisp, light and mineral, it doesn't compete with the cuttlefish ink or the fish, but simply refreshes the palate and makes you want to dive back in with your fork.

Cavatelli salsiccia e zafferano

page 36

+

Cannonau

Head to Sardinia with **Cavatelli salsiccia e zafferano**. Serve them with a **Cannonau** from the south-west of the island: black fruits, sweet spices and a hint of herbs. Full-bodied enough to rival the sausage and just the right amount of freshness to tame the saltiness of the pecorino.

Agnolotti del plin al coniglio

page 158

+

Barolo

Agnolotti del plin al coniglio calls for **Barolo**. And here, we have a more than perfect pairing. The rabbit, both delicate and deep, goes well with the fragrant and fresh Nebbiolo.

Busiate alla 'nduja page 106

+

Nero d'Avola

For **Busiate alla 'nduja**, nothing beats a well-structured **nero d'Avola**. Its juicy black fruits and velvety tannins soften the spiciness, whilst a touch of maturity tempers the heat of the chilli. The result is a real explosion of flavours.

Passatelli in brodo di carne page 104

+

Lambrusco di Sorbara

Passatelli in brodo carne is pure comfort food. Purists will say: no wine with a broth. But we reply: a dry **lambrusco di Sorbara**, please. Its pale pink, fresh and playful bubbles cleanse the palate after the broth and bring just the right amount of lightness.

Girella alla norma page 188

+

Nerello Mascalese

Girella alla norma calls for an Etna rosso. **Nerello mascalese**, nourished by volcanic soil, brings freshness, minerality and enough character to stand up to fried aubergine. The curious can explore the rosato version of the same grape variety, which is just as vibrant.

Bucatini all'amatriciana page 28

+

Rosso di Montalcino

Last but not least, for **Bucatini all'amatriciana**, it is impossible to overlook a **rosso di montalcino**. Sangiovese, with its cherry notes and pronounced acidity, balances perfectly with guanciale and tomato, as if it were created for this purpose. Juicy, earthy, delicious.

HOLY FRITTATA
Frittata di spaghetti

FOR 4 FRIENDS

- 300g (10½oz) spaghetti
- 4 eggs
- 80g (2¾oz) cooked ham
- 100g (3½oz) cheese of your choice (mozzarella, provolone, scamorza or Emmental)
- 40g (1½oz) grated Parmigiano Reggiano DOP
- 2 tbsp milk (optional, but why say no to a little sweetness?)
- Olive oil for cooking
- Salt and pepper QB

01 Cook the spaghetti *al dente* in a large saucepan of salted boiling water, then drain and leave to cool.

02 In a large bowl, beat the eggs with the Parmigiano, milk (for extra creaminess) and a little salt and pepper. Add the cold spaghetti and mix well so that it is coated in the sauce. Then stir in the ham, add the diced cheese and mix again.

03 Heat a generous drizzle of olive oil in a non-stick frying pan measuring 22–24cm (8½–9½in) in diameter. Pour in the mixture and spread it out evenly.

04 Cook over a medium-low heat for 6–8 minutes, until the base becomes crispy and golden brown.

05 Now, flip the frittata: using a large lid or plate, carefully turn it over, then continue cooking for another 4–5 minutes on the other side.

06 Allow the dish to cool slightly before cutting it into portions (equal portions – this is no time to spark drama at the table, sharing is caring!).
Next time, remember it's just as delicious served cold – perfect for a picnic on the beach or a lunch at the park. This frittata is here to make every moment special.

+ **On repeat in the kitchen:** For this typical Neapolitan dish, we hum 'Don Raffae' by Fabrizio de André whilst tapping our feet and clapping our hands. An ode to Naples and its dialect that resonates perfectly with this generous and sunny frittata.

PASTA MISTA CECI FAGIOLI E MOLLUSCHI

A love story between land and sea

FOR 4 FRIENDS

- 300g (10½oz) pasta mista, a delightful mix of pasta shapes that originated in the kitchens of southern Italy as a way to reduce waste. Today, it can be found ready-made in grocery stores, but there's nothing stopping you from making your own mix at home
- 500g (1lb 2oz) mussels
- 500g (1lb 2oz) clams (or cockles)
- 200g (7oz) cooked chickpeas (or from a jar)
- 200g (7oz) cooked cannellini beans (or other white beans)
- 1 shallot or small onion
- 1 stalk of celery (optional)
- 1 red chilli (fresh or dried, whatever you prefer)
- Extra virgin olive oil
- A bunch of fresh flat-leaf parsley
- Salt and pepper QB

01 Heat a generous dash of olive oil in a large, hot pan. Add the freshly rinsed mussels and clams, pour in a little water, cover and leave them to open gently. Without burning yourself, remove the shells from most of the seafood, but not all of them. We'll use them for a Michelin-starred presentation. Strain the cooking water and set aside this delicious, sea-salty liquid.

02 In a large saucepan or casserole dish (Dutch oven), sauté the finely chopped shallot (and a little celery if you like) with a drizzle of olive oil. Add the chilli, but only if you like spicy sauces. Fry gently and add the chickpeas and beans. Simmer for a few minutes.

03 Place the uncooked *pasta mista* directly into the pan and add the strained juice from the shellfish. Cook your pasta gradually, adding water ladle by ladle as it cooks, stirring over a medium heat for 12–15 minutes (the best way to check if it is cooked: taste it). Add a little hot water if you see that the liquid is evaporating too quickly and the mixture is becoming too dry. Be careful, it must not stick to the bottom of the pan. We're counting on you.

04 A few minutes before the end of cooking, add the shelled mussels and clams and stir gently to distribute the flavours evenly. Your kitchen should smell like the Mediterranean.

05 Remove from the heat, add a generous drizzle of olive oil, a sprinkling of fresh parsley and a twist of pepper. A little tip: taste before adding salt, since the shellfish and sea water may already be enough.

06 Arrange on pretty, deep plates, remembering to add the mussels and clams that still have their shells on top for decoration. *Bellissimo.*

\+ **On repeat in the kitchen:** The combination of beans and seafood originated in Campania and more specifically in Naples. A wonderful opportunity to play Pink Martini's 'Una notte a Napoli' and break into a few dance steps in the kitchen. Or not . . . you're the boss!

CHAPTER 2
STUFFED PASTA

LAMB-ORGHINI

Girelle alla polenta e mascarpone con ragù agnello

FOR 4 FRIENDS

For the girelle

- 200g (7oz) type 00 flour
- 150g (5¼oz) *semola rimacinata* (remilled durum wheat semolina)
- 8 egg yolks

For the filling

- 120g (4¼oz) fine cornmeal specifically for polenta
- 100g (3½oz) mascarpone
- 40g (1½oz) grated Parmigiano Reggiano DOP
- 500ml (2 cups) salted water
- Freshly ground black pepper QB

For the spicy lamb *ragù*

- 400g (14oz) boneless lamb shoulder, cut into small pieces
- 1 medium onion
- 1 carrot
- 1 stalk of celery
- 2 garlic cloves
- 300g (10½oz) crushed tinned or fresh tomatoes, peeled just before use for authenticity
- 1 glass of red wine
- 2 tbsp extra virgin olive oil
- 1 small fresh or dried red chilli pepper
- 1 sprig of rosemary
- Salt and freshly ground black pepper QB

For the *bagnetto verde* (delicious Piedmontese parsley sauce)

- 1 bunch of fresh flat-leaf parsley
- 1 small garlic clove
- 3 anchovy fillets in oil (optional)
- 1 tbsp desalted capers
- 80ml (⅓ cup) extra virgin olive oil
- 1 tbsp white wine vinegar
- A few sprigs of dill for the finishing touch
- Salt and freshly ground black pepper QB

01 Prepare the spicy lamb *ragù*. In a large saucepan, heat a generous dash of olive oil and sauté the onion, carrot and finely chopped celery over a low heat for 8 minutes. Add the minced garlic and chilli pepper (adjust the chilli according to your tolerance level). Add the lamb in small pieces, brown it over a high heat for a few minutes before deglazing with the red wine. Allow the alcohol to evaporate, add the crushed or peeled tomatoes and flavour with rosemary. Season with salt and pepper, cover and simmer for about 1 hour 30 minutes, until the meat is tender and the sauce has thickened.

02 On the work surface, pile the flour and semolina to create a small well. Place the egg yolks in the middle of the well, then beat them with a fork until you obtain a smooth dough. Knead by hand for 10–12 minutes: the dough should become supple, or even elastic. Cover with clingfilm and set aside for at least 30 minutes.

03 Bring 500ml (2 cups) of salted water to the boil and pour in the cornmeal in a fine stream whilst stirring. Cook for 20 minutes (or according to the instructions on the packet) until the polenta is nice and creamy. Remove from the heat, stir in the mascarpone and Parmigiano, season with pepper, then leave to cool until the mixture firms up. This is important because if the filling remains too runny, it may escape during cooking.

04 Next, make the *bagnetto verde*. In a mortar, for purists with the right equipment, or in a blender for the rest, purée the parsley, garlic, capers and anchovies. Then add the vinegar, followed by a drizzle of olive oil, until you obtain a silky green sauce. Taste and season with salt and pepper.

05 Once the dough has rested, roll it out thinly with a rolling pin or pasta machine on a floured work surface and turn to page 394 to learn how to fill and shape your girelles.

+ **On repeat in the kitchen:** A true ode to resilience, 'Combattente' by Fiorella Mannoia is a call to never give up. A song that is perfect for this recipe and, after all, for life in general. You are amazing, never forget that.

06 Cook the pasta in a large saucepan of simmering salted water for about 3 minutes and drain.

07 The final step, but we promise it's worth it: sauté the girelle in a little lamb *ragù* in a frying pan to coat them thoroughly. The melt-in-the-mouth mascarpone combined with the spicy *ragù* is what makes this recipe so magical.

08 Move on to plating. Arrange each girella on a plate, top with a ladleful of *ragù* and add a few drops of *bagnetto verde* for contrast and some sprigs of dill. It's a real work of art, so bring out your best dish – the idea is to make it look appealing. Right.

ANOLINI IN BRODO

A porcini opera in a bowl

FOR 4 FRIENDS

<u>For the anolini</u>
- 200g (7oz) type 00 flour
- 150g (5¼oz) *semola rimacinata* (durum wheat semolina)
- 8 egg yolks

<u>For the meat filling</u>
- 200g (7oz) minced beef (or a mixture of beef and veal, which we love)
- 50g (1¾oz) finely chopped mortadella or cooked ham
- 40g (1½oz) grated Parmigiano Reggiano DOP
- 1 small organic or free-range egg
- 1 shallot
- 1 tbsp breadcrumbs (optional)
- 1 tbsp olive oil
- A pinch of grated nutmeg (optional)
- Salt and black pepper QB

<u>For the mushroom stock</u>
- 25g (generous ¾oz) dried porcini mushrooms
- 1 carrot
- 1 stalk of celery
- 1 small onion
- 1 bay leaf
- Black pepper QB

01 Start by preparing the pasta. On your work surface, pile the flour and semolina and form a small well. Place the egg yolks in the middle of the well, then beat them with a fork until you obtain a smooth dough. Knead by hand for 10–12 minutes. The dough should become soft and elastic. Cover with clingfilm and set aside for at least 30 minutes.

02 Soak the dried porcini mushrooms in warm water for 20–30 minutes. Drain them, carefully reserving the soaking water, then strain the liquid through a fine sieve or chinois.

03 In a saucepan, add the chopped onion, carrot and celery, then add the rehydrated mushrooms, bay leaf, strained soaking water and a little cold water. Bring to the boil, simmer gently over a low heat for 40 minutes, then strain your mixture: you will obtain a clear and fragrant broth, which is exactly what we want here.

04 In a frying pan, sauté the finely chopped shallot in a generous drizzle of olive oil. Add the finely minced meat and allow it to brown. Remove from the heat and allow to cool.

05 In a salad bowl, combine the meat, chopped mortadella, Parmigiano, breadcrumbs, egg, a pinch of salt, pepper and a dash of grated nutmeg, making sure not to forget anything. Mix until you obtain a smooth filling that is neither too dry nor too wet – if necessary, add a few more breadcrumbs.

06 Roll out the dough thinly (with a rolling pin or pasta machine) and fill and shape the anolini (see page 393).

07 Bring the mushroom broth to a gentle boil, add the anolini and cook for 3–4 minutes, until they rise to the surface. Serve immediately in deep plates with the steaming broth. This dish is so comforting that you owe it to yourself to enjoy it whilst watching a film, reading a book, or a meaningful conversation such as 'Where should we go on holiday next summer?' or 'How does Inception really end?'

\+ **On repeat in the kitchen:** A nostalgic broth, gourmet anolini, the scent of the forest floor filling the house – could this be happiness? We listen to Marco Mengoni's 'L'essenziale', a reminder to focus on what really matters.

AGNOLOTTI DEL PLIN AL CONIGLIO

It's game on

FOR 4 FRIENDS

For the agnolotti del plin
- 300g (10½oz) type 00 flour
- 225g *semola rimacinata* (remilled durum wheat semolina)
- 300g (10½oz) egg yolks (fresh and free-range)

For the rabbit filling
- 400g (14oz) boneless rabbit meat (leg or saddle)
- 1 small carrot
- 1 stalk of celery
- 1 small onion
- 1 garlic clove
- 1 sprig of rosemary
- 2 tbsp dry white wine
- 1 egg
- 40–50g (1½–1¾oz) grated Parmigiano Reggiano DOP
- Extra virgin olive oil
- Salt and pepper QB

For the sauce
- 80g (2¾oz) unsalted butter
- Fresh sage
- Meat juices (those from cooking your rabbit will be perfect)
- Grated Parmigiano Reggiano DOP (optional)

01 On a clean work surface, form a well with the flour and semolina, then pour the egg yolks into the centre. Mix with a fork at first, and when the dough begins to form, knead by hand for a good 10 minutes until it is supple but not sticky. Cover with a tea towel or clingfilm and leave to rest for 30 minutes at room temperature.

02 Finely chop the carrot, onion and celery and gently fry them in a generous amount of olive oil with the whole or halved garlic clove. Add the rabbit cut into small pieces and the sprig of rosemary, and let everything brown gently. Deglaze with the white wine (and pour a glass for yourself. Cheers!). Cover and simmer over a low heat for about 25–30 minutes. Don't stray too far, you need to make sure it doesn't stick and add a little water from time to time if necessary.

03 Once the meat is cooked, leave it to cool, then remove the garlic and rosemary, which have now given all they have. Place the meat and vegetables in a large bowl and scrape the bottom of the pan (or casserole dish) to collect the caramelised juices. Strain this meat juice (liquid gold) through a sieve and set aside in a small bowl.

04 Finely chop the meat and vegetables, then mix them with the egg, Parmigiano and a little salt and pepper. Taste and adjust the seasoning.

05 Take your dough and roll it out thinly with a rolling pin or pasta machine. Using our guide on page 394, fill and shape your *agnolotti del plin* – small Piedmontese ravioli pinched by hand (the famous *plin*) – then place them on your floured work surface.

06 Melt the unsalted butter in a frying pan with a few sage leaves until it turns a nice hazelnut colour.

07 Cook the agnolotti for about 2 minutes in a large saucepan of salted water, drain, then toss them in the sage butter.

08 Serve the pasta in a deep plate and coat generously with your reduced rabbit juice. For those with a sweet tooth, add a final sprinkling of grated Parmigiano and it's ready. Well done, *maestro*.

\+ **On repeat in the kitchen:** Play 'Nuova ossessione' by the Piedmontese band Subsonica. A hit from the 2000s that perfectly matches the atmosphere of little '*agnolotti del plin*', which may well become your new culinary obsession.

FAMIGLIA CIUFO

Nino, Dafne & Iris

MINTURNO

YOU'RE MY LOBSTER

Cappellacci burrata e astice

FOR 4 FRIENDS

<u>For the capellacci</u>

- 200g (7oz) type 00 flour
- 150g (5½oz) *semola rimacinata* (remilled durum wheat semolina)
- 8 egg yolks

<u>For the lobster</u>

- 1 lobster weighing 600–700g (1lb 5oz–1½lb) (or 2 small lobsters weighing 400g/14oz each)
- Coarse salt for cooking

<u>For the filling</u>

- 250g (9oz) well-drained burrata (or stracciatella)
- 40g (1½oz) grated Parmigiano Reggiano DOP
- Salt and freshly ground black pepper QB

<u>For the tomato sauce</u>

- 300g (10½oz) fresh datterino tomatoes (or good quality tinned tomatoes)
- 2 tbsp extra virgin olive oil
- 1 garlic clove, squashed with the blade of a knife but kept whole
- A few fresh basil leaves
- Salt and pepper QB

01 Start by preparing the pasta dough. Tip the flour and semolina on your work surface and form a small well. Place the egg yolks in the middle and beat them with a fork until you obtain a smooth dough. Knead by hand for 10–12 minutes, the dough should become soft and elastic. Cover with clingfilm and set aside for at least 30 minutes. Just enough time to listen to the album *Half Hour of Power* by Sum 41 – let's face it: lucky you.

02 Bring a large pot of salted water to the boil and plunge the lobster(s) into it. Cook for about 8 minutes (feel free to adjust the cooking time according to its size, or even ask your fishmonger for advice). Drain, leave to cool, then shell the body and claws, and cut the flesh into even pieces. Set aside.

03 Heat 2 tablespoons of olive oil in a frying pan and gently fry the lightly squashed whole garlic clove. Add the halved tomatoes and sauté everything quickly over a high heat so that the tomatoes caramelise slightly. Reduce the heat and simmer for a further 5 minutes to obtain a silky, fragrant sauce. Season with salt and pepper, add a few basil leaves, then remove the garlic.

04 Now for the filling: mix the well-drained burrata (or stracciatella) with the Parmigiano, salt and pepper. Be careful: the filling should be creamy but not too soft, or it may escape during cooking.

05 Roll out the dough thinly with a rolling pin or pasta machine and turn to page 391 to find out how to fill and shape your pasta into hats (*cappello*, hat, voilà).

06 Cook the cappellacci for 3–4 minutes in a large saucepan of salted boiling water, drain them carefully then, over a low heat, sauté them in a frying pan with the tomato sauce. Add the pieces of lobster and mix gently, just long enough to heat them through without overdoing it. Overcooked lobster is a no-go.

07 Immediately arrange the cappellacci and tomato-lobster sauce in deep plates. Add a few leaves of fresh basil and a drizzle of extra virgin olive oil, then enjoy this exceptional dish by closing your eyes and reminding yourself how beautiful life is.

+ **On repeat in the kitchen:** You'll instantly fall in love with this recipe, so listen to 'Mi sono innamorato di te' by Luigi Tenco, a romantic song perfect for an intimate meal.

HEY, NICE MULLET

Bottoni al nero di seppia con guazzetto e triglie

FOR 4 FRIENDS

For the bottoni
- 1 tsp cuttlefish ink
- 200g (7oz) type 00 flour
- 150g (5½oz) *semola rimacinata* (remilled durum wheat semolina)
- 8 egg yolks

For the filling
- 250g (9oz) drained ricotta
- 30g (1oz) grated Parmigiano Reggiano DOP
- Grated zest of 1 organic or unwaxed lemon
- Salt and freshly ground black pepper QB

For the *guazzetto*
- 400g (14oz) ripe cherry tomatoes
- 2 whole garlic cloves, squashed with the blade of a knife but kept whole
- 4 tbsp extra virgin olive oil
- 1 small fresh or dried chilli pepper (for the hot and spicy team)
- 100ml (scant ½ cup) dry white wine
- Dill and basil
- Salt and black pepper QB

For the fish
- 4 fresh red mullet fillets, all bones removed
- Olive oil
- Fleur de sel

01 Start with the cuttlefish ink bottoni dough. On a clean work surface, pour the flour and semolina into a small mound, make a well in the centre and add the egg yolks and cuttlefish ink. Knead until you obtain a soft black dough. Cover with clingfilm and leave to rest for 30 minutes at room temperature.

02 Next, prepare the filling. Mix together the ricotta, Parmigiano, lemon zest, season with salt and pepper and set aside in the fridge.

03 Now prepare the guazzetto, a traditional sauce from southern Italy that has been adopted throughout the peninsula in various local forms. For this version, heat a generous dash of olive oil with the lightly squashed garlic cloves and a little chilli pepper in a frying pan. Add the halved cherry tomatoes and sauté them over a high heat. Deglaze with the white wine, allow it to evaporate, then simmer for about 10 minutes, until you obtain a light and fragrant sauce. Season with salt and pepper and sprinkle with chopped basil and dill. Remove the garlic before serving.

04 Once the dough has rested, roll it out very thinly with a rolling pin or pasta machine and go to page 393 for instructions on how to fill and shape your small buttons.

05 After that, cook the pasta in a large saucepan of salted boiling water for 3–4 minutes, drain it gently and coat the bottoni with *guazzetto*.

06 Last but not least: the red mullet. Drizzle the fillets with olive oil and season with a pinch of fleur de sel, then quickly sear them skin-side down in a hot non-stick frying pan. 1–2 minutes is enough: the flesh should remain pearly white, as red mullet is a delicate fish that does not tolerate high heat. Like many of us over the years, if we're being honest.

07 Now it's time to plate up. Arrange the bottoni in the centre of the plates, coat them with the fragrant *guazzetto*, then carefully place your red mullet fillets in small pieces on top of the pasta. A final drizzle of olive oil, a pinch of fleur de sel, a few sprigs of dill and basil leaves, and it's a feast.

\+ **On repeat in the kitchen:** Obviously, for these bottoni with squid ink, play 'Vedo nero' ('I see black') by Zucchero. Let's see you do a little dance as you serve the dish to your guests.

PEDAL TO THE NETTLE
Mezzelune all'ortica

FOR 4 FRIENDS

For the nettle mezzelune
- 290g (10¼oz) type 00 flour
- 290g (10¼oz) *semola rimacinata* (remilled durum wheat semolina)
- 6 egg yolks
- 200g (7oz) fresh nettle leaves (or young shoots)
- carefully washed

For the filling
- 250g (9oz) well-drained ricotta
- 40g (1½oz) grated Parmigiano Reggiano DOP
- A pinch of grated nutmeg (optional)
- 50g (1¾oz) finely chopped blanched nettles, if you want a more vegetal and aromatic filling (optional)
- Salt and freshly ground black pepper QB

For seasoning
- 80g (2¾oz) unsalted butter
- 60g (2oz) grated Parmigiano Reggiano DOP

01 Start with the dough. Bring a pan of water to the boil and blanch the nettles for 5 minutes to remove their sting. Drain them, refresh them in ice-cold water, then squeeze them thoroughly to remove any excess water. Next, blend them with the egg yolks until you obtain a smooth purée. On a clean work surface, pour the flour and semolina into a small mound, make a well in the centre and add the egg and nettle mixture. Knead the mixture until you obtain a smooth, elastic dough. Cover with clingfilm and leave to rest for 30 minutes at room temperature.

02 For the filling, mix the ricotta with the Parmigiano, a little salt, pepper and a pinch of nutmeg, if you like. If you have chosen the option with extra nettles, add your 50g (1¾oz) of finely chopped blanched nettles to this mixture.

03 Once the dough has rested, roll it out thinly with a rolling pin or pasta machine (if you don't have one, you can always knock on your handsome neighbour's door and check if he/she has one?), then go to page 393 to fill and shape your half-moons.

04 Next, cook the mezzelune for 3–4 minutes in a large saucepan of salted boiling water and drain them carefully.

05 In a large frying pan, gently melt the butter, add the mezzelune and coat them delicately. Serve immediately (to your neighbour or the neighbour across the street?) with grated Parmigiano. *Buon appetito.*

+ **On repeat in the kitchen:** Why not go and pick some nettles while humming 'Uno tranquillo' by Riccardo Del Turco?

AGNOLOTTI DEL PLIN ALLA VIGNAROLA

Spring it on me

FOR 4 FRIENDS

For the agnolotti del plin

- 200g (7oz) type 00 flour
- 150g (5¼oz) *semola rimacinata* (remilled durum wheat semolina)
- 8 egg yolks

For the filling

- 250g (9oz) well-drained ricotta
- 40g (1½oz) grated Parmigiano Reggiano DOP
- A pinch of grated nutmeg (optional)
- Salt and freshly ground black pepper QB

For the pea cream

- 250g (9oz) fresh peas (or frozen if you're making this recipe in November)
- 1 shallot
- 1 tbsp extra virgin olive oil
- 50ml (scant ¼ cup) vegetable stock (see page 317 for the homemade recipe)
- Salt and freshly ground black pepper QB

For the *vignarola* (a typical Roman spring vegetable stir-fry)

- 100g (3½oz) artichoke hearts
- 100g (3½oz) fresh broad beans
- 100g (3½oz) fresh peas
- 1 spring onion
- 3 tbsp extra virgin olive oil
- Fresh mint leaves
- Salt and freshly ground black pepper QB

For the crispy *guanciale*

- 100g (3½oz) *guanciale*, cut into thin strips

01 Tip the flour and semolina on the work surface and form a small well in the middle. Place the egg yolks in the well, then beat them with a fork until you obtain a smooth dough. Knead by hand for 10–12 minutes. Cover with clingfilm and set aside for at least 30 minutes.

02 Prepare the filling by mixing the ricotta with the Parmigiano, a little salt, pepper and nutmeg.

03 In a frying pan, sauté the chopped shallot in 1 tablespoon of olive oil, then add the peas and stock. Cook for 8–10 minutes. Blend thoroughly, season and pass through a sieve to obtain a smooth, silky sauce. Set aside. For the record, *vignarola* sauce takes its name from the *vignaroli* who worked in the vineyards and vegetable gardens around Rome and celebrated the arrival of spring by cooking the first vegetables of the season. Anyway, heat the 3 tablespoons of olive oil in a frying pan, add the chopped spring onion, then the cleaned and chopped artichokes. Sauté for 5 minutes. Add the broad beans and peas, and sauté quickly to keep the vegetables crisp. Season with salt and pepper and set aside.

04 Once the dough has rested, roll it out thinly with a rolling pin or pasta machine if you have one (if not, this is your chance to rekindle your *vignarole* solidarity with your kind neighbours), then turn to page 394 to fill and shape your plin.

05 Fry the strips of *guanciale* over a low heat until golden brown and crispy, then drain them on kitchen paper.

06 Cook the plin for 3–4 minutes in a large saucepan of salted boiling water and drain them gently.

07 Now it's time to plate up. Spoon a little pea cream into each dish, place the plin on top, sprinkle with *vignarola* and mint leaves. Add a few strips of crispy *guanciale* on top. Thank you, Romans.

+ **On repeat in the kitchen:** Giorgio Poi and Calcutta's 'La musica italiana', a tribute to all Italian songs which, when you're missing Italy, 'add a little nostalgia to your plate of pasta'. Their words, but we couldn't agree more.

GROW A PEAR

Cappellacci ricotta, gorgonzola e pere

FOR 4 FRIENDS

For the cappellacci
- 200g (7oz) type 00 flour
- 150g (5¼oz) *semola rimacinata* (remilled durum wheat semolina)
- 8 egg yolks

For the filling
- 200g (7oz) well-drained ricotta
- 100g (3½oz) mild gorgonzola
- 1 sweet pear, such as Williams or Comice
- Salt and freshly ground black pepper QB

For the pear crisps (chips)
- 1 firm pear, such as Conference or Williams
- A few drops of organic or unwaxed lemon juice

For the Parmigiano crumble
- 40g (1½oz) grated Parmigiano Reggiano DOP
- 20g (¾oz) plain flour
- 20g (¾oz) cold butter, cut into small cubes
- Black pepper QB

For the sauce
- 80g (2¾oz) butter
- 6–8 fresh sage leaves
- 40g (1½oz) whole hazelnuts, toasted and roughly chopped

01 Preheat the oven to 100°C fan/120°C/250°F/GM ¼. For the crisps, slice the firm pear very thinly – ideally with a mandoline – then sprinkle lightly with lemon juice. Place on a baking tray lined with greaseproof paper and dry in the oven for 1½–2 hours until the crisps are ultra-crunchy.

02 Next, prepare the pasta dough. Mix the flour and semolina on your work surface and form a small well. Place the egg yolks in the middle of the well, then beat them in with a fork until you obtain a smooth dough. Knead by hand for 10–12 minutes. The dough should become soft and elastic. Cover with clingfilm and set aside for at least 30 minutes.

03 Meanwhile, mix the Parmigiano, flour, cold butter and a little black pepper until you have a sandy texture for your crumble. Spread the mixture on a baking tray lined with greaseproof paper and bake in a preheated oven at 180°C fan/200°C/400°F/GM 6 for 8–10 minutes until the dough is golden brown. Leave to cool, then crumble.

04 For the filling, mix the ricotta with the crumbled gorgonzola, add the finely diced pear and season lightly. To help you be more precise when filling your cappellacci, we recommend putting the mixture into a piping bag.

05 Once rested, roll out your dough with a rolling pin or pasta machine and turn to page 391 to fill and shape your little gems.

06 Next melt the butter in a frying pan, add the sage and leave to infuse gently until the sauce takes on a lovely hazelnut colour and fills the kitchen with its aroma. In another pan, toast the hazelnuts then crush them coarsely.

07 Cook the cappellacci for 3–4 minutes in a large saucepan of salted boiling water, drain them, then coat in the sage butter.

08 Time to plate up: arrange the cappellacci on each plate, sprinkle with the Parmigiano crumble and toasted hazelnuts, and finish with 1–2 pear crisps on top for decoration.

+ **On repeat in the kitchen:** Like Tony Renis' hit song 'Quando, quando, quando', the combination of gorgonzola and pear is a timeless classic. Take the opportunity to improvise a little cha-cha-cha in the *cucina*.

KIND OF A BIG VEAL

Culurgiones al vitello e salsa verde

FOR 4 FRIENDS

For the culurgiones

- 200g (7oz) type 00 flour
- 150g (5¼oz) *semola rimacinata* (remilled durum wheat semolina)
- 8 egg yolks

For the filling

- 350g (12oz) veal (shoulder or neck, depending on what you can find at your butcher's)
- 1 small onion
- 1 garlic clove
- 1 sprig of rosemary
- 1 tbsp tomato paste
- 50g (1¾oz) grated Parmigiano Reggiano DOP
- Extra virgin olive oil
- Salt and pepper QB

For the green sauce

- 1 bunch of fresh flat-leaf parsley
- ½ garlic clove
- 2 anchovy fillets in oil (optional)
- 1 tbsp desalted capers
- 40ml (2½ tbsp) white wine vinegar
- 70ml (scant ⅓ cup) extra virgin olive oil
- 30g (1oz) breadcrumbs soaked in vinegar
- Salt QB

For the meat juices

- 200g (7oz) meat of your choice (or bones)
- 1 small carrot
- 1 shallot
- 1 garlic clove
- 1 tbsp tomato paste
- 200ml (generous ¾ cup) white wine
- 500ml (2 cups) meat stock of your choice (see recipe on page 316)
- 1 sprig of thyme
- 1 bay leaf
- 1 knob of butter

For the finishing touch

- 50g (1¾oz) butter
- 30g (1oz) toasted pine nuts
- A few fresh mint leaves

01 Pour the semolina and flour onto your work surface, make a small well in the middle and add the egg yolks. Mix with a fork at first, then with your fingers when the dough begins to form. Knead for 10 minutes until it becomes supple. Cover with a tea towel or clingfilm and leave to rest for 30 minutes at room temperature.

02 Meanwhile, start preparing your meat juices. In a hot pan with a drizzle of olive oil, brown the pieces of meat until they stick slightly to the bottom. Add the chopped shallot, carrot and garlic, and the tomato paste. Allow to caramelise for 1–2 minutes, then deglaze with the white wine. Scrape the bottom of the pan to collect all the juices, pour in the stock, add the herbs and simmer gently for 15–20 minutes. Strain, return to the heat, and reduce for another 5–10 minutes for maximum flavour. Remove from the heat and whisk in the knob of butter to obtain a silky, indulgent sauce.

03 Prepare the filling: in a frying pan, sauté the chopped onion, minced garlic and rosemary in a generous dash of olive oil. Add the diced veal and brown well. Stir in the tomato paste, season with salt and pepper and simmer for 30 minutes. Remove the rosemary, allow to cool, then finely chop the mixture with a knife or blender before mixing with Parmigiano. The filling mix should be smooth and compact.

04 Prepare the sauce by blending the parsley, garlic, the anchovies, capers, soaked breadcrumbs, vinegar and oil until you obtain a smooth cream. Adjust the seasoning and set aside.

\+ **On repeat in the kitchen:** These cheerful touches of colour make us long for lightness and freedom. So let's listen to 'La Rondine' ('The Swallow') by Mango to make every bite a little trip.

05 Once your dough has rested, roll it out thinly with a rolling pin or pasta machine and go to page 395 to fill and shape your culurgiones.

06 Cook the pasta in salted boiling water for 4–5 minutes then sauté in a frying pan with 50g melted butter.

07 Serve the pasta in a deep plate, add a few spoonfuls of green sauce and meat juice, sprinkle with toasted pine nuts and garnish with a few fresh mint leaves before the big tasting, during which you can boast about having made something as beautiful as it is delicious. Why not invite your mother-in-law?

MANTECARE

A word to remember, the method to adopt

Mantecare – behind this musical-sounding term lies an Italian cooking technique to adopt for all your pasta dishes, creating an almost magical binding agent that will make all the difference when you taste it.

The first step to mastering the art of *mantecatura* to perfection is to reserve a few ladles of the pasta cooking water before draining the pasta. This is the ultimate secret, as that cooking water contains all the starch needed to achieve the ideal texture.

After that, finish cooking the pasta in a frying pan with the ingredients of your recipe and add the cooking water. Then let everything bind together by moving your wrist backwards and forwards so that the contents of the frying pan are tossed into the air without losing a single drop. This small physical and technical gesture will elevate you to the rank of chef and turn your dish into a feast that no wooden spoon could ever match.

CULURGIONES SARDI

Braided treasures

FOR 4 FRIENDS

For the culurgiones

- 200g (7oz) type 00 flour
- 150g (5¼oz) *semola rimacinata* (remilled durum wheat semolina)
- 8 egg yolks

For the filling

- 500g (1lb 2oz) yellow floury potatoes
- 150g (5¼oz) mature Pecorino Sardo
- 2 tbsp Pecorino fresco or fresh sheep's cheese
- 2–3 tbsp extra virgin olive oil
- 1–2 small garlic cloves
- 8–10 fresh mint leaves
- Salt and black pepper QB

For the sauce

- 400g (14oz) *passata di pomodoro* (get motivated, we'll slip you the recipe on page 270)
- 2 tbsp olive oil
- 1 small garlic clove
- A pinch of salt
- A little grated pecorino cheese (optional, but why not?)

01 Pour the semolina and flour onto your work surface, make a small well in the middle and add the egg yolks. Mix with a fork first then with your fingers when the dough begins to form. Knead for a good 10 minutes until the dough is soft (but not sticky). Cover with a tea towel or clingfilm and leave to rest for 30 minutes at room temperature. This is a great opportunity to sort through your spices and condiments in the cupboards, as expiry dates can quickly pass and there are often some relics hanging around.

02 Next, make the filling. Boil the potatoes (with their skins on). Peel and mash them into a fine purée whilst still hot. Mix with the grated Pecorino, crushed garlic, chopped fresh mint and olive oil, then season with salt and pepper. Leave to rest in the fridge for 30 minutes.

03 Take your dough, roll it out thinly with a rolling pin or pasta machine and start filling and shaping the culurgiones. These Sardinian ravioli, braided by hand into the shape of a wheat ear, come straight from Ogliastra and mark the end of the harvest or large family celebrations. A recipe that has been passed down from generation to generation and requires a little dexterity. But don't panic: we explain how to do it on page 395.

04 For the sauce, fry the garlic in a large pan in a generous dash of olive oil. Add the *passata* and salt, then simmer for 15–20 minutes.

05 Next cook your culurgiones in a large quantity of salted boiling water (about 3–4 minutes).

06 Now it's time to plate up. Coat your serving dish or the bottom of each plate with a ladleful of tomato sauce, then place your little gems on top. A sprinkling of pecorino cheese, and you're done.

+ **On repeat in the kitchen:** Cesare Cremonini's 'Sardegna' is not a gimicky song, it's an intimate postcard, a summer memory frozen in emotion, like these little jewels of culurgiones.

CAPPELLACCI CON CONIGLIO ALLA CACCIATORA

Bunny and Clyde

FOR 4 FRIENDS

For the cappellacci

- 200g (7oz) type 00 flour
- 150g (5½oz) *semola rimacinata* (remilled durum wheat semolina)
- 8 egg yolks

For the filling

- 500g (1lb 2oz) boneless rabbit (legs or saddle)
- ½ onion
- 1 garlic clove
- A little rosemary
- 1 glass of dry white wine
- 1 tbsp tomato paste
- 1 dash of olive oil
- 50g (1¾oz) ricotta
- Salt and black pepper QB

For the beurre blanc

- 50ml (scant ¼ cup) dry white wine
- 1 tbsp white vinegar
- 1 shallot
- 100g (3½oz) cold butter
- Salt and white pepper QB

For the Pecorino *fonduta*

- 100ml (scant ½ cup) double cream
- 50g (1¾oz) grated Pecorino Romano DOP
- White pepper QB

For the olive powder

- 30g (1oz) black olives

For the finishing touch

- A few leaves of fresh marjoram

01 Start with the olive powder. Once washed, dried and pitted, spread the olives out on a baking tray lined with greaseproof paper, then bake in a preheated oven at 90°C fan/110°C/230°F/GM ¼ for 2–3 hours. Leave to cool, then blend finely in a food processor or spice mill until you obtain a very fine powder.

02 For the filling: sauté the whole garlic, roughly chopped onion and rosemary sprig with a generous drizzle of olive oil in a large saucepan. Add the chopped rabbit and tomato paste, then deglaze with the white wine. Cover halfway with water, lower the heat and simmer over a low heat for 1 hour and 15 minutes.

03 On a clean work surface, pour the flour and semolina into a small mound, make a well in the centre and add the egg yolks. Knead until you obtain a smooth dough. Cover with clingfilm and leave to rest for 30 minutes at room temperature.

04 Once cooked, drain the rabbit. Strain the cooking liquid (reduce it until you have a nice, fragrant syrup) and shred the meat. Mix it with the ricotta, season with salt and pepper and add 1 spoonful of the reduced rabbit stock.

05 Make a beurre blanc: in a saucepan, reduce the white wine, vinegar and chopped shallot over a low heat. Once only a syrupy base remains, remove from the heat. Add the cold butter, cut into cubes, little by little, whisking continuously: it's the emulsion that works the magic. Season with salt and pepper. Take off the heat and set aside.

06 For your Pecorino *fonduta*, pour the cream and grated Pecorino into a small saucepan, warm over a low heat and whisk gently until the sauce thickens. Be careful not to let it boil. Season generously with pepper and, if the texture is not perfectly smooth, blend in a mixer.

07 Retrieve your dough and proceed to the filling and folding workshop for these little hats, using our instructions on page 391. Cook your cappellacci for 2–4 minutes in a pan of salted boiling water. Drain and toss the pasta in the beurre blanc.

08 Time to plate up: arrange the cappellacci in a deep plate, top with the Pecorino *fonduta* and meat juices, and finish with black olive powder and a few fresh marjoram leaves. The hunt for the last cappellaccio is on.

TORTELLINI EMILIANI
An ode to Emilia-Romagna

FOR 4 FRIENDS

For the tortellini
- 200g (7oz) type 00 flour
- 150g (5¼oz) *semola rimacinata* (remilled durum wheat semolina)
- 8 egg yolks

For the filling
- 100g (3½oz) *lonza* or pork loin
- 100g (3½oz) Prosciutto di Parma
- 100g (3½oz) mortadella from Bologna IGP
- 1 egg
- 100g (3½oz) grated Parmigiano Reggiano DOP (aged at least 24 months)
- Nutmeg
- Black pepper QB

For the Parmigiano Reggiano DOP cream
- 200ml (generous ¾ cup) double cream
- 120g (4¼oz) finely grated Parmigiano Reggiano DOP (aged 24 or 30 months)
- Pepper QB

For the balsamic vinegar reduction
- 100ml (scant ½ cup) Modena IGP balsamic vinegar
- 1 tbsp honey (optional, but those with a sweet tooth will appreciate it)

01 On a work surface, pour the flour and semolina into a small mound, make a well in the centre and add the egg yolks. Knead until you have a smooth dough. Cover with clingfilm and leave to rest for 30 minutes at room temperature.

02 Finely chop all the meat. Add an egg, Parmigiano, a twist of pepper, a grating of nutmeg and mix everything together.

03 For the cream: gently heat the cream, add the grated Parmigiano and whisk without boiling. If necessary, use a hand blender to achieve a smooth texture. Season with pepper.

04 Pour the balsamic vinegar into a small saucepan, heat over a medium heat and reduce by half until it reaches a syrupy consistency. Add the honey for extra sweetness and set aside.

05 Take out your dough and roll it out very thinly with a rolling pin or pasta machine if you're lucky enough to have one handy. To fill and shape tortellino, the delicate little ring-shaped pasta from Emilia-Romagna, see page 392.

06 Cook the tortellini in a large saucepan of salted boiling water until they rise to the surface (usually after 3–4 minutes). Drain them carefullly with a slotted spoon.

07 Arrange your jewels in a deep plate. Drizzle with a generous amount of Parmigiano cream then with a little balsamic vinegar reduction and finish with a twist of pepper. Serve the family then hold for applause.

+ **On repeat in the kitchen:** Just a few notes of the popular anthem 'Romagna mia' by Casadei gets the crowds going at village festivals or weddings in Italy. Even the youngest know it, and it's often hummed by grandparents in their kitchens. So, shall we waltz?

PIRAMIDI ALL'AGNELLO E VERBENA

The best kind of love triangle

FOR 4 FRIENDS

For the piramidi
- 200g (7oz) type 00 flour
- 150g (5¼oz) *semola rimacinata* (remilled durum wheat semolina)
- 8 egg yolks

For the filling
- 2–3 tbsp extra virgin olive oil
- 400g (14oz) boneless lamb shoulder
- 1 carrot
- 1 stalk of celery
- 1 onion
- 1 shallot
- 1 glass of dry white wine
- 10g (¼oz) butter
- 1 tbsp sherry vinegar
- A few fresh mint and verbena leaves
- 30g (1oz) grated Parmigiano Reggiano DOP
- Your reduced lamb cooking juices (nothing is wasted, everything is transformed)
- Salt and pepper QB

For the Parmigiano *fonduta*
- 100ml (scant ½ cup) double cream
- 50g (1¾oz) grated Parmigiano Reggiano DOP

For the mint and parsley green sauce
- 1 bunch of fresh flat-leaf parsley
- 10 fresh mint leaves
- 2 tbsp extra virgin olive oil

01 Pour a generous dash of olive oil into a casserole dish (Dutch oven), add the boneless lamb shoulder, season with salt, and brown the meat on each side until it is golden brown. Remove the meat to sauté the roughly chopped carrots, celery and onion in the juices. Have they begun to take on a nice colour? Deglaze with the white wine, return the meat to the pan and cover partially. Cook in the oven at 80°C/180°F (or the very lowest setting) for several hours. Once cooked through, separate the meat from the juices, then strain the liquid and set aside in a small bowl in the fridge.

02 For the filling, shred the lamb shoulder very finely with a fork. Then, in a frying pan, sauté the shallot in the butter, add the meat and deglaze with the sherry vinegar. Remove from the heat, add the Parmigiano, a few chopped mint and verbena leaves, and a quarter of your strained meat juices (keep a little aside to serve). Mix everything together and set aside in a bowl in the fridge.

03 Next, focus on the piramidi. On a work surface, mix the semolina and flour together and form a small well in which to place the egg yolks. Mix with a fork, then, when the dough is smooth, knead by hand for 8–10 minutes. You should obtain a smooth, supple, even elastic texture. Cover with a cloth and set aside for 30 minutes at room temperature.

04 For the Parmigiano *fonduta*, heat the cream, stir in the Parmigiano and blend until smooth and creamy. For the green sauce, quickly blanch the herbs, blend with the olive oil and strain if necessary.

05 Roll out the dough thinly on your work surface, then fill and shape your pyramids. For a masterful folding techniques, please refer to page 392. Cook the piramidi in a saucepan of salted boiling water (about 3–4 minutes), then drain.

06 Arrange the piramidi in the centre of a deep plate, top with the Parmigiano *fonduta*, add the green sauce in delicate lines and a few drops of reduced lamb juice. Garnish with a few leaves of parsley and verbena.

\+ **On repeat in the kitchen:** While the lamb is slowly cooking in the oven, take a well-deserved break and play 'Primavera' by composer and pianist Ludovico Einaudi. Close your eyes and let yourself be lulled by this poetic and deeply meditative ballad.

BILLIE AUBERGINE

Cappellacci XXL alla parmigiana

FOR 4 FRIENDS

For the XXL cappellacci

- 200g (7oz) type 00 flour
- 150g (5¼oz) *semola rimacinata* (remilled durum wheat semolina)
- 8 egg yolks

For the filling

- 2 medium aubergines
- 1 mozzarella fior di latte (approximately 120g/4¼oz)
- 300g (10½oz) *passata di pomodoro* (see page 270 for the recipe if you're preparing from scatch, *maestro*)
- 50g (1¾oz) grated Parmigiano Reggiano DOP
- 4–5 fresh basil leaves
- 1 garlic clove
- Extra virgin olive oil
- Salt and freshly ground black pepper QB

For the Parmigiano *fonduta*

- 100ml (scant ½ cup) double cream
- 50g (1¾oz) grated Parmigiano Reggiano DOP

For the finishing touch

- Extra virgin olive oil

01 On a clean work surface, pour the flour and semolina into a small mound, make a well in the centre and add the egg yolks. Knead until you obtain a smooth dough. Cover with clingfilm and leave to rest for 30 minutes at room temperature. Just enough time to walk your dog or call your niece.

02 Wash the aubergines, cut them into thin slices and fry them in a pan with olive oil until they are tender. Season with salt and pepper, then drain them on kitchen paper.

03 In a frying pan, sauté the garlic clove in a drizzle of olive oil. Add the *passata*, season with salt and pepper and stir in a few basil leaves. Simmer over a low heat for 15–20 minutes.

04 Now roll up your sleeves and assemble the *parmigiana*: in an ovenproof dish, alternate layers of fried aubergines, tomato sauce, diced mozzarella and grated Parmigiano. Bake in a preheated oven at 180°C fan/200°C/400°F/GM 6 for about 20 minutes.

05 Once the dish is cooked and cooled, blend it until smooth – this is your filling – and refrigerate for at least 1 hour: the filling mix should be compact and easy to handle with a spoon or piping bag.

06 Roll out the dough very thinly with a rolling pin or pasta machine and make into XXL cappellacci, large plump ravioli that get their name from their shape, which resembles a small hat. All the instructions for folding and filling them successfully can be found on page 391.

07 For the Parmigiano *fonduta*: heat the cream, stir in the Parmigiano and blend until smooth and creamy.

08 Cook the cappellacci in a large quantity of salted boiling water for 3–4 minutes. Be very attentive during this step because overcooked ravioli falls apart, and then so do we.

09 Arrange the cappellacci in a deep plate, top with *fonduta* and finish with a drizzle of olive oil.

\+ **On repeat in the kitchen:** Because this recipe smells like endless summers, we're playing 'Dolce Vita' by Ryan Paris, THE ultimate Italo-disco hit. And while it's simmering, twirl in your apron as if you were on the dancefloor.

CASONCELLI OSSOBUCO

Carne diem

FOR 4 FRIENDS

For the casoncelli

- 200g (7oz) type 00 flour
- 150g (5¼oz) *semola rimacinata* (remilled durum wheat semolina)
- 8 egg yolks

For the filling

- 300g (10½oz) ossobuco (aka shredded braised veal shank cooked for a long time with 1 onion, 2 carrots, 1 stalk of celery, 1 glass of white wine, olive oil)
- 150g (5¼oz) fresh ricotta
- 1 tbsp grated Parmigiano Reggiano DOP
- Zest of 1 organic or unwaxed lemon
- Salt and pepper QB

For finishing the pasta

- 40g (1½oz) unsalted butter
- Zest of 1 organic or unwaxed lemon plus 1 tbsp juice

For the Parmigiano *fonduta*

- 100g (3½oz) grated Parmigiano Reggiano DOP (aged 24 months)
- 120ml (½ cup) double cream
- White pepper QB

For the gremolata

- Zest of 1 organic or unwaxed lemon
- Finely chopped flat-leaf parsley
- ½ garlic clove, grated

To finish

- Reduced meat juices (from your ossobuco)
- Fresh sage leaves (optional)
- Frying oil

01 Start by preparing the dough. On a clean work surface, tip the flour and semolina into a small mound, make a well in the centre and add the egg yolks. Knead lovingly until you obtain a soft, smooth and elastic dough. Cover with clingfilm and leave to rest for 30 minutes at room temperature.

02 Now prepare the base of the filling: the ossobuco. Finely chop the onion, cut the carrots and celery into small cubes. Lightly flour the shank and sear it in a casserole dish (Dutch oven) with a generous drizzle of olive oil until golden brown on both sides, then add the vegetables. Deglaze with the white wine, season with salt and pepper and simmer not quite covered for 1½–2 hours (the meat should be extremely tender, almost confit-like, the kind that falls apart with a fork). Reserve the meat juices and mix the shredded ossobuco with the ricotta, Parmigiano, lemon zest, salt and pepper. Then leave your mixture to rest in the fridge.

03 For the gremolata, an Italian parsley sauce, mix the finely grated garlic, lemon zest and finely chopped parsley in a bowl. Then place in the fridge for a few minutes.

04 Prepare the *fonduta*: heat the cream, stir in the Parmigiano, season with pepper, and blend until smooth and shiny.

05 In a frying pan, fry the fresh sage leaves in olive oil for 5–10 seconds, then drain them on kitchen paper.

06 Roll out the dough with a rolling pin or pasta machine, and fill and fold them into bonbon shapes using our guide on page 393.

07 Cook the casoncelli *al dente* in salted boiling water for 2–3 minutes. Drain and add your little treats to the melted butter with the lemon zest and juice to coat them gently.

08 Finally, it's time to plate up: put a few spoonfuls of *fonduta* in the centre of each plate, then arrange the casoncelli coated in lemon butter on top. Drizzle with reduced ossobuco juice and a pinch of gremolata. Finish with the crispy sage leaves. There you have it, all the warmth of Italy has invaded your *cucina*.

GIRELLA ALLA NORMA

For Norma-l People fans

FOR 4 FRIENDS

For the girelle
- 200g (7oz) type 00 flour
- 150g (5¼oz) *semola rimacinata* (remilled durum wheat semolina)
- 8 egg yolks

For the *alla norma* filling
- 1 large aubergine from the market (approximately 250g/9oz)
- 200g (7oz) ricotta
- 40g (1½oz) grated Parmigiano Reggiano DOP
- Zest 1 organic or unwaxed lemon
- Sunflower oil for frying
- Salt and black pepper QB

For the datterino tomato sauce
- 400g (14oz) fresh datterino tomatoes
- Extra virgin olive oil
- Salt and pepper QB

For plating
- A little crumbled *ricotta salata*
- 1 small aubergine to make the crisps (chips)

01 Start by preparing the girelle, which are stuffed pasta shapes rolled into a flower (or snail, if you prefer) shape. On your work surface, make a small well with the semolina and flour and pour in the egg yolks. Knead for 8–10 minutes until you obtain a smooth, supple and slightly elastic dough. Cover with clingfilm and leave to rest for 30 minutes at room temperature.

02 Prepare the crisps. Wash the aubergine, slice it into rounds using a mandoline and put them on a baking tray lined with greaseproof paper. Brush the slices with olive oil and bake for about 1 hour (in an oven preheated to 120°C fan/140°C/275°F/GM 1) until the crisps are crunchy. Remove from the oven and set aside at room temperature.

03 For the filling, dice the aubergine and fry in a generous amount of oil until golden brown. Drain on kitchen paper before mixing with the ricotta, Parmigiano and finely grated lemon zest. Season with salt and pepper, then pop in the fridge to cool.

04 Meanwhile, prepare your sauce by blending the tomatoes with a drizzle of olive oil, salt and pepper. Pass the mixture through a sieve to obtain a smooth texture. *Arrivederci* seeds. Before plating, heat this beautiful *sugo* over a low heat.

05 Next, move on to the more complex part of the recipe: filling and folding the girella, but don't panic. Roll out your dough thinly with a rolling pin or pasta machine, then follow the instructions on page 394.

06 Next, cook your pasta in salted boiling water for 4–5 minutes, then drain.

07 Place the girelle in the centre of each plate, sprinkle with salted ricotta, tomato sauce and aubergine crisps. *Mamma mia*, it's magnificent.

+ **On repeat in the kitchen:** 'La bambola' by Patty Pravo, with the lyrics 'You make me spin, you spin me around like I'm a doll' evokes the girella's spiral. Come on, let's twirl around the living room with our arms in the air.

THE GREAT WALL-NUT
Pansoti XXL salsa di noci

FOR 4 FRIENDS

<u>For the XXL pansoti</u>
- 200g (7oz) type 00 flour
- 150g (5¼oz) *semola rimacinata* (remilled durum wheat semolina)
- 8 egg yolks

<u>For the filling</u>
- 500g (1lb 2oz) *preboggion*, a mixture of cooked and drained herbs typical of Liguria (or 1.2kg/2.6lb fresh leaves to be cooked and drained). Depending on what you have picked or what you feel like: Swiss chard, red chard, borage, spinach, dandelion, nettles, chervil . . .
- 200g (7oz) cow's-milk ricotta (or a mix of cow's- and sheep's-milk ricotta)
- 50g (1¾oz) grated Parmigiano Reggiano DOP
- 1 egg
- A pinch of grated nutmeg
- Salt and pepper QB

<u>For the walnut sauce</u>
- 100g (3½oz) shelled walnuts, plus a few extra
- 1 mild garlic clove
- 30g (1oz) white breadcrumbs soaked in a little milk
- 20g (¾oz) pine nuts (optional, but common in Genoa)
- 40g (1½oz) grated Parmigiano Reggiano DOP
- Extra virgin olive oil
- Freshly chopped chives

<u>For the Parmigiano *fonduta*</u>
- 100ml (scant ½ cup) double cream
- 50g (1¾oz) grated Parmigiano Reggiano DOP

01 Start by preparing the pasta dough. On a clean work surface, pour the flour and semolina into a small mound, make a well in the centre and add the egg yolks. Knead until you obtain a smooth dough. Cover with clingfilm and leave to rest for 30 minutes at room temperature.

02 Now make the filling: if not already cooked, cook the herbs for 8 minutes in a little salted water or steam. Drain them gently, squeeze well to remove all the water, then chop finely with a knife. Then mix with the ricotta, Parmigiano, egg, a pinch of grated nutmeg, season with salt and pepper and pop it in the fridge.

03 For the walnut sauce, blanch the walnuts for 30 seconds in boiling water, then drain and blend with the garlic, breadcrumbs soaked in milk or water, pine nuts, a little grated Parmigiano and a drizzle of olive oil.

04 For the Parmigiano *fonduta*, heat the cream and Parmigiano over a low heat, whisking constantly, until you obtain a silky sauce.

05 Then roll out your dough thinly – use a pasta machine if you have one, or a rolling pin if not (good luck!) – then move on to filling and shaping the pansoti using our folding guide on page 391. The name *pansoti* comes from *pansa* (belly), a nod to their plump, rounded shape.

06 Plunge your pansoti into a large saucepan of salted boiling water for 3–4 minutes, until they rise to the surface. Remove and drain them carefully with a slotted spoon.

07 The final step: put your pansoti on plates and dress with Parmigiano *fonduta* and walnut sauce (twice rather than once, if you ask us). A little cloud of *Parmigiano*, a twist of the pepper mill, then a few crushed walnuts, chives and voilà. A vegetarian recipe that will make even the most ardent meat-eaters in the group salivate.

\+ **On repeat in the kitchen:** With 'Contro il mondo' by Baustelle, a sweet scent of nostalgia wafts through the air in the kitchen. As the smell of walnuts fills the house, we shape the pansoti as we reminisce about the past. Enjoy.

AGNOLOTTI XXL BOLOGNESE

We like big bolognese

FOR 4 FRIENDS

For the agnolotti del plin

- 200g (7oz) type 00 flour
- 150g (5¼oz) *semola rimacinata* (remilled durum wheat semolina)
- 8 egg yolks

For the firm béchamel filling

- 25g (¾oz) butter
- 25g (¾oz) plain flour
- 200ml (generous ¾ cup) whole milk
- 1 tbsp grated Parmigiano Reggiano DOP
- Nutmeg
- Salt and white pepper QB

For the *ragù alla bolognese*

- 200g (7oz) minced beef (or half beef, half pork)
- ½ carrot
- ½ stalk of celery
- ½ onion
- 1 tbsp double concentrate tomato paste
- 200ml (generous ¾ cup) *passata di pomodoro* or tomato pulp (we explain how to make it at home on page 270)
- 1 glass of whole milk
- ½ glass of red wine
- Olive oil
- Salt and pepper QB

For the Parmigiano *fonduta*

- 100ml (scant ½ cup) double cream
- 60g (2oz) grated Parmigiano Reggiano DOP (aged 24–30 months)
- White pepper

For the finishing touch

- Powdered bay leaf
- Pepper QB

01 On a work surface, pour the flour and semolina into a small mound, make a well in the centre and add the egg yolks. Knead lovingly until you obtain a smooth dough. Cover with clingfilm and leave to rest for 30 minutes at room temperature.

02 Now for the filling. Melt the butter in a saucepan over a low heat, add the flour and cook for 1 minute, stirring until you obtain a golden roux. Then pour in the milk in a thin stream, while whisking. Add a pinch of grated nutmeg, grated Parmigiano, salt, pepper and pop it in the fridge to cool.

03 Meanwhile, prepare a bolognese *ragù*: in a large saucepan, fry the finely chopped carrot, celery and onion with a drizzle of olive oil. Once the vegetables are tender, add the meat and brown it until it is coloured. Then deglaze with the red wine and let it evaporate. Next, add the tomato paste, *passata* and the milk. Season with salt and pepper and simmer over a low heat for at least 1 hour 30 minutes.

04 For the *fonduta*, heat the cream without boiling, then add the grated Parmigiano. Whisk gently until you obtain a smooth sauce. Blend if necessary. Add a twist of pepper and it's ready to use.

05 Take your pasta, roll it out very thinly (using a pasta machine or rolling pin, depending on what your arms feel up to), then turn to page 396 to make your XXL agnolotti with béchamel sauce filling.

06 Cook the agnolotti in a large saucepan of salted boiling water for 2–3 minutes, no more. Drain and arrange the pasta on warm plates, top with the steaming *ragù*, then add the *fonduta*. A twist of pepper, a sprinkling of bay leaf powder . . . *A tavola.*

\+ **On repeat in the kitchen:** 'It's wonderful, it's wonderful' – that's how you feel after the first bite of these little marvels. We are enthralled by the sound of Paolo Conte's 'Via con me', a joyful, slightly jazzy and deliciously retro classic.

TWICE AS NICE RAVIOLI

Ravioli ripieni di funghi, ricotta e spinaci

FOR 4 FRIENDS

<u>For the ravioli dough</u>

For the green dough

- 100g (3½oz) type 00 flour
- 75g (2½oz) *semola rimacinata* (remilled durum wheat semolina)
- 4 egg yolks
- 150g (5¼oz) spinach leaves
- 500ml (2 cups) water

For the yellow dough

- 100g (3½oz) type 00 flour
- 75g (2½oz) *semola rimacinata* (remilled durum wheat semolina)
- 4 egg yolks

<u>For the mushroom filling</u>

- 100g (3½oz) well-drained ricotta
- 150g (5¼oz) duxelles de champignons de Paris (chopped mushrooms cooked over a low heat for 10–15 minutes in a knob of butter with a chopped shallot)
- Nutmeg, salt, pepper QB

<u>For the ricotta and spinach filling</u>

- 150g (5¼oz) well-drained ricotta
- 100g (3½oz) cooked spinach, drained and finely chopped
- 5g (1 tsp) chopped parsley
- Fresh chives
- Nutmeg, salt, pepper QB

<u>For the melted mature *stracchino*</u>

- 120g (4¼oz) mature stracchino cheese (with a firmer texture than fresh stracchino, it gives the sauce a more pronounced depth)
- 100ml (scant ½ cup) double cream
- 20g (¾oz) unsalted butter
- Freshly ground black pepper QB

<u>For the finishing touch</u>

- 8–10 fresh sage leaves
- A knob of butter
- 2 tbsp toasted, crushed hazelnuts

01 Blanch the spinach leaves for the green dough in the water, drain and blend them in a food processor for 10 minutes. You will make a nice green liquid to mix with one of the two dough balls.

02 Prepare the ravioli dough. On the work surface, form two small volcanoes, one for each dough, with the semolina and flour. Pour the corresponding egg yolks into the hollow of each volcano. Add the spinach liquid to one of them. Mix with a fork and knead until you have two types of dough – one yellow and one green. Wrap them in clingfilm and leave to rest for 30 minutes at room temperature.

03 The magic of these ravioli lies not only in their two-coloured dough but also in their two-flavoured filling: two flavours, two colours, twice the pleasure. Prepare two bowls, one for each filling. In each bowl, mix all the ingredients until you obtain a smooth texture that is not too runny. Adjust the seasoning.

04 Roll out your pasta with a rolling pin or pasta machine, then arrange the sheets side by side, pressing them together firmly. Roll out again so that you have a single two-coloured dough. Then turn to page 395 to discover the guide to filling and folding these ravioli perfectly.

05 In a small saucepan, melt the *stracchino* cheese with the cream and butter over a low heat until you obtain a smooth sauce. Add a generous grinding of pepper to season.

06 In a frying pan, fry a few sage leaves in butter.

07 Cook your ravioli in a large saucepan of salted boiling water for 3–4 minutes. Drain and immediately toss them in the sage butter.

08 Arrange the ravioli on a plate, drizzle with sage butter and hot stracchino *fonduta*. Sprinkle with toasted hazelnuts, season with pepper . . . and voilà, you've created a dish worthy of the finest restaurants!

+ **On repeat in the kitchen:** With this vibrant and colourful recipe, turn up the volume with The Kolors and their hit song 'Italodisco'. If you don't start dancing around the table, frankly, we'll give up.

GET YOUR DUCKS IN A ROW

Ravioli anatra

FOR 4 FRIENDS

For the ravioli sheets
- 200g (7oz) type 00 flour
- 150g (5¼oz) *semola rimacinata* (remilled durum wheat semolina)
- 8 egg yolks
- 1 ravioli mould

For the filling
- 1 confit duck leg
- 20g (¾oz) pine nuts
- 20g (¾oz) sultanas
- Zest of 1 organic or unwaxed orange
- 20g (¾oz) grated Parmigiano Reggiano DOP (optional)
- Grated nutmeg
- Freshly ground black pepper QB

For the sauce
- 30g (1oz) butter
- A little powdered bay leaf
- A dash of orange juice (optional)
- Salt and freshly ground black pepper QB

01 Start with the ravioli dough. On your work surface, make a small well with the semolina and flour and pour in the egg yolks. Start by mixing with a fork, then knead by hand for 8–10 minutes until the ball becomes smooth, soft and slightly elastic. Cover the dough with clingfilm and leave to rest for 30 minutes at room temperature (this will make it easier to roll out).

02 Meanwhile, prepare the filling ingredients. Toast the pine nuts. Soak the sultanas in a little water. Boil the orange zest for 3 minutes before chopping it into very small pieces. Mix in a bowl with the finely shredded duck. Add a little pepper, nutmeg and Parmigiano, and your filling is ready.

03 Use a rolling pin (or pasta machine) and turn to page 396 to fill and shape your ravioli. You will need a ravioli board for this step (if you don't have one, this is the perfect opportunity to get to know your friendly neighbours).

04 In a small saucepan, melt the butter until it begins to foam and turn a nice hazelnut colour. Season with salt and pepper and add a dash of orange juice if you like.

05 Meanwhile, cook the ravioli sheets in a large saucepan of simmering salted water for 3 minutes. Then drain.

06 Arrange the ravioli by placing the sheet directly in the centre of the plate (it's more practical, plus an opportunity to show off!). Drizzle with hot brown butter and add a little orange zest, a sprinkling of Parmigiano, a little powdered bay leaf and a final twist of the pepper mill. *Buon appetito.*

\+ **On repeat in the kitchen:** Serve this dish to the sound of 'Nessuno mi può giudicare' ('Nobody can judge me') by Caterina Caselli. A great classic from the 1960s that will make you want to book your next trip to Italy.

AGNOLOTTI DEL PLIN ALLA VACCINARA

Small stuffed pasta that packs a punch

For a flavourful ragù, *the meat must simmer for 3–4 hours. We know it's a long time, but your* ragù *and the rest of the family will thank you for it.*

FOR 4 FRIENDS

For the agnolotti del plin

- 200g (7oz) type 00 flour
- 150g (5¼oz) *semola rimacinata* (remilled durum wheat semolina)
- 8 egg yolks

For the *alla vaccinara* filling

- 800g (1lbs 12oz) oxtail
- 1 onion
- 1 carrot
- 1 stalk of celery
- 2 tbsp tomato paste
- 1 glass of red wine
- 1 bay leaf
- A few cloves
- 20g (¾oz) bitter cocoa (optional, but traditional)
- 30g (1oz) grated Pecorino Romano DOP
- Salt and black pepper QB

For the pecorino *fonduta*

- 100g (3½oz) finely grated pecorino cheese
- 200ml (7floz) double cream

For the sauce

- 100ml (scant ½ cup) reduced cooking stock (made in step 02)
- 1 knob of butter

For the finishing touch

- 20g (¾oz) roasted pine nuts
- 20g (¾oz) raisins, soaked beforehand in a little warm water
- Chopped sorrel

01 On your work surface, form a small well with the flour and semolina and pour in the egg yolks. Mix with a fork, then knead for 8–10 minutes until you have a smooth dough. Cover the dough with clingfilm and leave to rest for 30 minutes at room temperature.

02 Pour a generous dash of olive oil into a casserole dish (Dutch oven) and add the finely chopped carrot, celery and onion. Add the oxtail and brown gently before adding the tomato paste, bay leaf and a few cloves. Season with salt and pepper and deglaze with the wine. Add enough water to cover and simmer covered over a low heat or in a prheated oven at 120°C fan/140°C/275°F/GM 1 for 3–4 hours.

03 Once the meat is tender and falling off the bone, remove it from the stock and set the liquid aside in a small bowl. Debone and finely chop the oxtail then in a large bowl, mix the meat, a little of your beef stock (but not all of it, some will be used for a sauce later), bitter cocoa and a sprinkling of grated pecorino. Mix, then leave to cool in the fridge.

04 On the work surface, roll out the agnolotti dough very thinly and turn to page 394, where we explain how to fill and shape it like a master. Cook the pasta for 2–3 minutes in salted boiling water and drain. While it is cooking, heat the remaining beef stock with a knob of butter in a frying pan over a low heat. For your pecorino *fonduta*, pour the cream and grated pecorino into a small saucepan, heat over a low heat and stir until the sauce thickens. Set aside.

05 Finally, it's time to plate up. Arrange the agnolotti in a dish, coat with the meat sauce, top with the raisins and pine nuts, a sprinkling of chopped sorrel, and finish with a little freshly ground black pepper.

+ **On repeat in the kitchen:** '50 Special' by Lùnapop, whose chorus 'Give me a Vespa and I'll take you on holiday' makes us want to plan a return trip to Rome.

SEEING ROSSO
Casoncelli ai gamberi rossi

FOR 4 FRIENDS

For the casoncelli
- 200g (7oz) type 00 flour
- 150g (5¼oz) *semola rimacinata* (remilled durum wheat semolina)
- 8 egg yolks

For the filling
- 100g (3½oz) *gambero rosso* (raw shell-on red prawns or red shrimps). If you can't find any, use large pink shrimp
- 50g *mazzancolle* (raw shell-on king prawns)
- 80g (2¾oz) well-drained ricotta
- A drizzle of extra virgin olive oil
- Salt and black pepper QB

For the red prawn tartare
- 100g (3½oz) raw red prawns
- Fresh chives
- Zest of 1 organic, unwaxed lime
- Juice of 1 organic or unwaxed lemon
- Extra virgin olive oil
- Salt QB

For the beurre blanc
- 1 shallot
- 80ml (⅓ cup) dry white wine
- 1 tbsp white wine vinegar
- 120g (4¼oz) cold butter
- Salt and white pepper QB

For the concentrated shellfish bisque
- Your prawn or king prawn shells
- 1 onion
- 1 carrot
- 1 stalk of celery
- 2 tbsp tomato paste
- Salt and pepper QB

01 On a work surface, pour the flour and semolina to make a small mound, make a well in the centre and add the egg yolks. Knead until you have a smooth dough. Cover with clingfilm and leave to rest for 30 minutes at room temperature.

02 Prepare the filling. Shell the red and king prawns, cut them into very fine pieces. In a bowl, mix them with the ricotta, salt, pepper and olive oil. Set aside in the fridge as is or put in a piping bag for more precision when shaping the casoncelli.

03 Take your dough, roll it out thinly with a rolling pin or pasta machine, fold it, then fill the casoncelli using our guide on page 393. Set aside on a floured work surface.

04 In a saucepan, sauté the chopped shallot, white wine and vinegar over a low heat until only 1 tablespoon of liquid remains. Then, over a very, very low heat (it must not boil), gradually add the diced cold butter while whisking. Season with salt and pepper.

05 Prepare your bisque. In a saucepan, sauté the chopped onion, carrot and celery in a drizzle of olive oil. Add the prawn shells, then leave on a low heat for 5 minutes. Add the tomato paste and a little water to thin the sauce. Season with salt and pepper and simmer for 30–45 minutes. Pass through a sieve or chinois and set aside.

06 In a large saucepan of salted boiling water, cook the pasta *al dente* (2–3 minutes), drain and toss in a frying pan with the melted butter and 10g (2 tsp) of bisque.

07 Prepare the tartare by seasoning the red prawns with lemon juice, olive oil, chopped chives and lime zest. Season with salt.

08 Arrange the casoncelli on a plate, drizzle with warm beurre blanc and a dash of reduced bisque. Add small dollops of tartare.

On repeat in the kitchen: Get in the mood with Tiziano Ferro's 'Rosso relativo', a must-have track since its release in 2001 in Italy, France and Spain. With his almost rap-like flow, the new prodigy of transalpine pop is rocking all the radio stations.

VENI, VIDI, VERDI

Culurgiones asparagi e piselli

FOR 4 FRIENDS

<u>For the two-colour culurgiones</u>

For the green dough

- 100g (3½oz) type 00 flour
- 75g (2½oz) *semola rimacinata* (remilled durum wheat semolina)
- 4 egg yolks
- 150g (5¼oz) spinach leaves

For the yellow dough

- 100g (3½oz) type 00 flour
- 75g (2½oz) *semola rimacinata* (remilled durum wheat semolina)
- 4 egg yolks

<u>For the filling</u>

- 300g (10½oz) well-drained cow's milk ricotta
- 50g (1¾oz) grated Parmigiano Reggiano DOP
- Salt and freshly ground black pepper QB

<u>For the minted pea purée</u>

- 200g (7oz) fresh shelled peas
- A few fresh mint and basil leaves
- Extra virgin olive oil
- Salt QB

<u>For the finishing touch</u>

- 100g (3½oz) fresh shelled peas
- 8 green asparagus tips
- A few mint leaves

01 Blanch the spinach leaves in the water, drain and blend them in a food processor for 10 minutes. You will obtain a nice green liquid to mix with one of the two dough balls. On a work surface, first pour the semolina and flour for the green dough into a small mound, place the egg yolks in the centre then pour in the green spinach liquid. Mix with a fork and knead by hand until you obtain a smooth green dough. Repeat the process for the yellow dough by forming a volcano shape, pouring in the egg yolks and mixing then kneading. Cover with clingfilm and leave your two dough balls to rest for 30 minutes at room temperature.

02 Prepare the filling. Mix together the ricotta, Parmigiano, season with salt and pepper, and set aside in a cool place.

03 Next, make the minted pea purée by cooking the peas in salted boiling water for 3 minutes before draining and rinsing under cold water. Blend with the mint, basil, a drizzle of olive oil and a little salt, until you have a really smooth sauce (we're nagging but this makes the dish so delicious, we promise!).

04 For a garnish *perfetta*, quickly cook the asparagus (2 minutes) and fresh peas in a pan of salted water, then rinse under cold running water.

05 Roll out each ball of dough with a rolling pin or pasta machine, then place them side by side, pressing them together firmly. Roll out again to create a single two-coloured dough. Fill and shape your culurgiones, Sardinian ravioli stuffed and hand-braided into the shape of an ear of wheat, using our guide on page 395.

06 Cook the pasta in a large saucepan of salted boiling water for 3–4 minutes.

07 On each plate, add a few dashes of pea purée. Arrange the culurgiones, add the crunchy vegetables and finish with a drizzle of olive oil and a few mint leaves. It's green, it's beautiful, it's delicious.

\+ **On repeat in the kitchen:** Here, asparagus and peas are two inseparable partners, two springtime flavours that bounce off each other as in Paolo Conte's 'Sparring Partner'.

IT'S EGG-STRAORDINARY

Raviolo con tuorlo, ricotta e spinaci

A true pioneer of signature cuisine in Italy, Nino Bergese has influenced generations of chefs. His famous 'Uovo in raviolo', with its runny egg yolk when cut, has become an icon of Italian cuisine. It's a technical dish, but don't panic, we'll guide you step by step and it's much simpler than it looks.

FOR 4 FRIENDS

For the ravioli
- 200g (7oz) type 00 flour
- 150g (5¼oz) *semola rimacinata* (remilled durum wheat semolina)
- 8 egg yolks

For the filling
- 40g (1½oz) fresh spinach
- 200g (7oz) sheep's or cow's milk ricotta
- 100g (3½oz) mature grated Parmigiano Reggiano DOP
- 1 egg yolk
- Grated nutmeg
- Salt and pepper QB

For the sauce
- 200g (7oz) butter (ideally artisanal Malga butter)
- 100g (3½oz) Parmigiano Reggiano DOP (to serve)
- A few sage leaves
- A little white or black truffle (optional)

01 On your work surface, mix the flour and semolina and form a small well. Place the 8 egg yolks in the well, then beat them first with a fork before kneading by hand for 10–12 minutes. The dough should become soft and elastic. Cover with clingfilm and set aside for at least 30 minutes.

02 Now for the filling. Cook the spinach, drain it thoroughly and chop it finely. Then mix it in a bowl with the ricotta, Parmigiano, a pinch of nutmeg, salt and pepper. For greater precision, you can use a piping bag for your filling, but a spoon will also do the trick if you don't have one to hand (and you refuse to go and knock on your neighbour's door).

03 Once your ravioli dough is ready, roll it out on a floured surface, separate your egg yolks and turn to page 394 to learn how to create your work of art.

04 Now it's time to pull out all the stops and concentrate. Cooking this requires a little attention. Place one raviolo at a time in a large saucepan of simmering salted water (definitely not boiling) for 2–3 minutes. The aim is to cook the pasta while keeping the yolk runny. Then gently remove your gem with a slotted spoon and place it on a warm soup plate.

05 Meanwhile, melt the butter in a frying pan until it turns golden brown. Add a few sage leaves. Sprinkle in a little Parmigiano, stir, and generously coat the ravioli with this delicious sauce.

06 Finish with a little more grated Parmigiano on top and, for special occasions, a few truffle shavings. There you have it, you've just served a five-star dish.

\+ **On repeat in the kitchen:** Carried by operatic voices and a spine-tingling melody, 'Grandeamore' by the trio Il Volo took Europe by storm at Eurovision 2015, winning the public vote hands down. A passionate, powerful and lyrical declaration, perfect to accompany this majestic ravioli.

CUTE AS A BUTTON

Bottoni caponata

FOR 4 FRIENDS

<u>For the bottoni</u>

- 200g (7oz) type 00 flour
- 150g (5¼oz) *semola rimacinata* (remilled durum wheat semolina)
- 8 egg yolks

<u>For the caponata filling</u>

- 1 large aubergine
- 1 stalk of celery
- 1 small shallot
- 1 peeled tomato or 1 tbsp tomato pulp
- 20g (¾oz) desalted capers
- 20g (¾oz) raisins, previously soaked in a little warm water
- 20g (¾oz) toasted pine nuts
- 1 tbsp white wine vinegar
- Extra virgin olive oil
- Salt and pepper QB

<u>For the datterino tomato sauce</u>

- 200g (7oz) fresh datterino tomatoes
- 1 dash of extra virgin olive oil
- 1 small garlic clove
- Salt QB

<u>For the stracciatella cream</u>

- 150g (5¼oz) buffalo stracciatella
- 80ml (3oz) double cream
- Salt and white pepper QB

<u>For the finishing touch</u>

- Basil leaves

01 Prepare the dough by mixing the flour and semolina on a work surface, then form a small well and pour the egg yolks into it. Mix first with a fork, then knead for 8–10 minutes until you obtain a smooth dough. Cover with clingfilm and leave to rest for 30 minutes at room temperature.

02 Pour a generous dash of olive oil into a frying pan, then fry the diced aubergine until it turns a nice golden colour. In another frying pan, sweat the shallot and finely chopped celery, add the peeled tomato cut into small pieces, then stir in the raisins, capers, pine nuts, vinegar, and finally, the stars of the show: the fried aubergines. Mix, season and cook for a few minutes over a low heat. Blend lightly or chop coarsely with a fork to obtain a texture suitable for stuffing, then leave to cool.

03 In another pan, sauté the minced garlic in a generous drizzle of olive oil and add the halved tomatoes. Simmer everything over a low heat for 15 minutes, adjust the seasoning then blend or sieve (*arrivederci* seeds). Keep the sauce warm.

04 Blend the stracciatella with the cream (it needs to be very cold) until you obtain a smooth, even cream. Season lightly with a pinch of salt and a twist of white pepper, then heat in a small saucepan over a very low heat (never, ever allow it to boil).

05 Take out your dough, roll it out thinly on your work surface and turn to page 393 to follow our filling and folding guide.

06 Cook the bottoni in a large quantity of salted boiling water for 3–4 minutes. Drain.

07 To serve, arrange the bottoni in the bottom of deep plates and pour a drizzle of tomato sauce around them. Add a few spoonfuls of stracciatella cream, a twist of pepper, some basil leaves for a touch of green, and it's ready. *Buonissimo.*

\+ **On repeat in the kitchen:** Aubergines mean summer, which means holidays . . . So let's turn up the volume with 'Una vita in vacanza' by Lo Stato Sociale, and off we go to Isola Bella, Ischia or Gallipoli . . . In short, any little corner of Italy where there is sunshine and warm sand.

RICOTTA GET THROUGH THIS

Cappellacci bicolore ricotta e spinaci

FOR 4 FRIENDS

For the two-coloured cappellacci

For the green dough

- 100g (3½oz) type 00 flour
- 75g (2½oz) *semola rimacinata* (remilled durum wheat semolina)
- 4 egg yolks
- 150g (5¼oz) spinach leaves
- 500ml (2 cups) water

For the yellow dough

- 100g (3½oz) type 00 flour
- 75g (2½oz) *semola rimacinata* (remilled durum wheat semolina)
- 4 egg yolks

For the filling

- 250g (9oz) well-drained ricotta
- 40g (1½oz) grated Parmigiano Reggiano DOP
- Zest of 1 organic or unwaxed lemon
- Salt and pepper QB

For the beurre blanc

- 1 shallot
- 80ml (⅓ cup) dry white wine
- 20ml (4 tsp) white wine vinegar
- 200g (7oz) cold butter
- Salt QB

For the finishing touch

- About 20 spinach leaves

01 Blanch the 150g spinach leaves, drain them and blend in a food processor for 10 minutes. You will obtain a nice green liquid to mix with one of the two dough balls.

02 On a work surface, pour the semolina and flour for the green dough into a small mound, place the egg yolks in the centre, then pour in the green spinach liquid. Mix with a fork and knead by hand until you obtain a soft green dough. Repeat the process for the yellow dough by forming a volcano shape, pouring in the yolks and mixing, then kneading. Cover with clingfilm and leave your two dough balls to rest for 30 minutes at room temperature.

03 In a bowl, mix all the ingredients for the filling and set aside in the fridge. Meanwhile, sauté the fresh spinach leaves in a little butter, which will be the finishing touch.

04 In a saucepan, sauté the chopped shallot, white wine and vinegar. Reduce over a low heat until there is almost no liquid left and then, over a very low heat, gradually add the diced butter, whisking continuously. Leaving on the heat, season with salt.

05 Take your dough pieces and roll them out separately on your work surface (using a rolling pin or pasta machine, whichever you prefer), then place them side by side, pressing them together firmly. Roll out again so that you have a single two-coloured dough. For two-colour filling and folding worthy of the greatest, see page 395.

06 Cook your pasta in a large saucepan of salted boiling water for 2–3 minutes. Drain and remember to keep a ladleful of the cooking water, your liquid gold. Pour the cappellacci into the pan with the beurre blanc, toss everything together for a few seconds and feel free to add a ladleful of cooking water if you want to thicken the sauce.

07 Time to plate up: arrange the cappellacci on a warm plate, coat with beurre blanc and add the spinach leaves. And there you have it! Well done, *Maestro*.

\+ **On repeat in the kitchen:** Who hasn't lost their voice singing at weddings, stadiums or other popular festivals to the sound of 'Sarà perchè ti amo' by Ricchi e Poveri? You don't need to speak Italian to sing along with this perfect little accompaniment for these little cappellacci delights.

RAGÙ ME TENDER

Pansoti XXL patate, ragù salsiccia e finocchietto

FOR 4 FRIENDS

For the pansoti

- 200g (7oz) type 00 flour
- 150g (5¼oz) *semola rimacinata* (remilled durum wheat semolina)
- 8 egg yolks

For the filling

- 400g (14oz) yellow floury potatoes
- 80g (23/4oz) ricotta (or fresh cheese such as robiola, if you can find it)
- 40g (1½oz) grated Parmigiano Reggiano DOP
- Grated nutmeg
- Salt and pepper QB

For the wild fennel sausage *ragù*

- 300g (11oz) sausage, skin removed and meat crumbled (preferably Italian, mild or spicy, depending on your preference)
- 1 small onion
- 1 garlic clove
- 200ml (generous ¾ cup) *passata di pomodoro* (a tomato purée, the homemade recipe can be found on page 270)
- 1 sprig of wild fennel (or, if unavailable, a few lightly crushed fennel seeds and fresh fennel)
- 100ml (scant ½ cup) dry white wine
- Olive oil QB
- Salt and pepper QB

01 On your work surface, form a well with the flour and semolina, add the egg yolks to the centre, then mix first with a fork before kneading by hand for a good 10 minutes. Cover with clingfilm and leave to rest for 30 minutes at room temperature.

02 Place the whole, unpeeled potatoes in a large saucepan of cold salted water. Bring to the boil and cook until tender. Peel them while still hot (taking care not to burn your fingers), then mash them with a fork.

03 In a large bowl, prepare your filling by mixing the potatoes, ricotta, Parmigiano, a little salt and pepper and a pinch of nutmeg then pop it in the fridge.

04 Meanwhile, in a large frying pan, sauté the chopped onion and garlic in a generous drizzle of olive oil. Add the sausage meat and brown until golden. Then deglaze with the white wine and leave until the *ragù* sauce reduces (perhaps even time to pour yourself a small glass? Double-check your selection from the wine merchant one last time, as not all cooking wines are suitable for drinking). Add the *passata*, wild fennel (or your mixture of fennel seeds and fresh fennel), a little salt, a twist of pepper, and simmer over a low heat for 30 minutes. The kitchen is starting to smell like a holiday!

05 Now it's time to shape the XXL pansoti. Roll out the dough thinly with a rolling pin – or a pasta machine if you have one – and go to page 391 for our filling and folding guide.

06 Plunge the pansoti into a large saucepan of salted boiling water and cook until they rise to the surface, which is your signal that they are ready.

07 Using a slotted spoon, place the pasta into the centre of deep plates. Top generously with the sausage *ragù*, fronds of fresh fennel and go, let's eat: this dish is best enjoyed piping hot.

+ **On repeat in the kitchen:** With these iconic Ligurian pansoti, put 'La città vecchia' by Fabrizio de André on in the background. You can hear the whole of Genoa: raw, beautiful and full of soul, just like your recipe.

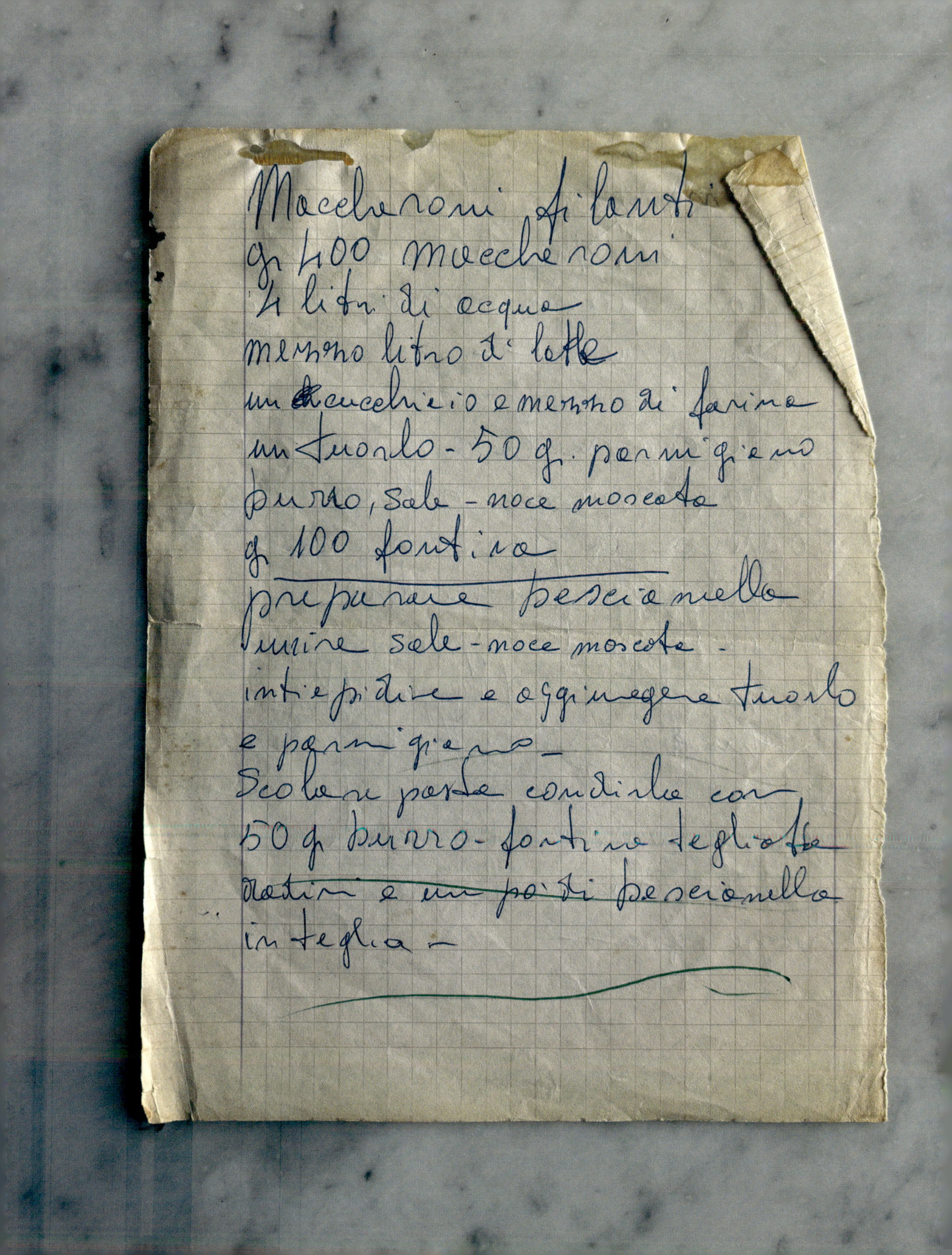

Maccheroni filanti
gr 400 maccheroni
4 litri di acqua
mezzo litro di latte
un cucchiaio e mezzo di farina
un tuorlo - 50 g. parmigiano
burro, sale - noce moscata
gr 100 fontina

preparare besciamella
unire sale - noce moscata -
intiepidire e aggiungere tuorlo
e parmigiano -
Scolare pasta condirla con
50 g burro - fontina tagliata a
dadini e un po' di besciamella
in teglia -

THE ART OF CHOOSING THE RIGHT PASTA

For the best results, and when it is better to use dry pasta rather than fresh, here are a few tips to help you make the right choice.

1 If you can, visit a small *alimentari* near your home. These neighbourhood Italian grocery stores are full of the best products from Italy and often offer plenty of advice. If there's one place to make friends, it's there.

2 In any case, wherever you are, look for the words 'trafilata al bronzo' on the packets which indicates the pasta has been extruded through a bronze die, giving them a rough texture that is ideal for holding onto sauce.

3 100% *semola di grano duro* is the Rolls-Royce of flours when it comes to pasta. A true guarantee of quality that is worth looking out for.

4 Finally, always choose packets that indicate long cooking times (10 minutes or more), as these are your allies for a quality meal. Good pasta cooked in 2 minutes is a false promise, *amici*.

CASONCELLI ALLA BERGAMASCA

Sweet and savoury sweeties

FOR 4 FRIENDS

For the casoncelli

- 200g (7oz) type 00 flour
- 150g (5¼oz) *semola rimacinata* (remilled durum wheat semolina)
- 8 egg yolks

For the filling

- 100g (3½oz) minced meat of your choice (traditionally pork, but you can opt for a mixture of pork and beef)
- 80g (2¾oz) crumbled sausage meat
- 60g (2oz) breadcrumbs, plus a few extra
- 30g grated Parmigiano Reggiano DOP
- 1 egg
- 1 garlic clove
- 30g (1oz) raisins, previously soaked in a little warm water or grappa (an Italian spirit made from grape pomace)
- 20g (¾oz) crumbled amaretti
- Grated zest of ½ organic or unwaxed lemon
- 1 tbsp parsley
- 1 tbsp pear or apple purée or, if you have it to hand, mostarda made from candied fruit of your choice (mostarda is a typical Italian fruit condiment, similar to Dijon mustard)
- Olive oil QB
- Salt and pepper QB

For the sauce

- 100g (3½oz) butter
- 100g (3½oz) pancetta (or smoked bacon), diced
- Fresh sage leaves

01 On a work surface, pour the flour and semolina into a small mound, make a well in the centre and add the egg yolks. Knead until you obtain a smooth dough. Cover with clingfilm and leave to rest for 30 minutes at room temperature.

02 In a frying pan, brown the minced meat and sausage meat in a generous dash of olive oil. Add the minced garlic and simmer until lightly browned.

03 Remove from the heat and add the breadcrumbs, grated Parmigiano, rehydrated raisins, crumbled amaretti biscuits, lemon zest, fruit purée (or mostarda), chopped parsley and egg. This sweet and savoury dish is a signature dish of Bergamo: every ingredient counts, it's impossible to leave any out. Season with salt and pepper, mix well and add a few more breadcrumbs if your filling mix is too wet.

04 Roll out the dough very thinly with a rolling pin or pasta machine, then follow our filling and shaping guide on page 393 to make your casoncelli bonbons.

05 Next, melt the butter in a frying pan with the sage leaves and pancetta. Heat gently until the butter turns a hazelnut colour and the pancetta becomes crispy.

06 Cook the casoncelli in small batches in a large saucepan of salted boiling water. Spoiler alert: they're ready when they float to the surface. Drain them gently.

07 Place the casoncelli in deep plates and top with the sage and pancetta butter sauce. These sweet and savoury treats are to be enjoyed without moderation.

\+ **On repeat in the kitchen:** As you taste these casoncelli with their unexpected flavour, (re)discover the song 'Pensiero stupendo' by Patty Pravo and let yourself be carried away by her deep, sensual voice.

FAZZOLETTI STRACHITUNT

Strachi-cool

FOR 4 FRIENDS

For the fazzoletti

- 200g (7oz) type 00 flour
- 150g (5¼oz) *semola rimacinata* (remilled durum wheat semolina)
- 8 egg yolks

For the filling

- 150g (5¼oz) well-drained ricotta
- 50g (1¾oz) grated Parmigiano Reggiano DOP
- Finely grated zest of 1 organic or unwaxed lemon
- White pepper (optional)

For the Strachitunt *fonduta*

- 120g (4¼oz) Strachitunt DOP (or, if unavailable, gorgonzola)
- 100ml (scant ½ cup) whole cream

For the green oil

- 1 small bunch of fresh herbs (basil, parsley, chives, tarragon, etc.)
- 5 tbsp olive oil

01 Start with the pasta dough. On a work surface, pour the flour and semolina into a small mound, make a well in the centre and add the egg yolks. Knead until you obtain a smooth dough. Cover with clingfilm and leave to rest for 30 minutes at room temperature.

02 Then prepare the filling. In a bowl, mix the ricotta with the Parmigiano and lemon zest. Add a little pepper, if you like, and set aside in the fridge.

03 Roll out the dough very thinly with a rolling pin or pasta machine, then refer to our filling and folding guide on page 394 to shape your mignonneries-fazzoletti. Place them on a floured work surface while you tackle the sauce.

04 Now it's time for your star attraction: Strachitunt. a blue cheese from Lombardy, the worthy ancestor of gorgonzola. In a small saucepan, melt it gently with the cream. Stir delicately until you obtain a smooth sauce, fragrant enough to tickle your nostrils, then set aside off the heat.

05 For the finishing touch, prepare a quick green oil: blend the fresh herbs with the oil until you obtain a beautiful bright green colour. Strain if necessary, for a perfectly smooth and shiny texture. It's simple, quick and impressive.

06 Finally, cook the fazzoletti for 2–3 minutes in a pan of salted boiling water. Drain them.

07 To serve, place the pasta in the centre of deep plates. Top with the Strachitunt *fonduta*, drizzle with green olive oil, add a final twist of pepper, and it's ready. A cheffy veggie dish that will bring everyone around the table together.

+ **On repeat in the kitchen:** Flashback to the early 1980s with 'Con il nastro rosa', one of Lucio Battisti's greatest hits, perfect to accompany this 100% comforting dish. *Chissàààààààà, chissà chi sei?*

CHAPTER 3

5-STAR PASTA

TUNA TURNER

Spaghettini peperoni e tonno

FOR 4 FRIENDS

For the spaghettini

- 320g (11¼oz) spaghettini (or capellini no. 1 or 2,
- the idea is to use thin, long pasta)
- Salt QB
- Extra virgin olive oil

For the reduced pepper juice

- 3 ripe red peppers
- Salt QB

For the filling

- 200g (7oz) fresh raw tuna (sashimi quality – your fish must be very fresh)
- 1 handful of capers in salt or brine
- 2 slices of wholemeal/sourdough bread or breadcrumbs
- A few fresh basil leaves
- Dried chilli flakes (optional)
- Olive oil
- Zest of 1 organic or unwaxed lemon (optional)

01 Start by preparing your pepper juice: wash, deseed, and chop the red peppers and extract the juice either by using a juicer or by blending with a little water. Strain through a fine sieve or cheesecloth to obtain a clear liquid, then pour into a small saucepan.
Simmer over low to medium heat until reduced to a light, slightly syrupy consistency (the holy grail). Season with salt to taste and leave to cool.

02 Cook the spaghettini in a large saucepan of salted boiling water (without breaking them, ever). Drain and immediately rinse under cold running water before drizzling with olive oil. Set aside in a cool place.

03 Cut the slices of bread into pieces – with love – and toast them in a frying pan with a drizzle of olive oil and, if desired, some dried chilli flakes. We all love crispy bread!

04 In another pan, fry the capers in a little hot oil until they are golden brown (if the capers were previously coated in salt, remember to wash them first, then drain them on kitchen paper).

05 Now it's time for the main character: fresh tuna. Dice it into small cubes, then season with olive oil, lemon zest, and a little pepper. Chill in the fridge until ready to use.

06 In a large bowl, mix the cooled pasta and pepper juice, then arrange everything on a pretty dish (make sure you make a good first impression). Scatter over the diced tuna, fried capers, crispy breadcrumbs, a few fresh basil leaves and drizzle with olive oil. Can you smell it? Summer is coming.

\+ **On repeat in the kitchen:** A true ode to Italian summer, this recipe pairs perfectly with the saline notes of Gino Paoli's 'Sapore di sale'. The goal: to make your dish as iconic as this hit song.

BENEFIT OF THE TROUT

Gnocchi con burro di acciughe, uova di trota e limone e menta

FOR 4 FRIENDS

For the gnocchi
- 500g (1lb 2oz) yellow floury potatoes, which, with their floury flesh, require less flour
- 150g (5¼oz) type 00 flour
- 1 tsp fine salt
- A pinch of pepper

For the topping
- 4 anchovy fillets in oil, drained
- 60g (2oz) unsalted butter
- 80g (2¾oz) trout roe (or salmon roe, depending on what you can find)

For the lemon-mint sauce
- 2 tbsp fresh lemon juice
- 1 tsp organic or unwaxed lemon zest
- 6 tbsp extra virgin olive oil
- 1 small shallot
- 8 fresh mint leaves
- Salt and freshly ground black pepper QB

For the finishing touch
- A few mint or basil leaves

01 Prepare the gnocchi: cook the whole potatoes, with their skins on, in a large saucepan of salted boiling water. Once tender, peel them while they are still hot (be careful not to burn yourself) and mash them with a potato masher. Leave to cool, then add the flour. Season with salt and pepper. Knead with the palms of your hands, a little but not too much, until you obtain a smooth, even dough. If it is a little sticky, add a pinch more flour. Then turn to page 399 to make your delicious gnocchi.

02 Cook your gnocchi in small batches in a large saucepan of salted boiling water. Spoiler alert: they are ready when they float to the surface. Drain them gently and set aside with a drizzle of olive oil to prevent them from sticking together.

03 In a large frying pan, gently melt the butter. Add the finely chopped anchovies and, still over a low heat, allow them to dissolve in the butter, stirring well.

04 In a small bowl, mix together the lemon juice and zest, chopped shallot and mint, and olive oil. Season with salt and pepper. Set aside.

05 Add the gnocchi to the pan with the anchovy butter and gently sauté to coat.

06 Put the gnocchi on deep plates, drizzle with lemon-mint sauce, and, for even more freshness, sprinkle with a few small mint or basil leaves. Last but not least, generously add the trout roe off the heat, without cooking it, to preserve its delicate flavour.

\+ **On repeat in the kitchen:** Iconic Italian duo Claudia Mori and Adriano Celentano singing 'Non succederà più', one of the biggest hits of the 1970s, which will melt your heart as gently as these eggs dissolve under your tongue.

FAMIGLIA VENTURO

Anna, Luigi & Giovanni

GIUGLIANO

BLACK AND GOLD

Lasagna zebra al ragù di salsiccia

FOR 4 FRIENDS

<u>For the lasagne sheets</u>
- 180g (6½oz) type 00 flour
- 180g (6½oz) *semola rimacinata* (remilled durum wheat semolina)
- 7 egg yolks

<u>For the squid ink linguine (or tagliolini)</u>
- 180g (6½oz) type 00 flour
- 180g (6½oz) *semola rimacinata* (remilled durum wheat semolina)
- 7 egg yolks
- 15g (½oz) squid ink

<u>For the sausage *ragù*</u>
- 330g (11oz) minced pork
- 640g (1lb 6¼oz) pork sausage, skinned and crumbled
- 1 carrot
- 1 stalk of celery
- 1 onion
- 1 garlic clove
- 375ml (generous 1½ cups) dry white wine
- 375ml (generous 1½ cups) vegetable stock (see page 317 for the recipe)
- 200ml (generous ¾ cup) *passata di pomodoro* (a homemade tomato pulp, the recipe for which can be found on page 270)
- 1 bouquet garni (bay leaf, sage, rosemary)
- 3 tbsp extra virgin olive oil
- Salt and pepper QB

<u>For the meat juices</u>
- 200g (7oz) meat of your choice (or bones)
- 1 small carrot
- 1 shallot
- 1 garlic clove
- 1 tbsp tomato paste
- 200ml (generous ¾ cup) white wine
- 500ml (2 cups) meat stock of your choice (see page 316 for the homemade version)
- 1 sprig of thyme
- 1 bay leaf
- 1 knob of butter

01 For the *ragù*, finely chop the vegetables and gently fry them in a large saucepan in a generous dash of olive oil. Add the meat and leave it to brown gently. Once it is nicely browned, deglaze with the wine and leave the liquid to evaporate completely. Then add the herbs, followed by the vegetable stock and *passata*. Simmer everything for at least 2½ hours over a very low heat until you have a fragrant, creamy sauce.

02 Meanwhile, start preparing your meat *jus*. In a hot pan with a drizzle of olive oil, brown the pieces of meat until they are slightly caramelised at the bottom – this is where the magic happens. Add the shallot, carrot, minced garlic and tomato paste, leave to caramelise for 1–2 minutes, then deglaze with the white wine. Scrape the bottom well to collect all the juices, pour in the meat stock, add the herbs and simmer gently for 15–20 minutes. Strain, return to the heat and reduce for another 5–10 minutes for maximum flavour. Remove from the heat and whisk in the butter until your sauce becomes silky smooth.

03 Now for the zebra-striped lasagne sheets – the artistic touch that will make an impression (if you prefer, classic lasagne sheets will work just as well). On a clean work surface, form a small volcano with the flour and semolina for the lasagne, make a well in the centre and add the egg yolks. Knead until you obtain a soft, smooth and elastic dough. Cover with clingfilm and leave to rest for 30 minutes at room temperature. Then move on to the tagliolini with squid ink. Same ritual: flour, semolina, egg yolks, but this time, squid ink is also added to obtain a black dough. Ten minutes of kneading later, cover with clingfilm and leave the ball of dough to rest.

+ **On repeat in the kitchen:** A nod to the artistic soul of this dish: play 'Monna Lisa' by Ivan Graziani, a pop rock ballad from the 1970s that begins with 'I would like to steal what belonged to me'.

04 Once your two types of dough are ready, roll them out thinly on a floured work surface using a rolling pin. What next? Turn to pages 389 and 396 for our guide to shaping lasagne sheets, tagliolini and zebra-striped sheets.

05 Now, cook your lasagne sheets (one by one) in a large saucepan of salted boiling water for 1–2 minutes max.

06 Finally, drain them, place the sausage *ragù* at the bottom of your plates, pour over the meat juices and then place the zebra lasagne sheets on top. Almost as beautiful as your summer crush.

HOUDINI SPAGHETTI
Spaghetti in bianco al pomodoro

For maximum flavour, the clear tomato sauce should be made the day before, guys.

FOR 4 FRIENDS

For the spaghetti
- 320g (11¼oz) durum wheat spaghetti
- 2–3 tbsp extra virgin olive oil
- Zest of 1 organic or unwaxed lemon (optional, for the finishing touch)
- White or black pepper (optional)
- Fleur de sel

For the clear tomato water
- 1kg (2lb 4oz) ripe tomatoes (datterino, beefsteak or heirloom tomatoes, we trust you as long as they are fragrant)
- 1 tbsp extra virgin olive oil
- A few basil leaves (optional)
- 5g (1 tsp) fine salt

01 Let's be clear, this dish is all about contrast: the absence of colour and the presence of intense flavour. To make it work, it's essential to follow each step carefully (we'll be the fun police today!). Wash and roughly chop the tomatoes, then blend them raw with the salt, a little olive oil, and basil if you like. Pour the purée into a sieve lined with a very fine, clean tea towel or cheesecloth set over a bowl. Leave to drain slowly in a cool place for at least 6–8 hours (ideally overnight), without pressing. By morning, you'll have a delicate, clear, intensely flavoured broth. Strain again if needed – you will want it almost transparent.

02 Cook the spaghetti *al dente*, without breaking it, in a pan of salted boiling water. Drain.

03 Pour a little of the tomato broth into a large frying pan and heat over a low heat. Add the spaghetti, a drizzle of olive oil, a little fleur de sel and even a dash of white pepper, and mix gently. Adjust the texture with a little more tomato broth if necessary until you obtain a nice light sauce that is completely colourless.

04 For a presentation worthy of the best Italian Trattorie, grab a fork and a ladle. Insert the fork into the steaming pasta and gently twist it against the ladle, as if winding thread. In just a few turns, you'll form a neat, tight nest, ready to be placed in the centre of the plate. If you're confident with tongs, now is the time to bring them out!

05 A drizzle of olive oil and some finely grated lemon zest for the finishing touch, and it's ready. We're going for a clean, almost monochrome look here – so the surprise comes with the first bite. Basil is allowed, but please, no small datterino tomatoes cut in half on the top. That's a red flag.

\+ **On repeat in the kitchen:** For this recipe, which plays on the dissonance between taste and sight, play Marco Mengoni's 'Due vite'. An emotional song – like your dish – that evokes the dialogue between the world of reason and the world of dreams. Fitting.

SPAGHETTI ALLA VITTORIO
Pasta that touches the stars

FOR 4 FRIENDS

- 320g (11¼oz) spaghetti
- ½ white or sweet onion
- 200g (7oz) tinned datterino tomatoes
- 200g (7oz) fresh datterino tomatoes (here, unity is strength)
- 40g (1½oz) butter
- 60g (2oz) grated Parmigiano Reggiano DOP
- 2–3 tbsp extra virgin olive oil
- Fresh basil
- Salt and freshly ground pepper QB

01 Heat a generous drizzle of olive oil in a saucepan, add the chopped onion and sauté over a low heat until translucent. Add the tinned datterino tomatoes, roughly crushed by hand, and the fresh tomatoes, cut in half. Simmer for 20–25 minutes over a medium heat until your sauce becomes thick and shiny. Then, you have two options: if you like a rustic texture, leave the pieces in; otherwise, strain and blend everything in a mixer until smooth for a top-quality sauce. Season with salt and pepper and set aside.

02 Meanwhile, cook the spaghetti (without breaking them, we're watching you) in a large quantity of salted boiling water until *al dente*. Drain, but as always, remember to keep a ladleful of the cooking water.

03 In a large frying pan, pour in the tomato sauce while it is still hot and add the spaghetti, a generous knob of butter (not all of it, we'll need some more later) and a handful of the Parmigiano. Sauté for a few seconds, add a dash of the cooking water and let the magic happen: the sauce should coat each strand of spaghetti.

04 Before serving, add the rest of the butter and Parmigiano, mix and serve immediately. A sprinkling of basil and you're done. *Buon appetito*, Chef.

\+ **On repeat in the kitchen:** This legendary recipe was born in the temple of gastronomy, the famous Da Vittorio restaurant, a little gem with a Michelin star located not far from Bergamo. A city described with love and poetry by Pinguini Tattici Nucleari in 'Bergamo'.

AND THE GOLDEN PASTA GOES TO . . .

On the big and small screen, Italian filmmakers film pasta as a reflection of society. Over there, around a steaming dish, anything can happen – settling of scores, bursts of laughter or grand declarations. It brings people together, tells stories and reveals truths, like a true headliner. Here are 10 examples to prove it.

I SOLITI IGNOTI

Persons Unknown

by Mario Monicelli, 1958

In this absurd heist comedy, Marcello Mastroianni, Totò, Vittorio Gassman and Renato Salvatori decide to rob a pawn shop. It's a bitter failure, as the wall they break through leads to . . . a kitchen. The prize? no treasure, just *pasta e ceci* (pasta and chickpeas) eaten straight from the pot as their loot. A failed heist, but an improvised feast of the highest quality.

IL GATTOPARDO

The Leopard

by Luchino Visconti, 1963

Among the most iconic scenes in *The Leopard*, a masterpiece with a royal cast – Burt Lancaster, Claudia Cardinale, Alain Delon – is the sumptuous banquet at the Donnafugata palace. On the menu: a baroque and majestic *timballo di maccheroni*, which Visconti elevates to the status of a cinematic icon.

MATRIMONIO ALL'ITALIANA

Marriage Italian Style

by Vittorio De Sica, 1964

Filumena Marturano (Sofia Loren), a former courtesan living with her wealthy client Domenico Soriano (Marcello Mastroianni), despairs of ever receiving a marriage proposal. After more than twenty years of patience, in an intense scene she nervously devours a plate of *pasta e fagioli* (pasta and beans). A true gourmet muse of Italian cinema, Sofia Loren has never hidden her love for cooking. In 1971, she even published *In cucina con amore*, a global bestseller in which she confides: 'Everything you see, I owe to spaghetti'.

C'ERAVAMO TANTO AMATI

We All Loved Each Other So Much

by Ettore Scola, 1974

In the popular Roman trattoria, Dal re della mezza porzione (The King of Half Portions), three friends who took part in the Italian Resistance – Vittorio Gassman, Nino Manfredi and Stefano Satta Flores – meet over *pasta e ceci* and a plate of *rigatoni con la pajata* to take stock and put the world to rights amid laughter, disappointment and nostalgia.

GOODFELLAS

by Martin Scorsese, 1990

In the Scorsese family, cooking is a serious business and, above all, a family affair. In *Goodfellas*, while in prison, members of the Lucchese clan (Ray Liotta and Robert De Niro) watch Vinnie – played by Charles Scorsese, the director's father – carefully prepare a meat tomato sauce. A *ragù* made with three meats and razor-thin slices of garlic, which is actually the real recipe of Catherine Scorsese, the filmmaker's mother of Sicilian origin.

RESPIRO

by Emanuele Crialese, 2002

Filmed on the island of Lampedusa, *Respiro* shows Grazia's (Valeria Golino) family gathered around large plates of pasta with tomato or fish sauce. Simple yet meaningful scenes convey a deep attachment to the land, the sea and blood ties. In this sunny and rugged southern Sicily, pasta is the compass.

IL DIVO

by Paolo Sorrentino, 2008

Il Divo, Giulio Andreotti's nickname, traces the career of this pillar of Italian politics. In one memorable scene, we see him (played by Toni Servillo) savouring *bucatini all'amatriciana*, Rome's iconic dish. A gourmet interlude where attention is briefly diverted from the political turmoil to focus on a profoundly human gesture.

MINE VAGANTI

Loose Cannons

by Ferzan Özpetek, 2010

In the Cantone family, wealthy pasta manufacturers from Puglia, the younger son Tommaso (Riccardo Scamarcio) wants to reveal his homosexuality during a family dinner. But his older brother, the designated heir to the factory, beats him to it . . . with the same announcement. A meal where pasta embodies both heritage and the weight of convention.

MIA MADRE

by Nanni Moretti, 2015

When Margherita (Margherita Buy) is devastated to learn that her mother is terminally ill, her brother (Nanni Moretti) gives up everything to be with her until the end. At the hospital, he brings her pasta *al pomodoro e basilico*, topped with a 'still warm' sauce and grated Parmigiano. The pasta becomes a final act of care, a moment of tenderness in the face of the inevitable.

C'È ANCORA DOMANI

There's Still Tomorrow

by Paola Cortellesi, 2023

In post-war Italy, Delia welcomes her daughter's fiancé's family for an 'engagement' lunch. On the menu: *pasta al forno* as the star dish, meat being a luxury item at the time. The Sunday meal becomes a symbol of class struggle, oscillating between biting irony and social criticism.

FELLINI, MAESTRO DELLA PASTA

In Fellini's films, we don't eat. We rejoice, we collapse, we dream. Pasta is a language in its own right, the embodiment of a noisy Italy, somewhere between tenderness and gluttony. As in *Roma* (1972), where meals become visual orgies and plates overflow with pasta in joyful chaos. Or in *Amarcord* (1973), where steaming tagliatelle is served in mountainous piles, reminiscent of childhood meals. Finally, in *La Strada* (1954), Il Matto, the moonstruck acrobat, eats his spaghetti while balancing on a tightrope. A Fellini-esque scene where a simple bite of pasta becomes vertigo and poetry.

CARBONARA WITH A SEA BREEZE

Tonnarelli alla carbonara di mare

FOR 4 FRIENDS

For the tonnarelli

- 180g (6½oz) plain flour
- 180g (6½oz) *semola rimacinata* (remilled durum wheat semolina)
- 7 egg yolks

For the carbonara

- 4 egg yolks
- 30g (1oz) grated Parmigiano Reggiano DOP
- 30g (1oz) grated Pecorino Romano DOP

For the concentrated shellfish or lobster bisque

- Lobster, langoustine (Dublin Bay prawn) or prawn shells (your fishmonger will no doubt give them to you with a smile)
- 1 onion
- 1 carrot
- 1 stalk of celery
- 2 tbsp tomato paste
- Olive oil
- Salt and pepper QB

For the seafood garnish

- 150g (5¼oz) fresh raw tuna, finely diced
- 150g (5¼oz) sea bass or swordfish (depending on your catch of the day), diced
- A few fresh mussels
- Extra virgin olive oil
- Fine salt QB

01 Start with the tonnarelli. On a clean work surface, pour the flour and semolina into a small mound, make a well in the centre and add the egg yolks. Knead until you obtain a smooth dough. Cover with clingfilm and leave to rest for 30 minutes at room temperature.

02 In a bowl, whisk the egg yolks with the Parmigiano, Pecorino and black pepper. The desired texture here is smooth but thick. Once you have achieved this, leave to rest at room temperature.

03 Prepare your bisque. In an oiled saucepan, put the chopped onion, carrot and celery. Add the shellfish shells, then sauté over a low heat for 5 minutes. Stir in the tomato paste and a little water to loosen the mixture. Season with salt and pepper, then simmer gently for 30–45 minutes. Strain through a fine sieve or chinois and set aside.

04 Pour a drizzle of olive oil into a frying pan and toast the sea bass or swordfish cubes for 30 seconds to 1 minute on each side, no more. Season lightly with salt. Place the mussels in a large saucepan after washing them. Leave them to open over a medium heat.

05 Get your dough, roll it out thinly with a rolling pin or pasta machine, and turn to page 389 for cutting instructions.

06 Cook the tonnarelli in a large saucepan of salted boiling water. *Al dente*, of course (3–4 minutes). Reserve a ladleful of the cooking water. In a stainless-steel mixing bowl or other large bowl, mix the drained tonnarelli with the egg cream and bisque. Add a little cooking water if necessary to bind everything together.

07 Serve the tonnarelli piping hot in deep plates.Place the seared sea bass or swordfish pieces on top, along with the mussels and finely diced raw tuna. Add a final pinch of pepper and *buon appetito*!

+ **On repeat in the kitchen:** With the hit 'Riccione' by Thegiornalisti, dive into the Adriatic coast in Romagna, the birthplace of *carbonara di mare*. Let yourself be carried away by the music and the smell of the beach, and book a ticket for your next holiday in this seaside resort that smells of suncream and summer romances.

RISOTTO ALLA MILANESE CON MIDOLLO

An icon for a reason

FOR 4 FRIENDS

- 320g (11¼oz) Carnaroli rice (avoid pre-cooked 'risotto rice' sold in sachets)
- 40g (1½oz) *midollo* (ideally 1 marrowbone, or 2 medium bones or 3 smaller bones)
- 1 small onion, finely chopped
- A pinch of saffron stems, infused in a little hot water
- 1 litre (4¼ cups) beef stock (see our recipe on page 316)
- 40g (1½oz) butter
- 50g (1¾oz) grated Parmigiano Reggiano DOP
- 1 small glass of dry white wine
- Fresh herbs (sage, parsley, rosemary)
- Zest of 1 organic or unwaxed orange or lemon
- Olive oil
- Salt and pepper QB

01 Start by preparing your veal marrow by soaking the bones in a large bowl of cold salted water for 1 hour. Stir occasionally to remove any impurities. Drain, discard the soaking water, rinse thoroughly with clean water, gently rubbing the ends of the bones to remove any residue, and repeat the process until the water is almost clear.

02 Place the herbs and zest of your chosen citrus fruit in a preheated oven at 60–80°C fan/80–100°C/175–210°F/GM ¼–½ to dry. Once dry, blend them into a powder: say hello to your *gremolata*.

03 In a saucepan, slowly reduce your hot beef stock over a low heat until you obtain a nice, syrupy base.

04 Roast the marrowbones in the oven for 7–8 minutes at 200°C fan/220°C/425°F/GM 7. Sprinkle with *gremolata* when finished in the oven.

05 Prepare your risotto. In a large saucepan, sauté the finely chopped onion in a drizzle of olive oil, add the rice and toast it for 2 minutes, stirring until it becomes pearly, not burnt. Deglaze with the white wine, let it evaporate completely, then pour in the hot stock ladle by ladle, stirring constantly. Halfway through cooking (around the eighth minute), add the saffron infusion: your risotto will then take on the colour of a sunset over the Piazza del Duomo.

06 After 16–18 minutes, remove from the heat and add the butter, Parmigiano, salt and pepper – this is the sacred moment of *mantecatura*, when the magic happens and the risotto becomes creamy and shiny.

07 Now it's time to plate up: spoon the risotto into a deep plate and pour your reduced beef stock around it. In Milan, they like it *a l'onda* (in waves), meaning that when you gently tilt the plate, the surface of the risotto – neither too thick nor too runny – should ripple like a small wave. Try it out and impress your guests with this little regional anecdote.

08 At the table, serve the risotto accompanied by roasted marrowbone sprinkled with *gremolata* and invite your guests to add it to their own plates: a truly experiential dinner.

\+ **On repeat in the kitchen:** In 'Il ragazzo della via Gluck', Adriano Celentano sings of his own journey: a working-class child in Milan, he grew up on Via Gluck, where nature gradually gave way to apartment buildings and asphalt. One of his greatest hits, still as relevant today as ever.

FAMIGLIA VENTURO

Antonio, Luigi, Anna, Giovanni

GIUGLIANO

RISOTTO ALL'AGLIO ORSINO E SCAMPI

Full langousteam ahead

FOR 4 FRIENDS

For the risotto

- 280g (10oz) Carnaroli rice (no compromises, it's the cream of the crop)
- 1 shallot, finely chopped
- 1 litre (4¼ cups) vegetable stock (see our recipe on page 317)
- 80ml (generous ⅓ cup) dry white wine
- 30g (1oz) cold butter
- 40g (1½oz) grated Parmigiano Reggiano DOP
- 2 tbsp extra virgin olive oil

For the wild garlic pesto

- 50g (1¾oz) fresh wild garlic leaves
- 30g (1oz) pine nuts or blanched almonds
- 55ml (1¾oz) extra virgin olive oil
- 20g (¾oz) grated Parmigiano Reggiano DOP (optional)
- Salt QB

For the filling

- 8 very fresh langoustines (Dublin Bay prawns), shelled and deveined
- 1 dash of organic or unwaxed lemon juice
- 1 dash of extra virgin olive oil
- Fleur de sel

For the spicy breadcrumbs

- 50g (1¾oz) breadcrumbs (use a little stale bread, blended; nothing is wasted, everything is transformed)
- 1 tsp tomato paste
- A pinch of chilli powder (such as peperoncino or smoked paprika)
- 1 tbsp olive oil
- Salt QB

01 Start with the pesto. Blend the wild garlic with the pine nuts or almonds, olive oil and Parmigiano (if using). The aim is to achieve a smooth texture that smells of the forest. Add salt to taste and keep cool.

02 Next, prepare the langoustines. Cut them in half lengthwise, then drizzle them lightly with olive oil, and season with a squeeze of lemon juice and a pinch of fleur de sel. Cover and set aside in the fridge.

03 In a small frying pan, heat a little olive oil, add the tomato paste and fry for a few seconds. Add the breadcrumbs and chilli powder, mix well to coat everything, then leave to brown over a low heat until it is crispy and nicely browned. Add a pinch of salt and leave to cool at room temperature.

04 Now for the risotto. In a saucepan, sweat the shallot in a drizzle of olive oil, add the rice and toast it for 2–3 minutes, stirring constantly. When the rice becomes pearly, deglaze with the white wine and pour in a ladleful of hot stock, then stir. Repeat this process several times as soon as the liquid evaporates, stirring continuously. This is important, otherwise the rice could stick or run out of water, which would be – between you and me – a disaster. After 15–18 minutes of cooking, remove from the heat and stir in the butter, Parmigiano and wild garlic pesto. The result: a perfectly creamy texture.

05 Spoon the risotto into the centre of a deep plate, arrange the langoustines on top and sprinkle with spicy breadcrumbs. Add a drizzle of olive oil and, between the chlorophyll green, paprika red and pearly langoustine, you have clearly created a work of art.

+ **On repeat in the kitchen:** Because this dish is a true declaration of love, we listen to 'Ti amo' by Umberto Tozzi: a legendary slow-dance song, full of intensity and passion, perfect to accompany this langoustine risotto. Is it time to pop the question?

RISOTTO DI MARE

Close your eyes and hear the ocean

FOR 4 FRIENDS

For the risotto

- 320g (11¼oz) Carnaroli rice (avoid pre-cooked 'risotto rice' sold in sachets)
- 1 shallot
- 1 glass of dry white wine
- 1 litre (4¼ cups) clear fish stock (fish stock is a broth made from fish heads and bones – ask your fishmonger nicely for some)
- 3 tbsp extra virgin olive oil
- Salt and black pepper QB

For the garnish

- 3 or 4 cockles or clams per person
- 1 red prawn (red shrimp) per person, as raw as it is fresh
- 100–120g (3½–4¼oz) branzino fillet (or European sea bass for the Frenchies)
- A few leaves of chervil (a chic touch that makes it look good)

01 In a large saucepan, boil the fish heads and bones in salted water. Simmer for 30–40 minutes, then carefully strain the liquid through a sieve. The aim is to obtain what is known as a clear stock. Set aside.

02 Clean your shellfish thoroughly if the fishmonger has not done it for you, then steam or boil them in a pan with a drizzle of olive oil. Cover and allow the *frutti di mare* to open gently for 3–5 minutes. As soon as they are open, remove them from the heat to prevent them from becoming rubbery and discard any that remain closed.

03 Cut the fish fillet into small cubes and sear them in a pan, skin-side down, until golden. Set aside.

04 In a sauté pan, fry the finely chopped shallot in a generous dash of olive oil. Add the rice and toast it for 1–2 minutes until it turns pearly. Deglaze with the white wine (and pour yourself a small glass with the rest, cheers). Gradually add the hot stock while stirring regularly. Repeat the process each time the liquid evaporates. The rice must not stick, so continue stirring throughout the process. Do this thoroughly, otherwise the rice will burn, and if it does we'll run away too.

05 After 16–18 minutes of cooking, remove from the heat, add a drizzle of olive oil, a twist of pepper and stir until the risotto becomes silky smooth.

06 Spoon the risotto into deep plates, place a few open cockles on top and add the red prawns to each plate. Finally, sprinkle with the diced fried branzino, sprinkle with chervil if you have made the wise decision to include it, and call the whole family to admire and taste your masterpiece.

+ **On repeat in the kitchen:** As your kitchen fills with the scents of the sea, set sail on 'In alto mare'. Can you smell the sea spray? That mist of freedom? It's the gravelly voice of Loredana Bertè carrying you away.

CACIO E PEPE CON SCAMPI

Spaghettoni cacio pepe, scampi e lime

FOR 4 FRIENDS

For the spaghettoni

- 320g (11¼oz) spaghettoni (note that size matters here: thicker than spaghetti, spaghettoni absorbs the sauce better)

For the cream

- 160g (5½oz) grated Pecorino Romano DOP
- 2 tsp freshly ground or crushed black pepper

For the scampi

- 8–12 very fresh langoustines (Dublin Bay prawns), shelled and deveined
- Finely grated zest of 1 organic or unwaxed lime
- 1–2 tbsp extra virgin olive oil
- Fine salt and black pepper QB

01 In a mixing bowl, combine the finely grated Pecorino and half of the black pepper coarsely crushed in a mill – or mortar, for purists. Set the other half of the pepper aside.

02 Cook the spaghettoni, *al dente* of course, in a large pot of lightly salted boiling water (the Pecorino will add salt). Drain, carefully reserving 2 ladles of cooking water, your liquid gold.

03 Now it's time for the crucial step to succeed like a *maestro*. Into your mixing bowl pour a ladleful of the cooking water; it should still be hot but not boiling, otherwise the cheese will split. This means that instead of obtaining a smooth and silky cream, you will end up with a grainy paste or, worse, lumps. Whisk and continue adding the hot water little by little until you obtain a creamy Pecorino, neither too runny nor too thick. Set aside at room temperature.

04 In a large frying pan, off the heat, pour in the cream and add the spaghettoni. Mix over a low heat, adding a little more cooking water to create a shiny emulsion. Finally, sprinkle with the rest of the crushed pepper.

05 For a presentation worthy of an Italian trattoria, place the spaghettoni in a ladle and twirl it with a fork into a neat nest, then transfer it to the centre of a deep plate. Arrange the chopped langoustines on top like precious jewels. Finish with a twist of pepper, a little lime zest, and a drizzle of olive oil. *Ci siamo!*

+ **On repeat in the kitchen:** Isn't this THE perfect recipe to impress your date? The irresistible creaminess of *cacio e pepe*, the gracefulness of scampi . . . an irresistible duo that makes you want to sing Alex Rossi's 'Tutto va bene quando facciamo l'amore'. The message is clear.

CAPELLINI AI RICCI DI MARE

Your guardian angel

FOR 4 FRIENDS

- 320g (11¼oz) capellini (nicknamed angel hair, this very fine pasta cooks extremely quickly)
- 80–100g (2¾–3½oz) fresh sea urchin uni, which you will find in the equivalent of 25–30 sea urchins (the uni are the five small orange tongues nestled in the heart of the shell, also called 'coral')
- 2 garlic cloves
- 1 small dried red chilli pepper, such as peperoncino (depending on how brave you are)
- 5 tbsp high-quality extra virgin olive oil
- Fine sea salt
- A few sprigs of flat-leaf parsley (optional, for garnish)

01 Start by preparing the sea urchins. If you are on good terms with your fishmonger, ask to have them opened in advance. If not, don't panic. The easiest way? Use scissors. Take the sea urchin in your hand (without pricking yourself), turn it over: you will see a small round area without spines. That's where you start. Slide the blade of your scissors along the edge, then cut in a circle all the way around. Once you have gone all the way around, the sea urchin will split in two. Once open, gently rinse the inside and collect only the orange parts. Drain them in a very fine sieve and set aside in a cool place.

02 In a large frying pan, heat the olive oil with the crushed garlic (and chilli, if you want to spice it up). As soon as the garlic is golden brown, remove it (and the chilli). Leave this fragrant oil to rest at room temperature.

03 Meanwhile, bring a large saucepan of lightly salted water to the boil (no need to add too much salt, as sea urchins are already quite salty) and cook the capellini *al dente*. Remove a ladleful of cooking water before quickly draining the pasta. Chef's secret.

04 Remove from the heat and stir the capellini into the flavoured oil in the pan. Add a little cooking water to create a nice emulsion: this is called *mantecatura*, an Italian technique that gives dishes a perfectly creamy texture. Then gently add the sea urchin coral, but above all, never cook it; it should always be added off the heat, just before serving. Mix gently.

05 Twirl the capellini into neat nests using a ladle and fork. If you like, add a little extra sea urchin on top. Finish with a drizzle of olive oil and a touch of chopped parsley and . . . it's ready. Just the sea, at its purest.

\+ **On repeat in the kitchen:** This dish of absolute purity deserves a soundtrack to match. The instrumental piece 'Spuma di mare' by guitarist Bruno Battisti D'Amario is a must: listen to it as if you were sipping a drink in Procida while a salty breeze caresses your cheek.

THE GOLDEN EGG PASTA

Spaghettini freddi al caviale

FOR 4 FRIENDS

- 320g (11¼oz) spaghettini (or capellini no. 1 or 2; the idea is to use thin, long pasta)
- 40–50g (1¼–1¾oz) caviar (ideally Italian: Calvisius, Ars Italica, but your favourite brand will always be the best)
- 1 organic or unwaxed lemon (optional but traditional)
- 4 tbsp extra virgin olive oil (Taggiasca, Garda or a light Tuscan oil, to enhance without overpowering), plus a little extra
- 2 tbsp double cream (optional)
- Fresh chives
- Fine salt QB
- Freshly ground white pepper (optional)

01 Cook the spaghettini in a large saucepan of salted boiling water (without breaking them, need we say more?) until *al dente*. Drain, rinse under cold water to stop the cooking process and add a generous drizzle of olive oil to prevent them from sticking together.

02 Once cooled, add the olive oil and a pinch of fine salt. If desired, add a small dash of cream for a slightly richer texture (use sparingly). Finely grate a little lemon zest – use a Microplane if you have one – then gently mix everything together.

03 Slowly and carefully, and off the heat, add two thirds of the caviar – it is a special guest, take care of it and stir gently.

04 For a presentation worthy of a Michelin star, grab a fork and a ladle. Stick the fork into the pasta and gently turn it in the hollow of the ladle, as if you were winding a thread. In a few quick turns, you will have a nice, tight nest, ready to be placed in the centre of the plate. Add a final spoonful of caviar on top, a touch of lemon zest, a drizzle of olive oil, and – for the daring – a twist of white pepper and a sprinkling of chopped chives. Simply chic.

+ **On repeat in the kitchen:** Exceptional dish, exceptional piece. We're playing Nicolas's 'Quei due' Godin (half of the duo Air), a soft and captivating sound that perfectly accompanies this subtle and elegant dish with its muted chords. Caviar for the ears.

BE OUR LOBSTER

Spaghetti all'freddi e lime

FOR 4 FRIENDS

- 320g (11¼oz) spaghetti
- 1 lobster or 250g (8¾oz) cooked, shelled lobster meat
- 150g (5¼oz) fresh tomatoes (datterino or cherry)
- 1 spring onion
- Juice and zest of 1 organic or unwaxed lime
- Zest of ½ organic or unwaxed lemon
- 6 tbsp extra virgin olive oil
- Fine salt and freshly ground white pepper QB

01 Start with the star of the dish: the lobster. Cook it in a large saucepan of salted boiling water for 6–7 minutes – no longer – as we want the shellfish to be tender. Once cooked, transfer it to an ice bath to stop the cooking process and preserve its beautiful texture. Next, it's time to cut it up: remove the claws, then crack them open with nutcrackers to extract the meat. Separate the tail from the thorax, break the rings and remove the meat with a small knife. A little tip from a friend: keep the shell, it will make a delicious homemade stock. Cut the meat into even pieces and set aside in the fridge.

02 Meanwhile, cook the spaghetti (without breaking it, we're watching you) then, as with the lobster, stop the cooking process by running it under cold water. Drain well and add a drizzle of olive oil to prevent it from sticking.

03 Dice the tomatoes and finely chop the spring onion.

04 In a bowl, emulsify the lime juice and zest, lemon zest, olive oil, and season with salt and white pepper. Taste, adjust, be bold – you're the chef.

05 In a stainless steel mixing bowl, combine the cold pasta with this sunny dressing, the tomatoes and spring onion, then gently add the pieces of lobster. Leave everything to rest for 5 minutes at room temperature, just long enough for the flavours to blend perfectly.

06 Arrange your plates elegantly – just like your cooking – in the style of a refined little nest using a fork and a ladle. Add some lemon zest here, a drizzle of olive oil there, and for the finishing touch, a twist of white pepper just before serving. Irresistible.

\+ **On repeat in the kitchen:** Lobster pasta is a must for special occasions, the party dish par excellence. So to set the right tone, turn up the volume and play Raffaella Carrà's 'Tanti auguri'. It's bound to be someone's birthday somewhere.

TAGLIOLINI AL GRANCHIO E ALL'ARAGOSTA

Plenty of fish in the sea

FOR 4 FRIENDS

For the tagliolini

- 180g (6½oz) type 00 flour
- 180g (6½oz) *semola rimacinata* (remilled durum wheat semolina)
- 7 egg yolks

For the bisque

- Lobster shells (negotiate a good price with the fishmonger)
- 1 shallot
- ½ fennel bulb
- 1 small carrot
- 1 stalk of celery
- 1 tbsp tomato paste
- 50ml (scant ¼ cup) white wine
- 250ml (1 cup) water
- 50ml (scant ¼ cup) double cream
- Extra virgin olive oil
- Salt and pepper QB

For the sauce

- 200g (7oz) cooked crab meat, shelled
- 150–200g (5¼–7oz) cooked lobster meat, shelled
- 1 garlic clove
- 1 small red chilli pepper (optional)
- 1 glass of dry white wine
- Fresh parsley
- Grated zest of ½ organic or unwaxed lemon
- 4 tbsp extra virgin olive oil
- Salt and pepper QB

01 On a clean work surface, pour the flour and semolina into a small mound, make a well in the centre and add the egg yolks. Knead until you obtain a smooth dough. Cover with clingfilm and leave to rest for 30 minutes at room temperature.

02 Prepare the bisque (ideally the day before, for maximum flavour). Heat a generous dash of olive oil in a saucepan. Add the lobster shells, then stir in the finely chopped shallot, fennel, carrot and celery. Fry for a few minutes before adding the tomato paste. Deglaze with the white wine, allow to evaporate, then pour in the water. Now close your eyes, take a deep breath, and imagine yourself in a small fishing port in Sicily. Simmer gently over low heat for 30 minutes, then strain, add the cream, season with salt and pepper, and set aside.

03 Once your dough has rested, roll it out thinly with a rolling pin (or a pasta machine if you have one in your cupboards or you can pinch one from your neighbours) and follow our guide on page 396 for cutting it.

04 In a large frying pan, heat the 4 tablespoons olive oil with the whole garlic clove and chilli pepper, chopped into small pieces, if you like it spicy. Add the crab and lobster meat, fry for 1–2 minutes. Deglaze with the white wine (and feel free to pour yourself a small glass), then allow it to reduce. Cheers. Add the lemon zest, a little chopped parsley, salt and pepper. Remove the garlic.

05 Cook the tagliolini *al dente* in a large saucepan of salted boiling water. Drain.

06 Mix the pasta with the seafood sauce.

07 Serve in a deep plate with 1 spoonful of hot bisque on top. All that's missing is the sound of the waves. How many days until we pack our bags?

+ **On repeat in the kitchen:** 'Amada Mia, Amore Mio' by El Pasador, a slow Italian disco number from the 1970s. Perfect for throwing a few shapes with your partner. Tango or mambo style, just make sure you swing those hips.

ASKING FOR TRUFFLE

Gnocchi con caciocavallo e tartufo

FOR 4 FRIENDS

For the gnocchi

- 500g (1lb 2oz) potatoes (preferably yellow floury potatoes: they contain less water, which means you can use less flour. The result? Light, delicious gnocchi. Tell everyone about it during drinks later on)
- 150g (5 ¼oz) type 00 flour
- 3g (0.1oz) fine salt
- A pinch of pepper

For the Parmigiano *fonduta*

- 400ml (1⅔ cups) double cream
- 20g (4 tsp) cornflour (always useful for thickening if needed)
- 300g (10½oz) grated Parmigiano Reggiano DOP

For the truffle clarified butter

- 100g (3½oz) clarified butter, as demonstrated in step 04 (who would even think to ask their personal digital assistant what that means?)
- A few drops of truffle oil

For plating

- Fresh truffle to grate on top when plating (optional)
- A few slices of caciocavallo (Caciocavallo Silano, a sharp semi-hard Italian) cheese

01 Start with your gnocchi: cook the whole potatoes, with their skins on, in a large saucepan of salted water. Once tender, peel them while they are still hot, then mash them with a potato masher. Leave to cool, then add the flour, salt and pepper. Knead with the palms of your hands until you obtain a smooth, even dough. If it sticks a little, add a pinch more 00 flour.

02 Next, make the Parmigiano *fonduta*. In a bowl, mix the cornflour with a little cold cream to prevent lumps from forming. In a saucepan, heat the remaining cream without bringing it to the boil. Remove from the heat and whisk in the Parmigiano until smooth. Return to a low heat, add the cornflour mixture, and cook for 2–3 minutes, stirring constantly, until slightly thickened.

03 Take your dough and shape your gnocchi using our guide on page 399.

04 Final step: melt the butter gently in a saucepan over a low heat without stirring. Skim the foam from the surface, remove the whey from the bottom, then flavour the clarified butter with a few drops of truffle oil. Sauté the gnocchi in the butter to give them a golden-brown colour.

05 To serve, arrange thin slices of caciocavallo on the plate. Add the golden gnocchi and spoon over the Parmigiano fondue. Finish with freshly grated truffle (celebrating anything?) and serve immediately.

\+ **On repeat in the kitchen:** For this emotional recipe, listen to 'La dolce vita'. by Christophe or its cover by Sébastien Tellier. There's no doubt that your truffle gnocchi will give you just as many thrills – if not more – as this song.

SEAS THE DAY

Lasagna aperta di mare

FOR 4 FRIENDS

For the lasagne

- 180g (6½oz) type 00 flour
- 180g (6½oz) *semola rimacinata* (remilled durum wheat semolina)
- 7 organic egg yolks

For the seafood

- 4 fresh langoustines (Dublin Bay prawns or large raw shrimps)
- 200g (7oz) sea bass fillet (branzino), whole or filleted
- 300g (10½oz) mussels
- Olive oil
- Salt and pepper QB

For the sauce

- 300ml (1¼ cups) fish stock (fish bones and carcasses)
- 1 small carrot
- 1 shallot
- 1 tbsp olive oil
- A little tomato paste (optional)

For serving

- Zest of 1 organic or unwaxed lemon
- Fresh chives

01 On your work surface, arrange the flour and semolina and form a small well. Place the egg yolks in the centre and beat them with a fork until you obtain a smooth dough. Knead by hand for 10–12 minutes: the dough should become soft and elastic. Cover with clingfilm and set aside for at least 30 minutes. Once your dough has rested, roll it out thinly with a rolling pin or pasta machine and follow our guide on page 389 for cutting lasagne sheets like a maestro.

02 Shell the langoustines or prawns. Cut the sea bass into small cubes, if whole, make sure to keep the bones and carcasses. You can use them to make a homemade fish stock. Set the shellfish and fish aside in a cool place.

03 In a saucepan, sauté the chopped carrot and shallot in 1 tablespoon of olive oil. Add the sea bass bones and langoustine or shrimp shells and brown everything. Deglaze with 300ml (1¼ cups) of cold water and add, if you like, a dash of tomato paste. Simmer for 20–25 minutes, then strain through a sieve (bones are very unpleasant in this sauce). Allow to reduce slightly to obtain a smooth, silky sauce, then set aside.

04 Open the mussels over a high heat in a saucepan with a little olive oil, remove them as soon as they open and set aside. Discard any that do not open. Quickly sear the sea bass cubes in a hot frying pan with a drizzle of olive oil until lightly browned. Season with salt and pepper and set aside. Finely chop your langoustines or prawns into a tartare, season with a little olive oil, salt and lemon zest, then set aside.

05 Next, cook the lasagne sheets one by one in a pan of salted boiling water, drain them and quickly rinse under cold water to stop them cooking.

06 Now it's time for plating! Place a warm lasagne sheet flat on each plate. Arrange the sea bass, mussels (without shells), and langoustine tartare on top. Spoon over the hot fish sauce and finish with a sprinkling of chopped chives and lemon zest.

\+ **On repeat in the kitchen:** Serve this dish with 'Tra te e il mare', one of Laura Pausini's biggest hits. A ballad to sing at the top of your voice while you prepare your sea-filled masterpiece.

CHAPTER 4

PASTA BAKES

LASAGNA DI ZUCCHINE

For courgette gluts and gluttons

FOR 4 FRIENDS

For the lasagne

- 180g (6½oz) type 00 flour
- 180g (6½oz) *semola rimacinata* (remilled durum wheat semolina)
- 7 egg yolks

For the sauce

- 2 medium green courgettes
- 2 medium yellow courgettes
- 500ml (2 cups) béchamel sauce (see recipe below)
- 200g (7oz) smoked mozzarella (or scamorza affumicata)
- 60g (2oz) grated Parmigiano Reggiano DOP
- 2 tbsp extra virgin olive oil
- Nutmeg (optional)
- Salt and freshly ground black pepper QB

For the béchamel sauce

- 40g (1½oz) butter
- 40g (1½oz) plain flour
- 500ml (2 cups) milk
- Salt, pepper, nutmeg QB

01 Start by preparing the pasta dough. On your work surface, mound the flour and semolina and make a small well in the centre. Add the egg yolks into the middle and beat with a fork to mix in the flour. Knead by hand for 10–12 minutes: the dough should become soft and elastic. Cover with clingfilm and set aside for at least 30 minutes.

02 Preheat the oven to 180°C fan/200°C/400°F/GM 6. While it's heating up, wash the yellow and green courgettes, cut off their ends, then slice them into thin rounds (ideally using a mandoline or, if you're feeling adventurous tonight, slice lengthways into strips for a more elegant look).

03 In a large frying pan, sauté the courgettes in a generous drizzle of olive oil over a medium heat for 5–7 minutes, until tender but not too browned. Season with salt and pepper.

04 For the béchamel sauce, melt the butter in a saucepan, then whisk in the flour gently. Gradually pour in the hot milk, whisking continuously to avoid lumps (we're counting on you), until the sauce thickens. Season with salt, pepper and a pinch of nutmeg, then set aside.

05 Cut the smoked mozzarella into thin slices or small cubes, as desired.

06 Grab your dough and refer to page 389 for our cutting guide.

07 Roll up your sleeves and start assembling the lasagna: spread a thin layer of béchamel sauce over the base of a lightly oiled baking dish, then start layering. Alternate between the lasagne sheets, courgette slices, smoked mozzarella, béchamel and grated Parmigiano. Repeat the process and finish with a generous layer of béchamel, a few courgette slices, and a sprinkling of smoked mozzarella and Parmigiano.

08 Bake for 30–35 minutes, until the top is a golden colour, then place it under the grill for 2–3 minutes (to get that mozzarella nice and crispy). Lasagna can be enjoyed hot, warm or cold – no rules here, just pure pleasure *Buon appetito*.

+ **On repeat in the kitchen:** Golden brown like a *ragazza* on Rimini beach, your lasagne comes out of the oven singing 'Abbronzatissima' by Edoardo Vianello. It smells like summer and melted Parmigiano.

COSY SAUSAGE BAKE
Lasagna salsiccia e friarielli

FOR 4 FRIENDS

For the lasagne sheets
- 180g (6½oz) type 00 flour
- 180g (6½oz) *semola rimacinata* (remilled durum wheat semolina)
- 7 egg yolks

For the filling
- 300g (10½oz) Italian sausage, skin removed and crumbled (mild or spicy, as desired)
- 300g (10½oz) friarielli, a type of winter cime di rapa (broccoli rabe) typical of Naples and Campania (or broccoli, if unavailable)
- 1–2 garlic cloves
- 80g (2¾oz) grated Parmigiano Reggiano DOP
- Extra virgin olive oil
- Chilli pepper (optional, depending on your mood)
- Salt and pepper QB

For the béchamel sauce
- 250ml (1 cup) milk
- 20g (4 tsp) butter
- 25g (generous ¾oz) plain flour
- Grated nutmeg
- Salt and pepper QB

01 Start with the lasagne dough. On a work surface, pour the flour and semolina into a small mound, make a well in the centre and add the egg yolks. Knead until you have a soft, elastic dough. Cover with clingfilm and leave to rest for 30 minutes at room temperature.

02 Then prepare the friarielli (or broccoli): wash then blanch for 3–4 minutes in a saucepan of salted boiling water. Drain well.

03 In a large frying pan, fry the halved garlic cloves in a generous dash of olive oil, then add the friarielli. Sauté for a few minutes, season with salt and pepper, and add a little chilli pepper (if you like a bit of heat).

04 In another frying pan, fry the crumbled sausage meat in a little olive oil until golden brown. Then add the friarielli, mix well and simmer for 5 minutes. It's a match made in Southern Italy.

05 Make your béchamel sauce. Melt the butter in a saucepan over a low heat, add the flour and cook for 1 minute, stirring constantly. Then gradually pour in the milk – whisking continuously – until the sauce thickens. Add a pinch of nutmeg, salt and pepper and set aside.

06 Roll out the dough very thinly using a rolling pin or pasta machine. Turn to page 389 and follow the steps for shaping lasagne sheets.

07 Assemble the lasagne. Spread a layer of béchamel over the base of your baking dish. Add a layer of lasagne sheets, then the sausage and broccoli mixture, a drizzle of béchamel, and a sprinkling of Parmigiano. Repeat until all ingredients are used up.

08 Bake in a preheated oven at 180°C fan/200°C/400°F/GM 6 for about 30 minutes until the top is nicely browned. Serve hot, but not too hot, to warm the body and soul.

+ **On repeat in the kitchen:** While you prepare this great Neapolitan classic, let yourself be carried away by 'Gigi l'amoroso', a delightful story of a small village near Naples told by Dalida. You can choose the language: Italian, French, Japanese . . . There are no fewer than six versions of this cult classic.

THE ONE AND CANNELLONI

Cannelloni ricotta e provola affumicata

FOR 4 FRIENDS

- 12 cannelloni, ready to fill (fresh lasagne sheets also work)
- 600ml (2½ cups) *passata di pomodoro* (the best? Yours, thanks to our recipe on page 270)
- 400g (14oz) ricotta
- 200g (7oz) smoked or mild provola cheese, diced into small cubes
- 1 organic or free-range egg
- 60g (2oz) grated Pamiggiano Reggiano DOP
- 1 garlic clove
- A few fresh basil leaves
- Mozzarella (optional)
- Extra virgin olive oil
- Nutmeg (optional)
- Salt and pepper QB

01 Prepare the tomato sauce. In a saucepan, sauté 1 clove of minced garlic in 2 tablespoons of olive oil. Add the *passata*, season with salt and pepper, and simmer over a low heat for 15–20 minutes. Add a few fresh basil leaves just before the end of cooking.

02 In a bowl, mix the ricotta, finely diced provola, egg, 40g (1½oz) Parmigiano (keep some back for later), salt, pepper and a pinch of nutmeg if you like. Mix gently until you have a smooth filling.

03 Preheat the oven to 180°C fan/200°C/400°F/GM 6.

04 Using a piping bag (or a spoon, which will also do the job nicely if necessary), fill the cannelloni tubes with the filling. If you opt for fresh lasagne sheets instead, simply pre-cook them for 1–2 minutes in salted boiling water, then roll them up with the filling like real homemade cannelloni. Spread a little tomato sauce on the bottom of a lightly oiled gratin dish, arrange the stuffed cannelloni side by side and cover with the remaining tomato sauce. Sprinkle the remaining Parmigiano on top and, for the real foodies, add a few slices of mozzarella on top.

05 A little tip: before putting it in the oven, remember to cover your dish with foil to help retain the heat and distribute it evenly. This helps avoid the rookie mistake of burnt Parmigiano on top and raw cannelloni underneath. Bake for 30–35 minutes and remove the foil for the last 10 minutes to brown the top nicely.

06 Leave to rest for a few minutes before serving. *Buon appetito*, Chef.

\+ **On repeat in the kitchen:** Alan Sorrenti's 'Tu sei l'unica donna per me', THE summer hit in Italy in 1979. A slightly cheesy declaration of love that became a classic of Italian romantic pop. Hum it to your lover, or to yourself, it's just as beautiful.

CONCHIGLIONI AL FORNO

Stuffed with herbs and ricotta

FOR 4 FRIENDS

For the stuffed pasta

- 300g (10½oz) conchiglioni – large, shell-shaped pasta
- 400g (14oz) fresh green vegetables (a small selection of seasonal vegetables of your choice: spinach, Swiss chard . . . be creative, but avoid lettuce)
- 400g (14oz) fresh ricotta
- 1 egg
- 50g (1¾oz) grated Parmigiano Reggiano DOP
- 1 garlic clove
- 30g (1oz) butter
- Extra virgin olive oil
- Grated nutmeg
- Salt and freshly ground pepper QB

For the béchamel sauce

- 250ml (1 cup) milk
- 20g (4 tsp or ¾oz) butter
- 25g (generous ¾oz) plain flour
- Grated nutmeg
- Salt and pepper QB

For the finishing touches

- Breadcrumbs (optional)

01 Wash your vegetables thoroughly. In a frying pan, gently sauté the halved garlic clove in a generous drizzle of olive oil, then add the Swiss chard or other goodies from your basket. Season lightly with salt, cover and leave to soften over a medium heat. Once tender, drain the vegetables thoroughly to remove excess water, then chop finely.

02 In a large bowl, mix the ricotta with the chopped greens, egg, grated Parmigiano, a pinch of nutmeg and a little salt and pepper. Knead until smooth and set aside.

03 Next, make your béchamel sauce. Melt the butter in a saucepan over a low heat, add the flour and cook for 1 minute, stirring constantly. Then gradually pour in the milk, whisking constantly, until the sauce thickens. Add a pinch of nutmeg, salt and pepper and set aside.

04 Cook the conchiglioni in a large saucepan of salted boiling water, removing them 1–2 minutes before the end of the indicated cooking time (they will finish cooking in the oven). Drain gently and leave to cool.

05 Using a small spoon – or a piping bag, for more precision – stuff each shell with the vegetable filling.

06 Preheat the oven to 180°C fan/200°C/400°F/GM 6. Pour half of the béchamel sauce into the bottom of a gratin dish and arrange the stuffed conchiglioni tightly together. Cover with the rest of the sauce and, for those who like a crispy gratin, sprinkle with breadcrumbs and a little grated Parmigiano.

07 Bake for about 25–30 minutes. Then leave to rest for a few minutes before serving. Perhaps the most difficult part of this recipe . . .

\+ **On repeat in the kitchen:** Listen to Lucio Corsi's very poetic song, 'Cosa Faremo Da Grandi? (What Will We Do When We Grow Up?), which gently and naively explores how shells are made and how they end up on beaches.

IT'S A PIECE OF CAKE

Rigatoni al forno con ragù di salsiccia

FOR 4 FRIENDS

For the sausage *ragù*

- 500g (1lb 2oz) rigatoni or paccheri, short pasta shaped like tubes
- 500g (1lb 2oz) sausages
- 350g (12oz) peeled tomatoes or *passata di pomodoro* (see page 270 to make your own)
- 1 carrot
- 1 stalk of celery
- 1 onion
- ½ glass of red wine
- Olive oil
- Salt QB

For the béchamel sauce

- 500ml (2 cups) milk
- 40g (1½oz) butter
- 50g (1¾oz) plain flour
- Grated nutmeg
- Salt and freshly ground black pepper QB

To finish

- 2 organic or free-range eggs
- 40g (1½oz) butter (for the dish and for finishing the gratin)
- 40g (1½oz) grated Parmigiano Reggiano DOP

01 In a large frying pan, start by sautéing the chopped carrot, celery and onion in a generous dash of olive oil. Once they are nicely browned, remove the skin from the sausages, crumble the meat into the pan and cook for 5 minutes with the vegetables. Deglaze with the red wine and allow to evaporate. This is also an opportunity to pour yourself a small glass, *salute*. Add the tomatoes and stir gently. If the sauce is a little too thick, feel free to add a little water to loosen it and achieve a smooth *sugo*. Simmer everything over a low heat for 50 minutes, until the aroma fills your home and the whole neighbourhood wants to come over for dinner. At least, that's what happens in our house.

02 Meanwhile, prepare the béchamel sauce. Melt the butter in a saucepan over a low heat, add the flour and cook for 1 minute, stirring constantly. Then gradually pour in the milk, whisking continuously, until the sauce thickens. Add a pinch of grated nutmeg, salt and pepper, and set aside.

03 Cook the rigatoni in a large saucepan of salted boiling water then drain 2 minutes before the end of the cooking time (they will finish cooking in the gratin).

04 In a large bowl, mix the drained pasta with the sausage *ragù* (keep a little aside to cover your gratin) and add 2 beaten eggs – these will bind your dish together (which will be useful when turning it out).

05 Preheat the oven to 200°C fan/220°C/425°F/GM 7 then butter a round 20cm (8in) springform tin. Then arrange the rigatoni 'standing up' and tightly packed together. You'll see, it makes quite an impression.

06 Pour the rest of the *ragù* and béchamel sauce over the top, add a few knobs of butter and grated Parmigiano as a finishing touch, then bake for 30 minutes, until your gratin-tart is golden brown.

07 Remove from the tin and cut into slices to serve your cake. Enjoy hot, so your Parmigiano is still melted to perfection.

\+ **On repeat in the kitchen:** Since this dish is perfect for sharing with family or friends, play Gianna Nannini and Edoardo Bennato's unifying hit 'Un'estate italiana'. Also known as 'Notti magiche', this iconic song from the summer of 1990 was the official anthem of the World Cup held that year in Italy. Classy.

UNE PASSATA E BASTA

We challenge you to search through the cupboards of a resident of The Boot without finding a bottle of *passata*. Because tomato sauce is the essential base for many (very) good Italian recipes, we'll pass on this little tip that has been secret among the inhabitants of Italy for generations: for this nectar to be absolutely perfect, it must be homemade in summer, when the *pomodori* are ripe and bursting with sunshine, then stored in bottles like a treasure to enjoy throughout the rest of the year.

Now that you know, you too can become the king of *passata* for all seasons to come.

For 2 bottles of *passata* (approximately):

- 2kg (4lb 4oz) datterino tomatoes
- 2kg (4lb 4oz) San Marzano tomatoes
- 1 bunch of fresh basil
- Salt QB

---

1 Wash your tomatoes under cold running water, drain well and cut into large pieces. Then tip them into a saucepan with a little salt and simmer over a low heat for 2½ hours.

2 Pass the tomato sauce through a food mill or a sieve to obtain a nice velvety texture. If you don't have one of these in your cupboards, use a whisk to thoroughly crush the pieces. This will remove the skin and give the sauce a silky smooth texture.

3 Once the mixture has been strained, add the basil leaves and voilà. You have just made the best tomato sauce in the world, your own.

4 If you want to bottle your precious harvest (we recommend this, given that there are no tomatoes in winter), don't forget to sterilise your jars for 45 minutes in boiling water before filling them with sauce (to about 2cm/¾in from the rim) and sealing them tightly.

TAGLIOLINI AL FORNO

A very naughty pasta bake

FOR 4 FRIENDS

For the tagliolini

- 180g (6½oz) type 00 flour
- 180g (6½oz) *semola rimacinata* (remilled durum wheat semolina)
- 7 egg yolks

For the sauce

- 50g (1¾oz) smoked cooked ham, cut into strips
- 50g (1¾oz) butter
- 30g (1oz) grated Parmigiano Reggiano DOP

For the béchamel sauce

- 250ml (1 cup) milk
- 20g (4 tsp or ¾oz) butter
- 25g (generous ¾oz) plain flour
- Grated nutmeg
- Salt and pepper QB

For the finishing touch

- 30g (1oz) grated Parmigiano Reggiano DOP

01 Start with the tagliolini (you can also use fresh tagliatelle if you are in a hurry). On a work surface, pour the flour and semolina into a small mound, make a well in the centre and add the egg yolks. Knead until you have a smooth dough. Cover with clingfilm and leave to rest for 30 minutes at room temperature.

02 Meanwhile, prepare your béchamel sauce. Melt the butter in a saucepan over a low heat, add the flour and cook for 1 minute, stirring constantly. Then gradually pour in the milk – whisking continuously – until the sauce thickens. Add a pinch of grated nutmeg, salt and pepper and set aside.

03 Once your dough has rested, roll it out very thinly with a rolling pin or pasta machine and shape the tagliolini according to the instructions on page 396.

04 Preheat the oven to 180°C fan/200°C/400°F/GM 6 on the grill setting.

05 In a large saucepan of salted boiling water, cook the pasta for 2–3 minutes. Drain and set aside.

06 In a large frying pan, melt 30g (1oz) butter, then add the strips of ham and fry for one minute.

07 Pour the drained pasta into the pan with the ham, add an additional 15g (1 tablespoon) of butter, sprinkle with grated Parmigiano and mix well. At this point, you should feel a wave of nostalgia as you stir – such is the power of this dish. If not, take a deep breath and enjoy its comforting aroma.

08 Butter a gratin dish, pour in the tagliolini or tagliatelle with ham, then generously coat with béchamel sauce. Sprinkle with grated Parmigiano and add a few knobs of butter on top for an ultra-cheesy result.

09 Bake for 3–4 minutes until the cheese is nicely browned, then leave to rest for a few more minutes before serving hot. *Buon appetito!*

\+ **On repeat in the kitchen:** Bring the children, grandchildren or little neighbours into the kitchen and sing 'Le tagliatelle di nonna Pina'. A nursery rhyme about a child who doesn't want to go to school anymore and finds comfort in this pasta, which is 'better than medicine'. How fitting, right?

RIGATONI AI 4 FORMAGGI

The pasta bake everyone loves

FOR 4 FRIENDS

- 320g (11¼oz) rigatoni
- 40g (1½oz) butter
- 40g (1½oz) plain flour
- 600ml (2½ cups) whole milk
- 150g (5¼oz) mozzarella – preferably *fior di latte* – cut into small pieces
- 100g (3½oz) crumbled Gorgonzola Dolce – or any other blue cheese, as long as it's mild
- 100g (3½oz) Fontina, diced
- 100g (3½oz) grated Parmigiano Reggiano DOP (or Pecorino DOP, for more character)
- A pinch of grated nutmeg
- Salt and freshly ground black pepper QB

01 Start by preparing your béchamel sauce. In a saucepan, melt the butter over a low heat, then add the flour to form a roux. Whisk for 1–2 minutes without letting it brown. Translation: the butter should never turn brown. Then slowly pour in the milk, whisking continuously to avoid lumps. Let it thicken until it reaches a nice velvety texture.

02 Add all the cheeses (except the Parmigiano), keeping a little mozzarella and Gorgonzola for a cheesy-crusty finish. Season with salt and pepper, grate a little nutmeg, mix . . . and you're done. Depending on the season (and your mood), feel free to vary the pleasure with the best cheeses Italy has to offer: a little Taleggio from Lombardy, Sicilian Caciocavallo, Scamorza from Puglia. In short, you're spoilt for choice.

03 Meanwhile, cook the rigatoni in a large saucepan of salted boiling water for 2 minutes less than the time indicated (it will finish cooking in the oven). Drain the pasta and immediately mix it with the cheese sauce. Pour everything into a well-buttered gratin dish and spread the remaining mozzarella and Gorgonzola on top – and a little Parmigiano too.

04 Then bake in a preheated oven at 200°C fan/220°C/425°F/GM 7 – for 20–25 minutes until the gratin is perfectly golden and the cheese is melted to perfection. It's quick, it's simple, it's delicious. You'll be asking for seconds.

\+ **On repeat in the kitchen:** In their 2017 album *Ti amo*, French band Phoenix fantasises about Italy and offers us 10 sun-drenched tracks, including 'Fior di latte', the perfect pop ballad to listen to while the mozzarella is baking.

ANELLETTI AL FORNO
Timballo style

FOR 4 FRIENDS

For the anelletti
- 300g (10½oz) anelletti, small ring-shaped pasta typical of Sicily
- 80g (2¾oz) *ricotta salata*, salted ricotta
- Extra virgin olive oil
- Salt and pepper QB

For the mould
- 2 aubergines
- Frying oil: peanut or sunflower
- A little plain flour, to coat the aubergines

For the sauce
- 700ml (2¾ cups) *passata di pomodoro* (homemade is even better, so if you're feeling brave, see page 270)
- 2 medium aubergines
- 2 garlic cloves
- Fresh basil
- Extra virgin olive oil
- Salt QB

01 Cut 2 aubergines lengthwise into thin slices using a mandoline. Cut the next 2 into small cubes. Season all the aubergine with salt and leave to drain for 30 minutes in a colander before draining on kitchen paper.

02 Fry the aubergines in plenty of hot oil until golden brown. Chef Alberto's tip: lightly flour the aubergines beforehand for extra crispness. Drain on kitchen paper and keep warm.

03 In a frying pan, sauté the garlic in a generous drizzle of olive oil, then add the *passata*, the diced aubergines and a little salt, and simmer gently for 30 minutes–1 hour, adding a few basil leaves at the very end.

04 Cook the anelletti in a large saucepan of salted boiling water (2–3 minutes less than the time indicated, as they will finish cooking in the oven). Drain and mix with the tomato sauce, half of the crumbled salted ricotta, a few hand-torn basil leaves and a drizzle of olive oil.

05 Preheat the oven to 180°C fan/200°C/400°F/GM 6. Grease a mould with high sides, such as a charlotte, savarin or soufflé mould – in short, any round mould. Then line it with the fried aubergine slices, leaving them to hang slightly over the edges: they will be used to close your timballo once it has been assembled.

06 Pour half of the pasta into the mould, sprinkle with the rest of the crumbled salted ricotta, then add the second half of the pasta on top. Press down firmly so that the cake holds together. There will be no meal if it collapses when unmoulded. Finally, fold the aubergine slices towards the centre to close your precious creation.

07 Bake for 25–30 minutes, then leave to rest for about 10 minutes at room temperature before carefully removing from the mould. You should have a beautiful crown, or rather a charlotte lined with aubergines to present to your guests. Let's just say it's the height of chic.

\+ **On repeat in the kitchen:** Like this iconic dish that delights all generations around the table, we suggest playing 'La notte vola' by Lorella Cuccarini. It'll get young and old dancing before dessert, or just set the mood in the kitchen while you prepare your feast.

FAMIGLIA PROTA

Paola & Manuel

FORMIA

GIRELLE DI LASAGNE

Our kind of green flag

FOR 4 FRIENDS

For the green lasagne sheets

- 290g (10¼oz) type 00 flour
- 290g (10¼oz) *semola rimacinata* (remilled durum wheat semolina)
- 6 egg yolks
- 350g (12oz) spinach leaves
- 500ml (2 cups) water

For the spinach béchamel sauce

- 500ml (2 cups) milk
- 40g (1½oz) butter
- 40g (1½oz) plain flour
- 150g (5¼oz) fresh spinach (or Swiss chard or rocket, depending on the season)
- Grated nutmeg
- Salt and freshly ground pepper QB

For the gratin

- 500g (1lb 2oz) fresh ricotta
- 60g (2oz) grated Parmigiano Reggiano DOP
- 1 egg yolk
- Grated nutmeg
- Salt and pepper QB

For the finishing touch

- 30g (1oz) grated Parmigiano Reggiano DOP

01 Wash the spinach for the lasagne, blanch it (1 minute in boiling water), then blend it with the water for 10 minutes. Strain through a sieve. On your work surface, arrange the flour and semolina to create a small well. Place the egg yolks in the centre, then beat them with a fork until you get a smooth paste. Pour the green liquid into the paste and knead by hand for a good 10 minutes. Cover with clingfilm and leave to rest for 30 minutes at room temperature.

02 Meanwhile, wash the spinach for the béchamel sauce and blanch for 1–2 minutes in salted boiling water. Drain and immediately plunge into iced water. Squeeze out any excess water and blend with 2–3 tablespoons of milk (which you can take from the 500ml) until you obtain a smooth, even cream.

03 Then make your béchamel sauce. Melt the butter in a saucepan over a low heat, add the flour and cook for 1 minute, stirring constantly. Then gradually pour in the milk. Add a pinch of nutmeg, salt and pepper, and stir in the spinach cream. Mix well and set aside.

04 In a large bowl, mix together the ricotta, egg yolk, grated Parmigiano, a pinch of salt, pepper and grated nutmeg.

05 Butter a gratin dish and pour a thin layer of béchamel sauce on the bottom.

06 Take your dough, roll it out very thinly with a rolling pin or pasta machine, and turn to page 389 to learn how to shape each lasagne *sfoglia* (sheet).

07 Bring a large pan of salted water to the boil and cook the lasagne sheets one by one for 1 minute. Drain gently, then add a strip of filling to each sheet and roll up into a spiral. Cut the rolls into pieces about 4–5 cm (1½–2in) wide.

08 Place the rolls close together in the greased gratin dish, cover with the remaining béchamel sauce, sprinkle with grated Parmigiano and bake in a preheated oven at 180°C fan/200°C/400°F/GM 6 for 25–30 minutes. A veggie, cheesy and 100% comforting dish.

+ **On repeat in the kitchen:** Turn up the volume and play 'Felicità' by Al Bano & Romina Power. A hit that needs no introduction, perfect for celebrating, just like your dish.

FORZA SCAMORZA!

Lasagna con zucca e scamorza affumicata

FOR 4 FRIENDS

For the lasagne sheets

- 180g (6½oz) type 00 flour
- 180g (6½oz) *semola rimacinata* (remilled durum wheat semolina)
- 7 egg yolks

For the filling

- 700g (1lb 9oz) squash (butternut or pumpkin)
- 200g (7oz) smoked *scamorza* cheese (or plain, as preferred)
- 250g (8¾oz) ricotta
- 50g (1¾oz) grated Parmigiano Reggiano DOP
- 1 small onion
- 1 sprig of rosemary or a few sage leaves
- 2 tbsp extra virgin olive oil
- Salt and pepper QB

For the béchamel sauce

- 500ml (2 cups) whole milk
- 40g (1½oz) butter
- 40g (1½oz) plain flour
- Grated nutmeg
- Salt and pepper QB

01 On a work surface, pour the flour and semolina in a small mound, make a well in the centre and add the eggs and a pinch of salt. Knead until your dough is smooth. Cover with clingfilm and leave to rest for 30 minutes at room temperature.

02 Now for the squash. Peel and dice your butternut squash or pumpkin into small cubes. In a large frying pan, sauté a chopped onion in a generous dash of olive oil with the rosemary or sage. Add the squash, season with salt and pepper, and simmer over a medium heat for 15–20 minutes. Roughly mash the mixture with a fork, then set aside.

03 In the meantime, make your béchamel sauce. Melt the butter in a saucepan over a low heat, add the flour and cook for 1 minute, stirring constantly. Then gradually pour in the milk. Add a pinch of grated nutmeg, salt and pepper, and set aside.

04 On your work surface, cut the *scamorza* into thin slices. Then, in a bowl, mix the ricotta with a little salt, pepper and Parmigiano.

05 Next, take your dough, roll it out very thinly with a rolling pin or pasta machine, and turn to page 389 to follow the steps for shaping your lasagne sheets.

06 Finally, assemble the lasagne. Spread a layer of béchamel sauce on the bottom of a lightly oiled baking dish to form the base. Then add a layer of lasagne sheets, a little squash, a little ricotta and a few pieces of *scamorza*. Add a drizzle of béchamel sauce then repeat the process until all your ingredients are used up. Finish your lasagne with a layer of pasta, béchamel sauce, a little *scamorza* and grated Parmigiano.

07 Bake in a preheated oven at 180°C fan/200°C/400°F/GM 6, for 30–35 minutes until the top is crispy and melted. Leave to rest for 5–10 minutes before serving and say cheeeeeeese.

\+ **On repeat in the kitchen:** 'Add a place at the table' exclaims Johnny Dorelli in the song 'Aggiungi un posto a tavola'. An omen that is likely to come true when the smell of smoked gratin has filled the entire stairwell. Be prepared.

SCRIGNO DI VENERE
Tortellini in pastry

The Scrigno di Venere (Venus's Casket) is a small puff pastry case containing a divine treasure: tortellini with béchamel sauce. A symbol of special occasions in Emilia-Romagna, this dish requires a fair amount of patience, but we promise it's worth the effort!

FOR 4 FRIENDS

For the tortellini
- 200g (7oz) type 00 flour
- 150g (5½oz) *semola rimacinata* (remilled durum wheat semolina)
- 8 egg yolks

For homemade puff pastry (the winning team)
- 200g (7oz) type 00 flour
- 100g (3½oz) cold butter
- 70ml (scant ⅓ cup) very cold water
- A pinch of salt
- A pinch of sugar

For the béchamel sauce
- 500ml (2 cups) cold whole milk
- 40g (1½oz) butter
- 40g (1½oz) plain flour
- Grated nutmeg
- Salt and pepper QB

For the tortellini filling
- 300g (10½oz) minced beef and pork mixture
- 100g (3½oz) grated Parmigiano Reggiano DOP
- 200g (7oz) mortadella
- 200g (7oz) cured ham

For the finishing touches
- 50g (1¾oz) grated Parmigiano Reggiano DOP
- 1 egg yolk for glazing

01 Pour the flour and semolina onto a work surface to form a mound, with a well in the centre. Add the egg yolks to the middle, whisk them lightly with a fork, then knead by hand for 10–12 minutes, until you have a soft, elastic dough. Cover with clingfilm and leave to rest for 30 minutes at room temperature.

02 For the puff pastry, mix the flour and the very cold cubed butter, water, salt and sugar. Knead quickly, form a ball, cover with clingfilm and put it in the fridge for 30 minutes–1 hour.

03 In a frying pan, brown the minced meat in oil, then mix in with the chopped mortadella and ham in a bowl to form the filling mix. Set aside.

04 For the béchamel sauce, melt the butter in a saucepan, add the flour and whisk to form a roux. Pour in the cold milk, add a pinch of grated nutmeg and salt and pepper and stir over a low heat until thickened. Set aside.

05 Roll out the tortellini dough very thinly with a rolling pin or pasta machine, then turn to page 392 for instructions on how to shape your little wonders.

06 Once ready, cook the tortellini for 1–2 minutes in a large saucepan of salted boiling water. Drain. Mix with the béchamel sauce and half the Parmigiano. Leave to cool.

07 Butter a soufflé or springform tin with high sides. Roll out the puff pastry to a thickness of about 3mm and place it in the dish, making sure to leave a wide rim all around the edge to close your Venus casket. Fill with your pasta mixture and sprinkle over the rest of the Parmigiano. Fold the edges over, brush with egg yolk and prick the surface lightly so that the steam can escape.

08 Bake in a preheated oven at 180°C fan/200°C/400°F/GM 6 for 40 minutes until the pastry is golden brown. Leave to rest a few minutes before turning out your divine creation.

+ **On repeat in the kitchen:** A heavenly soundtrack to accompany a dish fit for the gods. We're listening to Alan Sorrenti's 'Figli delle stelle', a cross-generational disco-pop hit which, like this dish, has stood the test of time without going out of fashion.

LASAGNA AL PESTO

A very best of Portofino

FOR 4 FRIENDS

For the lasagne
- 180g (6½oz) type 00 flour
- 180g (6½oz) *semola rimacinata* (remilled durum wheat semolina)
- 7 egg yolks

For the pesto *alla genovese*
- 50g (1¾oz) fresh basil
- 1 or 2 garlic cloves
- 30g (1oz) pine nuts
- 60g (2oz) grated Parmigiano Reggiano DOP
- 20g (4 tsp or ¾oz) grated Pecorino DOP
- 100ml (scant ½ cup) extra virgin olive oil
- A pinch of coarse salt

For the béchamel sauce
- 500ml (2 cups) milk
- 40g (1½oz) butter, plus extra for the dish
- 50g (1¾oz) plain flour
- Grated nutmeg
- Salt and pepper QB

For assembly
- 150g (5¼oz) mozzarella (for a deliciously creamy texture)
- 40g (1½oz) grated Parmigiano Reggiano DOP

01 Start by preparing the pasta dough. On your work surface, mix the flour and semolina and make a small well. Place the egg yolks in the middle, then beat them with a fork until it forms a smooth paste. Knead by hand for 10–12 minutes. The dough should become soft and elastic. Cover with clingfilm and set aside for at least 30 minutes. That gives you time to sort through your cupboards to make space for your next culinary adventure. Once your cupboards are sorted and your dough has rested, roll it out thinly with a rolling pin and follow our guide on page 389 to cut the lasagne sheets.

02 We suggest you complete this Italian journey by preparing a Genovese pesto – typical of Portofino, a small town with colourful houses in Liguria – the star of this dish, using our recipe on page 289.

03 Then move on to the béchamel sauce. Melt the butter in a saucepan over a low heat, add the flour and cook for 1 minute, stirring to avoid lumps. Then gradually pour in the milk, whisking constantly, until the sauce thickens. Add a pinch of grated nutmeg, salt and pepper, and set aside.

04 Generously butter a gratin dish, then spread a thin layer of béchamel sauce in it before alternating layers of lasagne sheets, béchamel, pesto, mozzarella and Parmigiano. Repeat until all the ingredients are used up, finishing with a generous layer of béchamel sauce, a few basil leaves, pesto and a little Parmigiano. A little tip from our chef Alberto for even more indulgence: mix two thirds of the béchamel sauce with a third of the pesto and save the rest for the final layer and plating.

05 Bake in a preheated oven at 180°C fan/200°C/400°F/GM 6 for 25–30 minutes until the lasagne is nicely browned and smelling delicious. After that, there's just one more step, and it's the hardest one: wait 20 minutes for the dish to cool. That's perfect, because that's exactly how long you need to set the table AND serve yourself a little *aperitivo* at the corner of the coffee table, a real treat.

+ **On repeat in the kitchen:** Play an obvious choice for this recipe, 'Love in Portofino' by Dalida. After one (or two) Spritzes, you'll be trilingual, humming along to this hit without missing a note.

PRESTO PESTO

It's no coincidence that this sauce from Genoa is called 'green gold'. What equipment do you need? Ideally, a white Carrara marble mortar, smooth enough to preserve the sauce's bright green colour, and a fruit-wood pestle to avoid overheating the basil. But any similar item you have is acceptable in the kitchen. The most important thing, written in bold, is to never, EVER, cook pesto. It is a raw sauce that is served cold on your pasta. A word to the wise, *bon appétit.*

Pesto alla genovese for 4 friends:

- 50g (1¾oz) fresh basil
- 1 or 2 garlic cloves
- 30g (1oz) pine nuts
- 60g (2oz) grated Parmigiano Reggiano DOP
- 20g (4 tsp or ¾oz) grated Pecorino DOP
- 100ml (scant ½ cup) extra virgin olive oil
- A pinch of coarse salt

---

1 In a mortar, gently crush the garlic with the coarse salt, then gradually add the torn basil leaves.

2 Add the pine nuts, then the grated Parmigiano and Pecorino, continuing to crush.

3 Finish with a thin stream of olive oil until you obtain a beautiful green and fragrant paste.

PS: Don't have a mortar? Don't panic: blend all the ingredients little by little in a blender, gradually adding the olive oil, and you're sorted.

SHE SELLS SEASHELLS

Conchiglioni al forno con ragù di carne

FOR 4 FRIENDS

For the conchiglioni

- 16–20 conchiglioni (shell-shaped pasta)
- 300g (10½oz) minced meat (beef or a mixture of beef and pork, as you prefer)
- 1 carrot
- 1 stalk of celery
- 1 small onion
- 400ml (1⅔ cups) *passata di pomodoro* (go on, give it a try – we explain how to make your own on page 270)
- 100ml (scant ½ cup) red wine
- 100g (3½oz) fresh peas
- 2 tbsp olive oil
- 100g (3½oz) grated Parmigiano Reggiano DOP
- Butter for the dish
- Salt and pepper QB

For the béchamel sauce

- 250ml (1 cup) milk
- 20g (4 tsp or ¾oz) butter
- 25g (¾oz) plain flour
- Grated nutmeg
- Salt and pepper QB

01 Start by sautéing the chopped celery, carrot and onion in a saucepan in olive oil for 5 minutes. Add the minced meat, brown it for a few moments, then deglaze with the red wine (shall we pour ourselves a glass? Yes, cheers!). Once evaporated, add the *passata* and fresh peas, then season with salt and pepper and simmer over a low heat for 30–40 minutes. Can you smell the pride of a homemade sauce wafting into the living room?

02 Next, make your béchamel sauce. Melt the butter in a saucepan over a low heat, add the flour and cook for 1 minute, stirring constantly. Add a pinch of nutmeg, salt and pepper, then gradually pour in the milk – whisking constantly to avoid lumps, which no one likes – until the sauce thickens. Set aside.

03 Cook the conchiglioni in salted boiling water, stopping the cooking 2 minutes before the indicated time – they will finish cooking in the oven. Drain and leave to cool on a clean tea towel, spacing them apart from each other. Feeling a bit lazy? Do it anyway, it's important.

04 Generously butter a gratin dish and cover the bottom with a ladleful of your lovely béchamel sauce.

05 Stuff each conchiglione with *ragù* and béchamel sauce, then arrange them neatly in the dish before sprinkling generously with Parmigiano.

06 Bake in a preheated oven at 180°C fan/200°C/400°F/GM 6 for 20–25 minutes, until the top is golden brown and cheesy-crispy. Symbols of love, these shells will melt hearts. Be smart, choose carefully who you serve them to tonight.

+ **On repeat in the kitchen:** Play 'A fare l'amore comincia tu' by Raffaella Carrà, a disco gem from the 1970s. Your kitchen will become the hottest dancefloor in town.

PASTISS ALLA PIACENTINA

The *pièce de résistance*

Pasticcio di Maccheroni – or Pastiss alla Piacentina – is a traditional dish from Piacenza, once reserved for banquets and noble tables during the Renaissance. This sweet and savoury timballo may or may not pique your guests' curiosity. Either way, you now know how to present it properly.

FOR 4 FRIENDS

<u>For the sweet shortcrust pastry</u>

- 500g (1lb 2oz) plain flour
- 160g (5½oz) butter, at room temperature
- 120g (4¼oz) caster sugar
- 8g (1½ tsp) baking powder
- 4 egg yolks + 2 whole eggs

<u>For the maccheroni filling</u>

- 400g maccheroncini or maccheroni rigati
- 2 pigeons weighing about 500g (1lb 1½oz) each, cut into quarters (you can substitute another type of poultry or beef, as long as you don't hunt your own prey in the city)
- 100g (3½oz) butter
- 60g (2oz) onions
- 4 bay leaves
- 60g (2oz) crumbled amaretti biscuits
- 2 whole eggs
- 100g (3½oz) grated Grana Padano DOP
- Oil and flour for the mould
- Salt and pepper QB

01 Start by mixing the softened butter with the flour, sugar and baking powder. Add the eggs and egg yolks, then knead until you have a smooth dough. Wrap it in clingfilm and leave to rest in the fridge for 30 minutes.

02 Meanwhile, in a saucepan, fry the diced onion in butter with the bay leaves. Add the pieces of meat and brown them. Add salt, cover with cold water and simmer over a low heat for about 2 hours. Take this opportunity to watch Ettore Scola's *Maccheroni*, in which Jack Lemmon and Marcello Mastroianni become friends against the backdrop of Italian cuisine.

03 Remove the meat, debone it if necessary and shred. Reserve half of the cooking juices and stir the shredded meat into the rest of the juices.

04 Cook the maccheroni until *al dente*, then drain and leave to cool. Mix with the meat, crumbled amaretti biscuits, beaten eggs and Grana Padano.

05 Grease and flour a high-sided baking tin, roll out three quarters of the shortcrust pastry to a thickness of 5–6mm and place it in the tin, keeping enough pastry to seal the *pastiss*. Pour in the maccheroni mixture, press down lightly, then cover with a disc of pastry and seal the edges well. Make three small holes in the top to allow moisture to escape during baking.

06 Bake in a preheated oven at 170°C fan/190°C/375°F/GM 5 for about 1 hour and 10 minutes.

07 Finally, leave to rest for 20 minutes before turning out and serving with the reserved juice. If your guests don't give you a standing ovation, take the dish with you – they don't deserve it.

+ **On repeat in the kitchen:** Is your *pastiss* the most beautiful thing you've ever seen? The perfect opportunity to hum Eros Ramazzotti's 'Più bella cosa' while you immortalise your masterpiece on camera.

FAMIGLIA PROTA

Paola & Manuel

FORMIA

A WHOLE NEW BALL GAME

Lasagna con polpettine

FOR 4 FRIENDS

For the lasagne

- 180g (6½oz) type 00 flour
- 180g (6½oz) *semola rimacinata* (remilled durum wheat semolina)
- 7 egg yolks

For the filling

- 6 tbsp grated Parmigiano Reggiano DOP
- Olive oil
- Salt and pepper QB

For the meatballs

- 300g (10½oz) minced meat (beef or beef and veal mixture)
- 1 egg
- 30g (1oz) grated Parmigiano Reggiano DOP
- 1 slice of bread soaked in milk
- 1 garlic clove
- Parsley QB
- Olive oil for cooking
- Salt and pepper QB

For the béchamel sauce

- 500ml (2 cups) milk
- 40g (1½oz) butter
- 50g (1¾oz) plain flour
- Grated nutmeg
- Salt and pepper QB

For the tomato sauce

- 500ml (2 cups) *passata di pomodoro* (we give you a foolproof homemade version on page 270)
- 1 garlic clove
- 1 tbsp extra virgin olive oil
- A few basil leaves (optional)
- Salt QB

01 On your work surface, arrange the flour and semolina to form a mound with a small well. Place the egg yolks in the middle, then beat them with a fork until you obtain a smooth dough. Knead by hand for 10–12 minutes, the dough should become soft and elastic. Cover with clingfilm and set aside for at least 30 minutes. Once your dough has rested, roll it out thinly with a rolling pin or pasta machine and follow our guide on page 389 to cut the lasagne sheets.

02 Now for the meatballs. Mix the minced meat, egg, bread, chopped garlic and parsley, Parmigiano, salt and pepper. Shape into small balls with your hands and fry in a little oil until golden brown. Drain on kitchen paper.

03 Next, make the béchamel sauce. Melt the butter in a saucepan over a low heat, add the flour and cook for 1 minute, stirring constantly. Gradually pour in the milk, whisking continuously to prevent lumps from forming, until the sauce thickens. Add a pinch of nutmeg, salt and pepper and set aside.

04 Prepare the tomato sauce. Heat the olive oil in a saucepan with the whole garlic, add the *passata* and simmer for 15–20 minutes over a low heat. When the timer goes off, add salt and basil.

05 Cook the lasagne sheets in a saucepan of salted boiling water, drain them and quickly rinse them under cold running water to stop them cooking. Tip: brush them with a little olive oil to prevent them sticking together.

06 In a baking dish, spread a first layer of béchamel sauce, then alternate layers of lasagne sheets, tomato sauce, béchamel sauce, meatballs and Parmigiano. For the final layer: layer the lasagne sheets, tomato sauce, meatballs and Parmigiano, but no béchamel sauce.

07 Bake in a preheated oven at 180°C fan/200°C/400°F/GM 6 for 30–35 minutes until the top is nicely crispy. Leave to rest for 10 minutes before serving. After that, enjoy every last drop of sauce.

\+ **On repeat in the kitchen:** As a tribute to the Italian immigrants who introduced us to meatballs in New York, play Renato Carosone's 'Tu vuo' fa' l'americano' while savouring these.

ZITI STARDUST
Ziti alla vodka al forno

FOR 4 FRIENDS

- 320g (11¼oz) ziti or penne (ziti is a type of very long pasta that looks a lot like long penne, so we'll let you choose whichever shape you like best)
- 1 small onion
- 1 garlic clove
- 80ml (⅓ cup) vodka (we'll leave the measurements down to you . . .)
- 250g (9oz) *passata di pomodoro* (we give you a foolproof homemade version on page 270)
- 200ml (generous ¾ cup) double cream
- 40g (1½oz) grated Parmigiano Reggiano DOP
- 60–80g (2–2¾oz) grated or diced mozzarella
- Extra virgin olive oil
- Chilli flakes (for those who like it hot)
- Salt and pepper QB

01 A cool-kitsch dish emblematic of the 1980s, penne *alla vodka* has gradually established itself as a staple of Italian cuisine. Here, we revisit it in a gratin version for an extra dose of enjoyment. Start by sautéing the finely chopped onion and garlic in a generous drizzle of olive oil. When they are translucent, deglaze with the vodka and leave to reduce for another 2 minutes. Add your incredible homemade *passata*, season with salt and pepper and simmer for 10–15 minutes. Stir in the cream, then the grated Parmigiano and mix well. Taste and adjust the seasoning if necessary, adding a little chilli for those who like it hot.

02 Cook the ziti or penne for 2 minutes less than the indicated time, in a large quantity of salted water (the pasta will finish cooking in the oven). Drain and mix directly into the pan with the vodka sauce.

03 Pour the mixture into a lightly oiled gratin dish and sprinkle the grated or diced mozzarella on top.

04 Bake in a preheated oven at 200°C fan/220°C/425°F/GM 7 for 15–20 minutes until the top is ultra cheesy. After that, wait the recommended time to enjoy the dish without burning your palate, i.e. about 20–30 minutes. This is the ideal time to make a list of a few restaurants where you can try this recipe and say that yours is better.

+ **On repeat in the kitchen:** With a nod to the scent of vodka and sometimes foggy mornings, we're playing 'Paracetamolo' by Calcutta. An indie-pop prescription to be listened to without moderation.

POMO-ADORO

Pomodori con risoni

FOR 4 FRIENDS

- 200g (7oz) risoni (small rice-shaped pasta)
- 8 large, medium-sized round vine-ripened tomatoes
- A little *passata di pomodoro* (you can make your own using our recipe on page 270, it's even better)
- 50g (1¾oz) grated Pecorino DOP or Parmigiano Reggiano DOP, whatever you prefer
- 1 bunch of fresh flat-leaf parsley
- 6–8 fresh basil leaves
- Extra virgin olive oil
- Breadcrumbs (optional, but they can make all the difference)
- Fine salt and freshly ground black pepper QB

01 Wash and cut the tops off each tomato. Do not discard them, as they will be useful later. No tops, no finishing touch. Using a spoon, scoop out the flesh of the tomatoes and place in a large bowl, then lightly salt the inside of the tomatoes. Turn the tomatoes over onto a plate to drain for 15–20 minutes.

02 Meanwhile, prepare the filling that will make your taste buds dance by mixing the tomato pulp with a little of your *passata*, grated Pecorino, the uncooked risoni, finely chopped parsley and basil. Add a pinch of salt, a twist of pepper, a generous drizzle of olive oil and mix. Leave to rest for about 30 minutes. Be patient, the risoni needs time to absorb the juice so that it cooks more easily . . .

03 Preheat the oven to 180°C fan/200°C/400°F/GM 6. Place the tomatoes in an oiled gratin dish and stuff them with the filling without pressing down too much (the pasta will become plump during cooking). For a crispy twist, sprinkle with a few breadcrumbs before replacing the top of each tomato. Drizzle with a little olive oil and bake for 45–50 minutes.

04 Serve your delicacies warm or at room temperature, just long enough to tidy up the kitchen and set the table before your guests arrive.

\+ **On repeat in the kitchen:** A must-have for beach picnics and large summer gatherings, enjoy this sunny dish to the tune of Jovanotti's 'L'estate addosso'. Dancing allowed.

CHAPTER 5

ALTERNATIVE PASTA DISHES

SPAGHETTI DI FARRO ALLA GRICIA

50 shades of gricia

Before we begin, here's a little cultural tidbit to impress your guests. Gricia, a rustic dish originating in the Amatrice region, is actually said to be the ancestor of the famous amatriciana sauce – but without the tomatoes, which were only added later. Hence its nickname: 'amatriciana bianca' (white amatriciana). Right, now we're ready to begin.

FOR 4 FRIENDS

- 320g (11¼oz) spaghetti *di farro* (an ancient grain, farro is rich in fibre and has a pleasant nutty flavour)
- 160g (5½oz) *guanciale* (Italian cured pork cheek, is essential to the traditional recipe. If you don't have any on hand, you can replace it with artisan pancetta – cured pork belly – but our chef Albi tells us that the taste will be slightly less authentic)
- 100g (3½oz) grated Pecorino Romano DOP
- Freshly ground black pepper QB
- Salt, for the cooking water (use sparingly, as the *guanciale* and Pecorino are already quite salty)

01 First, cut the *guanciale* into nice strips, then gently fry it in a large frying pan over a low heat, without any oil or butter. Let it slowly render all its fat until it becomes crispy on the outside and tender on the inside: this takes about 8–10 minutes. When it is ready, remove the pan from the heat and set it aside.

02 Meanwhile, cook your spaghetti *di farro* in a large saucepan of lightly salted boiling water. Farro takes slightly longer to cook than traditional wheat (check the packet, usually 9–11 minutes). Once *al dente*, drain the pasta but remember to keep a generous ladleful of the cooking water, liquid gold, as chefs say.

03 Return the pan with your *guanciale* to low heat. Add the well-drained spaghetti, 1 tablespoon of cooking water and mix so that each spaghetto is coated with the melted fat.

04 Remove from the heat and gradually stir in the grated Pecorino, stirring vigorously to prevent lumps from forming: the aim is to achieve a creamy, coating sauce, like those made in the best Roman trattorias.

05 Add a generous amount of freshly ground black pepper to bring out the flavours. If your sauce seems a little too thick, feel free to add a little more cooking water.

06 Serve immediately, piping hot, with a final sprinkling of Pecorino on top and a final twist of the pepper mill. Just to be clear: there's no need for olive oil here – the fat from the *guanciale* brings everything together.

\+ **On repeat in the kitchen:** Simple and delicious, spaghetti *alla gricia* has stood the test of time without ever going out of style, like Tony Dallara's late 1950s hit 'Come prima'. Often imitated, never equalled.

POLPO PICASSO

Fusilli integrali alla Luciana

FOR 4 FRIENDS

- 320g (11¼oz) wholemeal fusilli (wholemeal pasta has a slightly more rustic flavour and a slightly firmer texture)
- 600g (1lb 5oz) *moscardini* (mini octopus)
- 300g (10½oz) cherry tomatoes (can be replaced with 250g/8¾oz crushed peeled tomatoes)
- 2 tbsp pitted black olives
- 1 small garlic clove, squashed with the blade of a knife but kept whole
- 1 small red chilli pepper (fresh or dried, according to taste)
- ½ glass of dry white wine
- 4 tbsp extra virgin olive oil
- Fresh parsley
- Salt and pepper QB

01 Rinse the *moscardini* thoroughly under cold running water. Remove the beak located in the centre of the tentacles and empty the sac. If you're squeamish, you can ask your favourite fishmonger to do this for you. If you find them a little too plump, feel free to cut them into pieces: we want the bites to be balanced, similar in size to the pasta.

02 In a large frying pan, heat a generous dash of olive oil with 1 crushed garlic clove and a small chilli pepper. Then sauté the *moscardini* for 2–3 minutes over a high heat. Once seared, deglaze with the white wine and allow the alcohol to evaporate slowly. If you have any wine left over, pour yourself a small glass – you've earned it. Cheers!

03 Add the tomatoes and olives, season with salt and pepper, cover and simmer over a low heat for about 30–35 minutes. A lovely Italian aroma should fill your home. It is cooked when the *moscardini* are tender and the sauce has reduced. Remember to remove the garlic clove.

04 Cook the wholemeal fusilli in a large quantity of salted boiling water until *al dente* (the cooking time is usually a little longer than for regular pasta). Drain, reserving a ladleful of the cooking water.

05 Add the fusilli to the pan with the *moscardini* sauce and stir over a medium heat for 1–2 minutes, adding a little of your pasta water to bind everything together. Is it sizzling in the pan? *Va bene*, that's a good sign.

06 Serve hot, with a sprinkling of chopped parsley and a drizzle of olive oil.

+ **On repeat in the kitchen:** Because 'à la Luciana' evokes the fishermen of the Santa Lucia neighbourhood. In Naples, people throw open their windows and sing the most famous Neapolitan song in the world: 'O sole mio'. Whether you prefer Dalida's or Pavarotti's version, we trust you to sing your heart out!

MAGIC MUSHROOMS
Gnocchi di farina di castagne ai funghi

FOR 4 FRIENDS

For the chestnut flour gnocchi
- 400g (14oz) potatoes (preferably yellow floury potatoes: they contain less water, which means you can use less flour. The result? Lighter, more delicious gnocchi)
- 100g (3½oz) chestnut flour
- 50–70g (1¾–2¼oz) type 00 flour (adjust the amount depending on the moisture content of your dough)
- Salt QB

For the mushroom sauce
- 300–400g (10½–14oz) fresh mushrooms (ideally a forest mix with porcini, oyster mushrooms or chanterelles)
- 1 garlic clove
- 3 tbsp extra virgin olive oil
- 1 knob of butter (optional, but recommended for added flavour)
- Fresh parsley
- Salt and pepper QB

01 Make your gnocchi: cook the whole potatoes, with their skins on, in a large saucepan of salted boiling water. Once tender, peel them while still hot (be careful not to burn your fingers) and mash them with a potato masher – do not use a blender, as this will turn your mixture into an elastic purée, which is not the desired result. Leave to cool, then add the sifted chestnut flour, a little 00 flour for consistency and a pinch of salt. Knead with the palms of your hands until you obtain a smooth, even dough. If it sticks a little, add a pinch more 00 flour.

02 Then it's time to shape them, so roll up your sleeves, take a look at page 399, and let's get started. Line up your gnocchi on a clean, floured tea towel, without stacking them – they need space, just like everyone else.

03 Meanwhile, prepare the sauce. Clean the mushrooms by brushing them and wiping them with a damp cloth. Cut them into strips and fry them in a large frying pan with a generous dash of olive oil and the crushed garlic for 6–8 minutes over a medium heat until they release their water and brown slightly. Add a knob of butter, salt, pepper and finish with the parsley.

04 Your kitchen should start to smell like the forest floor. Cook the gnocchi in a large saucepan of simmering salted water. Tip: they are ready when they rise to the surface (allow about 2–3 minutes). Drain them gently with a slotted spoon – taking care to keep a ladleful of cooking water – and add them directly to the pan with the mushrooms. Mix gently, adding a little of your pasta water to bind the sauce if necessary.

05 This rustic dish, typical of the Tuscan Apennines, is true Italian comfort food: simple, generous and deeply comforting. Serve immediately to lift your spirits, sprinkling a little chopped parsley on top before tasting.

\+ **On repeat in the kitchen:** Like a balm for the soul, Giorgia's song 'La cura per me' ('My remedy' in English) gently envelops, warms the heart and heals with every word. A perfect antidote to the autumn gloom.

1

SPAGHETTI CACIO E PEPE AL TOVAGLIOLO

From Rome with love

FOR 4 FRIENDS

- 320g (11¼oz) spaghetti no. 5 or 7 – ideally *trafilata al bronzo*, meaning 'bronze die-cut'. They are rougher and better at catching the sauce
- 160g (5½oz) mature Pecorino Romano DOP
- 8–10g (1½–2 tsp) black peppercorns
- Salt QB
- 1 *tovagliolo* (a clean, slightly dampened cotton tea towel; this dish is a rustic reinterpretation of the legendary Roman *Cacio e Pepe* where the spaghetti is rolled in a tea towel to absorb the sauce, without direct cooking. The result is an ultra-creamy texture and a nod to Lazio)

01 Start by preparing the pepper, the star of the dish. The secret here is to dry toast the peppercorns in a large frying pan over a low heat for 1 minute, until they fill your kitchen with their aroma. Then, coarsely crush the peppercorns in a mortar or with a coarse pepper mill. Set aside while you prepare the spaghetti.

02 In a large saucepan of lightly salted boiling water (the Pecorino takes care of the rest), cook the spaghetti until very *al dente*, about 2 minutes less than the time indicated. Drain, carefully reserving at least 300ml (1¼ cups) of the cooking water.

03 Pour a small ladleful of this liquid into the frying pan with the pepper to infuse it. Set aside off the heat.

04 Spread your best slightly damp tea towel on a wooden board. Place the well-drained spaghetti in a line in the centre. Immediately sprinkle with finely grated Pecorino (like a thin veil) and drizzle with your pepper-infused water and the rest of your cooking water, which acts as a magical binding agent. Roll everything up, squeezing the cloth tightly: the pasta will absorb the heat and moisture, and the cheese will melt gently, without lumps or thermal shock. Leave to rest for 3–5 minutes and savour the fact that you are making an Italian chef's dish, like a Roman.

05 Then carefully unroll the tea towel and serve it as it is to your guests (it should make quite an impression!). At the table, add a sprinkling of Pecorino and a twist of pepper. Above all: no butter, no cream, no olive oil. Just the magic of cheese, pepper and water.

\+ **On repeat in the kitchen:** Play Nino Rota's 'La dolce vita' because it's Rome in black and white, Anita Ekberg in the Trevi Fountain . . . Listen to it while the spaghetti strands roll in their tea towel like Vespas in the cobbled streets of Trastevere.

RIGATONI AL RAGÙ DI CAVOLFIORE
Caul me maybe?

FOR 4 FRIENDS

- 320g (11¼oz) rigatoni (or penne rigate)
- 1 small cauliflower (approximately 500–600g/1lb 2oz–1lb 5oz)
- 1 onion
- 1 carrot
- 1 stalk of celery
- 2 tbsp tomato paste
- 400ml (1¾ cups) tomato pulp or *passata di pomodoro* (find out how to make your own on page 270)
- 1 small glass of dry white wine (and a second one for the chef, cheers)
- 5–6 tbsp extra virgin olive oil
- Rosemary or bay leaf (optional)
- Salt and black pepper QB

For the finishing touch (optional)

- Chopped or crushed almonds
- Grated *ricotta salata*
- A few marjoram leaves

01 Cut the cauliflower into florets, then grate it coarsely or blend it quickly to obtain a brunoise-style texture, a bit like minced meat. This is the basis of our vegetarian *ragù*: a flavourful meatless bolognese sauce. Set aside.

02 In a large frying pan, prepare the *soffritto*: sauté the chopped onion, carrot and celery in a generous drizzle of olive oil for about 10 minutes, until they start to colour a little. Then add the cauliflower, stir and leave to brown gently over a low heat. After that, deglaze with the white wine, leave to reduce, then add the tomato paste. Stir, pour in the tomato pulp and a little water if necessary to obtain a nice creamy sauce, and the herbs of your choice. Can you smell it? Italy is invading your kitchen. Simmer over a low heat for 25–30 minutes, until the magic happens: the sauce will become thick and fragrant. Take the opportunity to pour yourself a glass of white wine, you deserve it. Cheers.

03 Cook the rigatoni – *al dente ovviamente* (that means 'obviously', in case you were wondering) – in a large saucepan of salted boiling water. Drain and mix immediately with the cauliflower *ragù*.

04 Serve hot, drizzled with olive oil, a sprinkling of *ricotta salata* or, for the vegan version, a few almond breadcrumbs. A twist of pepper, a few marjoram leaves and it's ready. Have any leftovers? Recycle your veggie bolognese sauce in lasagne or gnocchi the next day. You'll thank us later.

\+ **On repeat in the kitchen:** 'I open my eyes and think of you. Every morning, every evening, every night, I think of you.' The lyrics of 'Io ho in mente te' by Equipe 84 perfectly sum up our relationship with this cauliflower *ragù*: a persistent, almost romantic obsession.

ON THE FREGOLA

Paella di fregola con coniglio e gamberi

FOR 4 FRIENDS

- 300g (10½oz) fregola sarda, mini wheat balls straight from Sardinia
- 350g (12oz) boneless rabbit (legs or saddle), cut into pieces
- 8–10 raw prawns (or large shrimps), half-shelled (keep the heads only), straight from the fishmonger if you can, the fresher, the better
- 80g (2¾oz) peas
- 1 fresh red pepper, finely chopped
- 1 ripe tomato, chopped
- ½ onion
- 1 garlic clove
- A pinch of saffron stems, infused in a little hot water
- 1 sprig of rosemary or thyme
- 1 bay leaf
- 1 litre (4¼ cups) stock (chicken or fish, choose your favourite recipe on page 316)
- 1 small glass of dry white wine
- 1 organic or unwaxed lemon
- 5 tbsp extra virgin olive oil
- Salt and pepper QB

01 Start by cooking the meat: heat the olive oil in a large sauté or paella pan, add the rabbit pieces and brown them until they take on a nice amber colour. Then add the minced or whole garlic, the diced onion, the rosemary (or thyme), the bay leaf, the pepper and tomato. Simmer for a good 5 minutes. Deglaze with the white wine (take the opportunity to pour yourself a glass, *cin-cin amici*), let it reduce gently, then add the saffron. Season with salt and pepper, breathe in: that's the smell of (very) good food cooking.

02 Pour the uncooked fregola directly into the pan (yes, unexpected) and mix well so that it absorbs all the *sugo*. Add the hot stock little by little, as you would for a risotto, stirring occasionally. This will take about 12–15 minutes. Be careful to keep an eye on the grains; the balls should never burn . . .

03 Halfway through cooking, add the raw prawns and peas to the pan.

04 When the fregola is tender, the liquid has been almost completely absorbed and the prawns are pearly white, turn off the heat. Cover and leave to rest for 2–3 minutes. Just long enough for everything to blend together perfectly.

05 Finish with a drizzle of olive oil, a little lemon zest and a lemon wedge on the side, for those who like a touch of acidity. Then serve directly from the pan if you're part of the 'I've just finished, it's ready in a minute' team or arrange everything elegantly on a large platter. *Buon appetito.*

+ **On repeat in the kitchen:** A nod to our Iberian friends, this Italian-style surf and turf paella is best enjoyed to the sound of Zucchero's 'Baila morena', which mixes Italian, Spanish and English and makes you want to dance.

(GOOD) BROTHS

Because no stock cube, even the most magical one, can replace the unique flavour and aroma that homemade stock brings to your recipe, here we share with you how to make some really good ones.

BRODO DI CARNE

For 1 litre (4¼ cups) of meat stock:

- ½ chicken (or 400–500g/14oz to 1lb 2oz of pieces + carcass), or 300g (10½oz) beef (shank, shoulder or rib), according to your preference
- 1 carrot, cut into large pieces
- ½ stalk of celery, cut into pieces
- ½ onion, peeled
- ½ bay leaf
- 2 or 3 black peppercorns
- Coarse salt (to be adjusted at the end of cooking)
- 1 litre (4¼ cups) cold water

1 Place all the broth ingredients in a saucepan, add the cold water, then cook for about 1 hour in simmering but not boiling water.

2 Turn off the heat and leave to cool in the saucepan. When the stock is cold, strain out any impurities using a ladle and a sieve.

BRODO VEGETALE

For 1 litre (4¼ cups) of vegetable stock:

- 1 litre (4¼ cups) cold water
- 1 medium carrot, peeled and cut into large pieces
- 1 stalk of celery with leaves, cut into pieces
- 1 medium onion, peeled and halved
- 1 bay leaf
- A few sprigs of parsley (or thyme, sage or rosemary)
- 2 or 3 black peppercorns
- Salt QB

1 Place all the washed and chopped vegetables, herbs and peppercorns in a large saucepan.

2 Add the water and bring gently to the boil.

3 As soon as it boils, reduce the heat to low and simmer for 45–60 minutes, partially covered.

4 Skim off any impurities that rise to the surface, then add a pinch of salt.

5 Finally, strain the stock through a sieve.

HARDER, BETTER, FETA, STRONGER

Fazzoletto XXL feta e zucca

FOR 4 FRIENDS

For the fazzoletti

- 200g (7oz) type 00 flour
- 150g (5¼oz) *semola rimacinata* (remilled durum wheat semolina)
- 8 egg yolks

For the filling

- 300g (10½oz) squash (butternut, pumpkin or Crown Prince squash, as long as the flesh is firm and not too watery, it's up to you)
- 100g (3½oz) feta
- 1 tbsp grated Parmigiano Reggiano DOP (optional, but why not?)
- A pinch of grated nutmeg
- Olive oil
- Black pepper QB

For the smooth squash cream

- 400g (14oz) squash (butternut, Delica or musquée)
- 1 shallot
- 2 tbsp extra virgin olive oil
- 300ml (1¼ cups) vegetable stock (homemade recipe on page 317)
- 20g (¾oz) butter
- Salt and black pepper QB

For the parsley oil

- 1 bunch of fresh flat-leaf parsley
- 80ml (generous ⅓ cup) extra virgin olive oil
- Salt QB

For the finishing touch

- 60g (2oz) unsalted butter
- Zest of 1 organic or unwaxed lemon
- Salt and black pepper QB

01 Start by preparing the pasta dough. On your work surface, place the flour and semolina in a pile, then create a small well in the centre. Place the egg yolks in the middle of the well and beat with a fork. Once the dough is smooth, knead it by hand. After 10–12 minutes, the dough should be soft and elastic. Cover with clingfilm and set aside for at least 30 minutes.

02 Now for the filling. Cut the squash into cubes, place in a baking dish, drizzle generously with olive oil and bake in a preheated oven at 180°C fan/200°C/400°F/GM 6 for 30–40 minutes. It should come out nice and soft. Mash it roughly with a fork (we don't want a purée here), then add the crumbled feta, a little pepper, a pinch of nutmeg and, why not, a little Parmigiano if you're feeling generous. Mix well: the filling should be soft, fragrant and dry.

03 Now make the smooth squash cream. In a saucepan, sauté the chopped shallot in olive oil, add the diced squash, cover with stock and simmer for 20 minutes. Blend until smooth, then add the butter to make an ultra-creamy sauce.

04 In another saucepan, blanch the parsley leaves for 10 seconds in boiling water, then plunge them into iced water. Drain, dry and blend with the olive oil and a pinch of salt. Strain through a sieve to obtain a smooth oil.

05 Take your dough, roll it out thinly with a rolling pin or pasta machine on your work surface and fill and fold it. We tell you everything on page 392.

06 Cook the fazzolletti in a large saucepan of salted boiling water for 2–3 minutes. They should rise to the surface when they are *al dente*, which is the ideal time to drain them (and taste them too, if you want to check that they are still a little *al dente*).

07 Melt the butter in a frying pan until it begins to smell like roasted hazelnuts.

08 Arrange the fazzolletti in the bottom of deep plates, drizzle with the brown butter, a few spoonfuls of squash cream and a few drops of parsley oil, then sprinkle with lemon zest for freshness and a twist of pepper from the mill for more personality. A must-have for autumn, ideal for prolonging summer without getting depressed.

+ **On repeat in the kitchen:** Let Giorgio Poi whisper of timeless afternoons to you in 'I Pomeriggi'. A song like a ray of late summer sunshine, perfect for welcoming the shortening days.

DUCK IT

Maltagliati al cacao e ragù d'anatra

FOR 4 FRIENDS

<u>For the cocoa maltagliati</u>

- 300g (10½oz) type 00 flour
- 30g (1oz) bitter cocoa powder (yes, you need cocoa; and no, this is not a dessert)
- 3 eggs

<u>For the duck *ragù*</u>

- 1 whole duck leg (or 2 small ones)
- 1 carrot
- 1 stalk of celery
- 1 onion
- 1 small glass of red wine
- 400ml (1⅔ cups) chicken or vegetable stock (see our recipes on pages 316–317)
- 1 sprig of rosemary
- Extra virgin olive oil
- Salt and pepper QB

<u>For the finishing touch</u>

- Grated Parmigiano Reggiano DOP
- A few fresh sage leaves
- A little orange zest (optional)

01 Start by preparing the pasta dough. On your work surface, mix the flour and sifted cocoa powder (the little twist in this unusual recipe), then make a well and break the eggs into the centre. Add a pinch of salt and . . . get to work. Start by beating with a fork, then knead by hand until you obtain a smooth, supple, chocolatey dough. Let the dough rest at room temperature for 30 minutes under a clean cloth while you impress your date with a glass of red wine. Then roll out the dough thinly with a rolling pin or pasta machine (maybe you have one at home, you never know), then turn to page 389 to learn how to cut the dough.

02 In a hot casserole dish (Dutch oven), heat a generous dash of olive oil and add the duck leg. Brown it on all sides – it should be well coloured. Then set it aside.

03 In the same casserole dish, sauté the winning trio – finely chopped onion, carrot and celery – until the whole kitchen is filled with their aroma, then deglaze with the red wine. Return the duck to the pan, add the rosemary, moisten with the stock of your choice and simmer gently, covered, for 1½ hours until the meat falls off the bone. Patience: the longer and slower the cooking, the tenderer the meat . . .

04 Once cooked, shred the duck, return it back into the sauce and let it reduce a little more. The *ragù* should be thick and silky.

05 Cook the maltagliati in a large pan of salted boiling water for 2–3 minutes, no more. Drain and mix immediately with the hot *ragù*. Add a drizzle of olive oil to make everything shine and serve with a few sage leaves, a sprinkling of Parmigiano or some orange zest – if you have some to hand – for a little surprise effect.

+ **On repeat in the kitchen:** The sensuality of cocoa, the melt-in-the-mouth deliciousness of duck . . . this recipe has everything you need for a romantic dinner. Let's get started with 'L'appuntamento' ('the date') by Ornella Vanoni playing in the background, and everything is set for a cosy atmosphere, perfect for seduction.

FAMIGLIA PROTA

Paola & Manuel

FORMIA

THE GREEN GODDESS

Mafalde al pesto di rucola

FOR 4 FRIENDS

- 320g (11¼oz) mafalde, a long pasta with wavy edges named after Princess Mafalda of Savoy, their curls resembling the lace on her royal dress
- 100g (3½oz) fresh rocket
- 50g (1¾oz) grated Parmigiano Reggiano DOP
- 30g (1oz) pine nuts (or walnuts)
- 1–2 garlic cloves
- 100–120ml (scant ½–½ cup) extra virgin olive oil
- 1 dash of lemon juice (optional, but why say no to lemon?)
- Salt and freshly ground black pepper QB

01 To make the pesto: in a blender (or a mortar, if you're a purist), place the well-washed and dried rocket, pine nuts, garlic, a pinch of salt and a generous sprinkling of freshly grated Parmigiano. Blend gently, pouring in the olive oil in a thin stream until you obtain a smooth sauce that is neither too runny nor too thick. If the pesto lacks flavour, a little lemon juice can liven it up. And for even more character, consider lightly toasting the pine nuts before blending them, as this is a great way to boost flavours.

02 Meanwhile, boil a large pot of well-salted water. Add the mafalde and cook until *al dente* (usually 8–10 minutes, but we trust you to keep an eye on it, or taste it, and check regularly). Drain and remember to keep a ladleful of water (your liquid gold).

03 Mix the pasta with the pesto in your best large bowl and feel free to thicken your sauce with a little of your magic water.

04 Serve piping hot, with a final sprinkling of grated Parmigiano, a few toasted pine nuts on top, a twist of pepper for good measure, and you're ready to enjoy!

+ **On repeat in the kitchen:** 'Il cielo in una stanza' by Gino Paoli, a romantic and intimate song that has become a cult classic, which transforms every bite into something timeless.

THE MOUNTAINS ARE CALLING YOU

Pizzoccheri della Valtellina

FOR 4 FRIENDS

<u>For the pizzoccheri</u>

- 300g (10½oz) buckwheat flour
- 150g (5¼oz) type 00 flour
- 150ml (⅔ cup) lukewarm water

<u>For the dish</u>

- 300g (10½oz) firm potatoes, such as Charlotte or Yukon Gold
- 300g (10½oz) curly kale or Swiss chard (or a mixture of both, if you're feeling adventurous)
- 200g (7oz) Casera cheese (or, if unavailable, Fontina, Reblochon or farmhouse Raclette)
- 2–3 garlic cloves, lightly squashed with a knife blade or the palm of your hand
- 60g (2oz) grated Parmigiano Reggiano DOP
- 80g (2¾oz) butter
- A few sage leaves (optional)
- Freshly ground black pepper QB

01 On a clean work surface (as always, right?), mix the two types of flour, gradually add the water and knead until you have a smooth, even dough. Cover with a clean cloth and set aside for 30 minutes.

02 Once your dough has rested, go to page 399 for instructions on how to shape your pizzoccheri.

03 Peel the potatoes, dice them and cook them in a large saucepan of salted boiling water. After 5 minutes, add the chopped kale or Swiss chard, then, 5 minutes later, the pizzoccheri. Cook for another 7–8 minutes.

04 Drain and plate up. In a large dish (or directly on each plate), alternate layers: a layer of pasta with vegetables, slices of cheese, a sprinkling of Parmigiano. Repeat until all the ingredients are used up.

05 In a small saucepan, melt the butter with the sage leaves if you like, and the garlic cloves. Allow the garlic to turn golden, then remove.

06 Drizzle the dish or plates with this hot flavoured butter, add a few twists of pepper, then quickly cover with a tea towel to allow the cheese to melt gently. These pizzoccheri, a typical dish from Valtellina, are best enjoyed piping hot to ward off the cold. Remove the tea towel, serve and savour while watching the snow fall.

\+ **On repeat in the kitchen:** Just as comforting as this recipe, the song 'Gianna' by Rino Gaetano makes you want to sing loudly in an Alpine chalet and nod your head. Turn up the volume and smile.

CURVE E LENTICCHIE

It's the lentil things in life

FOR 4 FRIENDS

- 320g (11¼oz) elbow macaroni, small semi-circular pasta
- 200g (7oz) green or Puy lentils
- 1 medium onion
- 1 carrot
- 1 stalk of celery
- 2 garlic cloves
- 1 tbsp tomato paste
- 1.2–1.5 litres (5–6⅓ cups) hot vegetable stock (see page 317 for the recipe)
- 2 tbsp extra virgin olive oil
- Salt and freshly ground black pepper QB
- Grated Parmigiano Reggiano DOP (optional, but why say no?)

01 Pour a generous dash of olive oil into a large saucepan and sauté the finely chopped onion, carrot and celery over a low heat for 5–7 minutes. Add the minced garlic, fry for a minute and then stir in the tomato paste. Mix well until the sauce turns a Tuscan red.

02 Rinse the lentils in cold water, drain them and pour them into the saucepan. Stir, then pour in 500ml (2 cups) of hot vegetable stock. Cover and simmer over a low heat for about 20 minutes, keeping an eye on the mixture. Add stock regularly until the lentils are almost tender – but still firm.

03 Pour the macaroni directly into the saucepan. Continue adding hot stock, ladle by ladle, and stir until the pasta is *al dente* (allow about 10–12 minutes). Never take your eyes off your precious creation, as the pasta could stick. If this happens despite your vigilance, don't panic, just add a little broth and stir gently. Taste, season with salt and pepper, and when the pasta and lentils are cooked through and the texture is creamy, remove from the heat.

04 Serve hot, with a drizzle of olive oil and grated Parmigiano for those who like to live a little. A comforting dish that warms the body and the heart, ideal for winter days. Or any other time of year, because every day is a good day to treat yourself.

+ **On repeat in the kitchen:** 'Lenticchie a capodanno, fortuna tutto l'anno' (Lentils on New Year's Eve, good luck all year round). In Italy, they say that eating lentils on 31 December promises prosperity for the coming year. All you have to do is enjoy your New Year's Eve meal with Mahmood's 'Soldi' playing in the background – who knows, you might just tempt a little extra fortune your way.

CHAPTER 6

PASTA SALADS

CAPRESE DI TUFFOLI

Caprese me if you can

FOR 4 FRIENDS

- 320g (11¼oz) tuffoli (or other short pasta: rigatoni, mezzi paccheri, etc.)
- 300g (10½oz) multicoloured cherry tomatoes
- 300g (10½oz) multicoloured beefsteak tomatoes
- 250g (8¾oz) buffalo mozzarella
- 6–8 fresh basil leaves
- 4–5 tbsp extra virgin olive oil
- Fine salt and freshly ground black pepper QB

01 Wash the tomatoes thoroughly. Cut the cherry tomatoes in half or quarters, depending on their size, and dice the beefsteak tomatoes. Mix everything together in a large bowl, season with salt and pepper, add a generous drizzle of olive oil and the basil leaves, torn by hand. Mix gently and leave to marinate at room temperature for 30–40 minutes. The tomatoes should release their juice and develop their full flavour.

02 Meanwhile, cook the tuffoli in a large saucepan of salted boiling water. This sunny dish, typical of Rome, is a summer must-have that is best eaten cold. So rinse your pasta under cold water after draining it. Add a drizzle of olive oil, just enough to keep the pasta from sticking.

03 Drain the buffalo mozzarella well, then slice it.

04 Add the cooled pasta to the bowl with the marinated tomatoes. Mix gently to coat them well with the juice and oil. Add the mozzarella and stir one last time before serving. *Delizioso.*

+ **On repeat in the kitchen:** Don't hesitate to take a nap while the pasta cools. Close your eyes to Andrea Laszlo De Simone's languid 'Immensità' and wake up on a terrace in Capri, in your mind at least.

GOLDEN BALLS

Fregola sarda con ceci, erbe fresche e limone

FOR 4 FRIENDS

- 250g (8¾oz) fregola sarda, those wheat balls straight from Sardinia (if you don't have any, giant couscous will do the job, but don't tell the Sardinians)
- 200g (7oz) cooked chickpeas (homemade or tinned, we won't judge)
- Zest of 1 preserved lemon
- Juice of 1 fresh organic or unwaxed lemon
- 1 very ripe tomato (optional, but she loves gatecrashing)
- 1 bunch of fresh flat-leaf parsley
- 1 bunch of fresh mint
- 1 small bunch of fresh coriander (optional)
- 2 spring onions or 1 small shallot, whichever you prefer
- 4–5 tbsp extra virgin olive oil
- Salt and freshly ground black pepper QB

01 Cook the fregola in a large quantity of salted boiling water for 10–12 minutes. Drain, rinse under cold water, drizzle with olive oil and leave to cool completely.

02 Finely chop the parsley, mint and coriander (if you feel like it – we know there are two camps here). Mince the spring onions or shallot. Dice the preserved lemon peel (if you've found a whole preserved lemon, you can reuse the pulp in a vinaigrette with a little olive oil, chopped fresh herbs, salt and pepper, ideal for accompanying your pan-fried vegetables). Then, if using one, finely dice the tomato, taking care to remove the seeds first – we want to avoid a swimming-pool effect in the salad bowl.

03 In a large salad bowl, combine the cooled fregola with the chickpeas, fresh herbs, onions, preserved lemon and tomato, if you gave in to temptation. Season with lemon juice, olive oil, a little salt and a little pepper, then leave to rest in the fridge for at least 30 minutes to allow all the flavours to blend.

04 Serve very chilled, on its own as a vegetarian dish or as an accompaniment to grilled fish, for example. *Buon appetito.*

\+ **On repeat in the kitchen:** 'Tin, tin, tin . . .' To the mischievous rhythm of 'Tintarella di luna' by the enchanting Mina, we swear you can hear the fregola balls dancing in the salad bowl. And honestly, who's stopping you from dancing along with them in the kitchen?

WHERE TO EAT LIKE A TRUE ITALIAN?

Our chef Alberto has concocted the holy grail: a small selection, region by region, of the must-try restaurants and dishes to discover in Italy. Buon appetito.

NORD ITALIA

PIEMONTE

Agnolotti del Plin
Albergo Ristorante Trattoria del Castello, Serralunga d'Alba

Tajerin with rabbit *ragù*
Repubblica di Perno, Monforte d'Alba

Tagliolini with truffles
La Piola, Alba

LOMBARDIA

Casoncelli alla Bergamasca Trattoria
Visconti, Ambivere

Paccheri alla Vittorio
Da Vittorio, Brusaporto

Pizzoccheri
Quattro Stagioni Restaurant, Mantello

Tagliatelle with butter and Parmigiano Reggiano
Trippa, Milan

TRENTINO-ALTO ADIGE

Canederli
Ristorante Boivin, Levico Terme

FRIULI-VENEZIA GIULIA

Gnocchi made from leavened dough with rabbit *ragù*
Lokanda Devetak, San Michele del Carso

EMILIA-ROMAGNA

Traditional lasagne
Ristorante Al Cambio, Bologna

Tortelli with herbs
Ai Due Platani Restaurant, Coloreto

Fried pasta
Trattoria Oppici, Montevaca

Rice bomb
Ostreria Fratelli Pavesi, Podenzano

Pastiss alla Piacentina
Isa Mazzocchi, La Palta, Bilegno, Borgonovo

LIGURIA

Trofie al pesto
La Brinca, Ne

Ravioli al tuccu
Baccicin du Caru, Pontedecimo

CENTRO ITALIA

LAZIO

Carbonara
Luciano Cucina Italiana, Rome

Cacio e Pepe
Roscioli Salumeria con Cucina, Rome

UMBRIA

Tagliatelle with pigeon *ragù*
Il Capanno, Torrecola

TOSCANA

Pici with garlic
Al Convento, Scarlino

Rasnal soup
Ristorante Maggese, San Miniato

SUD ITALIA

CAMPANIA

Spaghetti alla Nerano Quattro
Passi, Nerano

Pasta allo Scarpariello
Lido Lo Schiacchetiello, Bacoli

Spaghetti with tomato sauce
George Restaurant (Grand Hotel Parker's), Naples

Minestra di pasta mista e crostacei
La Torre del Saracino,Vico Equense

PUGLIA

Spaghetti all'Assassina
Al Sorso Preferito, Bari

SICILIA

Busiate
Il Duomo Restaurant, Ragusa Ibla

SARDEGNA

Culurgiones
Hotel Ristorante Ispinigoli, Dorgali

LIVE BY THE SWORD

Calamarata con pesce spada, melanzane e menta

FOR 4 FRIENDS

- 320g (11¼oz) calamarata (or paccheri, or mezze maniche, as long as it holds the sauce)
- 300g (10½oz) swordfish fillet, cut into 1.5cm (½in) cubes (skin and bones removed, please)
- 1 medium aubergine
- Juice of ½ organic or unwaxed lemon
- 200g (7oz) cherry tomatoes
- 6–8 fresh mint leaves
- A few fresh basil leaves
- 3–4 tbsp extra virgin olive oil
- Salt and freshly ground black pepper QB

01 Cut the aubergine into small cubes. Salt the cubes and leave them to rest in a colander for 20–30 minutes. They will release their juices and cook perfectly. Then fry them in 3 tablespoons of olive oil over a medium heat until they turn a beautiful golden colour. The goal is to achieve a crispy-melting result. Drain on kitchen paper.

02 In a bowl, mix your swordfish cubes with the lemon juice, a little fine salt, pepper and extra virgin olive oil, and set aside to allow the fish to marinate slightly.

03 Cook the calamarata in a large saucepan of salted boiling water for 10 minutes until *al dente.* Drain, rinse under cold water and set aside in a cool place, drizzling with olive oil to prevent it from sticking.

04 In a salad bowl, mix the cooled pasta, halved cherry tomatoes, fried aubergine, chopped mint, roughly chopped basil and marinated swordfish. Keep a little basil and swordfish aside for the finishing touch.

05 Time to plate up. Serve your dish on individual plates or in a large dish for a more convivial effect, and top with the remaining diced swordfish, a few basil leaves and a drizzle of olive oil. Voilà, you've just passed the *pasta maestro* test.

+ **On repeat in the kitchen:** The sun is shining, the olive oil is glistening, the mint is dancing, and here you are on a culinary road trip to the sound of Negrita's 'Rotolando verso Sud'. Head to Taormina, Syracuse or Cefalù, where *pesce spada* reigns supreme.

BASIL INSTINCT

Spaghetti integrali e zucchine trombetta, basilico, mandorle

FOR 4 FRIENDS

- 320g (11¼oz) wholemeal spaghetti (wholemeal pasta has a slightly more rustic flavour and a slightly firmer texture)
- 2–3 trombetta courgettes (trombetta or tromboncino courgettes are the long, thin stars of the vegetable garden: low in water content and slightly sweet, they are ideal for flavouring this sauce)
- 1 garlic clove
- 30g (1oz) fresh basil
- 40g (1¼oz) almonds (whole or flaked, depending on what you have in your cupboard)
- 4–5 tbsp extra virgin olive oil
- Salt and freshly ground black pepper QB

01 Wash the courgettes, then use a vegetable peeler to cut about ten long strips lengthwise. These will be mixed with the spaghetti when plating to create a pretty trompe l'oeil effect. Cut the rest of the courgettes into thin rounds.

02 In a large frying pan over a medium heat, gently brown the whole garlic in olive oil. As soon as it begins to turn a nice colour, add the courgette slices. Cook for 8–10 minutes, until they are tender. Season lightly with salt, then remove the garlic to retain only its flavour. Remove the courgette from the heat and blend with the basil leaves to obtain a smooth pesto. Set aside.

03 Meanwhile, dry-toast the almonds in a small frying pan until lightly browned. Leave to cool, then crush them (if they were whole) coarsely by hand or with a knife.

04 Now cook the wholemeal spaghetti in a large quantity of salted boiling water (without breaking them). Drain, then rinse under cold water and drizzle with olive oil to prevent it from sticking together. Set aside in a cool place.

05 In a large bowl, mix the cooled spaghetti with the pesto, the courgette strips, half the crushed (or flaked) almonds and a drizzle of olive oil if you want an even silkier sauce. Stir gently.

06 Time to plate up: place the spaghetti in deep plates (shaped in small nests, Italian trattoria-style), sprinkle with the remaining toasted almonds and a sprig of fresh basil. A twist of the pepper mill, a final drizzle of extra virgin olive oil, and it's ready. Sunshine on your plate, a smile from ear to ear.

+ **On repeat in the kitchen:** Erlend Øye's 'La prima estate' is a sunny celebration of youth, love and shared moments. A hymn to joie de vivre and small victories to be listened to in good company to preserve the moment.

FAMIGLIA DI FUSCO-CARAFA

Viviana & Flavia

BAIA

PIMP MY POLPO

Calamarata polpo e patate

FOR 4 FRIENDS

- 320g (11¼oz) calamarata
- 600g (1lb 5oz) fresh octopus, straight from your fishmonger
- 2 medium firm potatoes (approximately 300g/10½oz)
- 1 garlic clove
- Juice of ½ organic or unwaxed lemon, and its zest
- A little fresh flat-leaf parsley
- 4 tbsp extra virgin olive oil
- Desalted capers (optional)
- Pitted black olives (optional)
- Datterino tomatoes (optional; yes, that's a lot of options, but we suggest and you decide)
- Fine salt and freshly ground black pepper QB

01 Start by rinsing your octopus under cold water before plunging it into a large saucepan of boiling water. Leave it to cook over a low heat for 40–50 minutes. Flavia's grandmother's secret? Leave it to cool in the water: tenderness guaranteed. Once at room temperature, cut it into small pieces.

02 Peel and dice the potatoes then cook in a saucepan of salted boiling water for 10–12 minutes; they should be tender but not mushy (we want some texture). Once cooked, drain and leave to cool.

03 Place the calamarata in a large saucepan of salted boiling water and cook for 30 seconds to 1 minute longer than the time indicated on the packet. Why? Because after draining them, you will rinse them under cold water, which will stop them cooking. A little tip to keep in mind for your next salads. Drizzle with a little olive oil before setting aside at room temperature.

04 In your finest salad bowl, mix the finely chopped garlic, fresh lemon juice, chopped parsley, a little salt, pepper and a generous drizzle of olive oil. Then add the octopus pieces and potatoes. Mix gently.

05 Add the cooled calamarata and stir to coat each ingredient. Taste and adjust the seasoning to your liking, because it's only really good if you say so.

06 Then pop it in the fridge for about an hour, giving you time to freshen up and the salad to rest, or vice versa. Be careful to not let the salad get too cold and lose its flavour. Remember to take it out 10 minutes before serving. Want to switch things up? You can add a few halved tomatoes, olives or capers when plating up – you're the chef. Add the lemon juice and zest just before serving your masterpiece, and now all that remains is to enjoy it.

+ **On repeat in the kitchen:** This cold dish from Puglia, which is found on the coast between Gallipoli and Otranto, is best enjoyed while listening to the song 'Estate' by Negramaro, the region's leading band.

FREGOLA LA LA LAND

Fregola con agrumi, finocchio e trota

FOR 4 FRIENDS

For the gravlax trout (which ideally needs to marinate for 48 hours, so be warned, this isn't a last-minute dish)

- 1 salmon or trout fillet weighing 150–200g (5¼–7oz) (skinless and boneless)
- 30g (1oz) coarse salt
- 25g (generous ¾oz) caster sugar
- 1 tsp pink peppercorns
- Zest of ⅓ organic or unwaxed lemon
- Zest of ⅓ organic or unwaxed orange
- 2 tsp gin
- A few sprigs of dill

For the fregola

- 250g (8¾oz) fregola sarda, those wheat balls from straight from Sardinia
- 1 orange and 1 organic or unwaxed lemon
- 1 fennel bulb, with a few of the green fronds for the finishing touch
- 1 tsp mild or wholegrain mustard
- 5–6 tbsp extra virgin olive oil
- A few mint or dill leaves, as desired
- Fine salt and black pepper QB

01 Prepare the gravlax trout. Spread half of the salt and sugar on a baking tray in an even layer. Place the trout fillet on top, flesh side up. Add the pink peppercorns, grated lemon and orange zest, gin and dill to the fillet. Cover the fish with the remaining salt and sugar, making sure to coat all the other ingredients with them. Wrap up tightly in clingfilm and place a light weight on top – yesterday's Tupperware, yoghurts, a small tray . . . we trust you to find the perfect thing to weigh down the fish. Transfer the gravlax to the fridge and leave to marinate for at least 48 hours, turning the fillet halfway through. Once marinated, rinse the fish under cold water.

02 Cook the fregola in a pan of salted boiling water for 10–12 minutes. Drain, rinse under cold water, drizzle with olive oil and leave to cool completely.

03 Next, prepare the garnish. Remove a few orange segments, squeeze the rest of the fruit and collect the juice in a small bowl. Zest the orange and lemon and set aside. In another bowl, finely slice the raw fennel – ideally using a mandoline. Combine some of the fennel with the orange segments and zest in a large bowl and bake the rest of the fennel in a preheated oven at 180°C fan/200°C/400°F/GM 6 in the oven until it browns nicely.

04 In the bowl of orange juice, add the mustard, olive oil, a pinch of salt and a twist of freshly ground pepper. Mix well, then pour this dressing into a salad bowl. Next, add the cooled fregola, raw fennel and orange, chopped mint and dill, then thin slices of gravlax trout (keep some for the finishing touch). Mix together.

05 Adjust the seasoning and serve in deep plates or in a large dish to share. Finish with a sprinkling of fennel fronds and a little lemon juice. fresh citrus zest, orange segments, roasted fennel, a few slices of trout and, if you feel like it, a few more mint or dill leaves. This salad is ideal as a light starter, a single dish for sunny days, or as part of a buffet to impress your guests.

+ **On repeat in the kitchen:** Light, danceable, with a touch of retro, the song 'Guarda come dondolo' by Edoardo Vianello dances like the fregola balls on your taste buds. You're bound to find yourself 'twisting, twisting' in the cucina.

FAMIGLIA DI FUSCO-CARAFA

Giorgio, Luca, Viviana, Flavia, Alessandro, Alessio, Federica & Daniele

BAIA

ALL UP IN MY GRILL

Lumache con verdure grigliate e feta

FOR 4 FRIENDS

<u>For the snails</u>

- 400g (14oz) lumache, small snail-shaped pasta
- 4 tbsp basil pesto (homemade, preferably using our recipe on page 289)

<u>For the grilled vegetables</u>

- 1 aubergine
- 1 courgette
- 1 red pepper
- 6 small carrots or baby carrots (the smaller the better)
- Extra virgin olive oil
- Salt and pepper QB

<u>For the sun-dried tomatoes</u>

- 300g (10½oz) cherry or datterino tomatoes
- 2 tbsp extra virgin olive oil
- 1 sprig of thyme
- 1 garlic clove
- A pinch of salt
- A pinch of sugar

<u>For serving</u>

- 120g (4¼oz) feta cheese
- A few fresh basil leaves

01 Preheat the oven to 120°C fan/140°C/275°F/GM 1. Cut the cherry tomatoes in half, place them on a baking tray with the olive oil, thyme, garlic, a little salt and a pinch of sugar. Bake for about 1 hour 30 minutes until they are well caramelised (but still a little juicy).

02 Wash the vegetables, then slice the aubergine, courgette and pepper into even slices. Peel the carrots and cut them in half lengthwise if they are a little too large. Brush all the vegetables with olive oil, season with salt and pepper and grill them on a hot griddle or grill until they brown. Arrange them harmoniously – we insist – on a large platter and leave them to cool.

03 Cook the lumache in a large saucepan of salted boiling water for 9–10 minutes until *al dente*, then drain them, remembering to reserve a ladleful of the cooking water. As this is a cold dish, rinse the pasta under cold water to stop it cooking.

04 Mix the pasta with the basil pesto, adding a little hot water to bind everything together if necessary. Set aside and wait for the mixture to cool.

05 Arrange the lumache with pesto on a bed of roasted vegetables, add the sun-dried tomatoes in small dollops and sprinkle with crumbled feta and chopped fresh basil. There you have it, it looks beautiful, but you know we don't eat with our eyes, so *a tavola*!

+ **On repeat in the kitchen:** Isn't this the perfect recipe to enjoy after a hot summer's day, sitting outside under the moonlight? The perfect moment to listen to Fred Buscaglione's 'Guarda che luna'.

PASTA DI LENTICCHIE CON MELANZANE, YOGURT E TAPENADE

Is this gluten-free? Yes, it is!

FOR 4 FRIENDS

For the pasta

- 360g (12½oz) lentil pasta (fusilli or penne, depending on what you find on the shelves)

For the aubergines

- 2 large aubergines
- Olive oil (for baking) or frying oil (depending on which cooking method you choose)
- A pinch of salt

For the tomato tapenade

- 200g (7oz) fresh cherry tomatoes
- 150g (5¼oz) sun-dried tomatoes
- 1 garlic clove
- 1 handful of fresh basil leaves
- 2 tbsp extra virgin olive oil
- Salt and pepper QB

To serve

- 200g (7oz) plain Greek yoghurt
- A few sun-dried tomatoes
- 40g (1½oz) toasted flaked almonds
- A few basil leaves

01 Two ways to cook your aubergines here – we suggest, you decide. First option, in the oven: cut the aubergines into even cubes, place them on a baking tray lined with greaseproof paper, drizzle with olive oil, season with salt, then bake at 200°C fan/220°C/425°F/GM 7 for about 25 minutes until golden brown. Second option, frying: dice the aubergines in the same way, fry them in hot oil until they are nicely browned, then drain them thoroughly on kitchen paper before salting them lightly. Two methods, two results, immediate success in both cases.

02 For the tomato tapenade: blend the fresh and sun-dried tomatoes with the olive oil, garlic, basil, a little salt and a little pepper.

03 Cook the lentil pasta in a large saucepan of salted boiling water following the instructions on the packet. Drain, then immediately mix in some of the tapenade and the diced cooked aubergine.

04 To serve, spread a thin layer of seasoned Greek yoghurt (a little salt and pepper or other spices to taste) on the bottom of each plate, arrange the pasta on top, add a few spoonfuls of tapenade, sun-dried tomatoes for extra flavour, toasted flaked almonds and a few fresh basil leaves. After that, we hope you've made extra, otherwise there'll be a flurry of forks around the table during the meal.

+ **On repeat in the kitchen:** Is this dish so good that it leaves you speechless? Then there's no need to search for words: it's the perfect moment to listen to 'Senza parole' by Vasco Rossi.

CHAPTER 7

DESSERTS

PASTA PUDDING
Childhood memories

FOR 4 FRIENDS

- 250g (9oz) gramigna pasta (or, if unavailable, small childhood pasta such as coquillettes or ditalini)
- 1 litre (4¼ cups) whole milk (or 100g/3½oz double cream)
- 80g (2¾oz) sugar (adjust according to taste)
- 1 vanilla pod (or 1 tsp vanilla extract)
- A pinch of salt
- Zest of 1 organic or unwaxed orange or lemon (optional, just to add flavour according to your childhood memories)

01 Heat the milk in a large saucepan with the split vanilla pod (or vanilla extract), the sugar and a small pinch of salt – just enough to awaken the taste buds.

02 When the milk begins to simmer gently, sprinkle in the pasta. Now, lower the heat and keep a close eye on your precious creation: stir often and gently so that it doesn't stick, thinking about your childhood, your grandmother or your great-uncle, whom it would be nice to call soon. Simmer for 15–20 minutes, until the little curves become melt-in-the-mouth. If the milk evaporates too quickly, add more (preferably warm) to maintain a creamy texture.

03 Once the dessert is as creamy as you like, remove from the heat and pour into a large bowl or several small individual ramekins. You can then grate a little lemon or orange over the top, as you wish.

04 Enjoy hot, warm or cold, dipping your spoon in as if it were a childhood memory.

+ **On repeat in the kitchen:** And since this dessert has the magical power to take us back to our childhood, we listen to it along with Olly's 'Balorda nostalgia', a real musical comfort blanket.

SEADA SARDA

Doughnuts with melted sheep's cheese and lemon

An iconic Sardinian dessert, seada sarda are small fried doughnuts filled with melted sheep's cheese and topped with honey. They smell of the scrubland and sunshine.

FOR 4 FRIENDS

For the dough

- 250g (8¾oz) plain flour
- 50g (1¾oz) cold butter
- 50ml (scant ¼ cup) lukewarm water
- Salt QB

For the filling

- 360g (12½oz) fresh sheep's cheese, such as pecorino
- Grated zest of 1 organic or unwaxed lemon

For frying and the finishing touch

- Peanut oil
- Honey (traditionally heather honey, but any type of honey will do)

01 In a mixing bowl, combine the flour, salt and butter cut into small pieces (don't let it soften; the cold helps the dough's elasticity) and mix with your fingers until you obtain a sandy texture. Gradually, add a little lukewarm water and knead until you form a smooth, even ball. Cover and leave to rest at room temperature for 30 minutes under a clean tea towel.

02 Meanwhile, prepare the filling: grate the fresh sheep's cheese with a coarse grater and form small flattened balls. If the cheese is too dry, soften it gently over a low heat with a drop of milk so that you can shape it. Mix it with the grated lemon zest.

03 Roll out the dough very thinly (2mm) and cut out circles 10–12 cm (4–4¾in) in diameter (a wide glass or cookie cutter will do). Place 90g (3oz) of filling in the centre of half of the circles, cover with the remaining circles and seal the edges well, first with your fingers and then with a fork. Leave your little wonders to rest for 10–15 minutes at room temperature.

04 Heat a generous amount of peanut oil in a frying pan and, when it is hot (around 170°C/375°F), add one *seada* at a time. If you don't have a thermometer at home, follow Chef Flavia's advice and dip a small piece of dough in to test: it should immediately start to bubble. Fry until they are golden brown on both sides and slightly puffed up. Drain on kitchen paper, away from little thieving hands . . .

05 Drizzle generously with honey while they are still hot (feel free to quickly heat your honey in a pan to make it as liquid as possible). For those of you with a sweet tooth – no icing sugar or spread in this recipe, just the ultimate nectar: fragrant honey.

06 Serve warm, when the cheese is still melted in the centre. Purists can sprinkle a little freshly ground black pepper on top for an even more traditional and rustic version.

\+ **On repeat in the kitchen:** 'Miele' by Gigi d'Alessio is a light and romantic ballad that invites you to take a gourmet break. Simply honey for your ears.

FAMIGLIA DI FUSCO-CARAFA

Luca, Viviana & Flavia

BAIA

FIG MAMMA

Casoncelli dolci ai fichi

FOR 4 FRIENDS

<u>For the shortcrust pastry</u>

- 250g (8¾oz) plain flour
- 125g (scant 4½oz) cold butter
- 50ml (scant ¼ cup) cold water
- A pinch of salt

<u>For the filling</u>

- 300g (10½oz) dried figs
- 50g (1¾oz) sugar
- 50ml (scant ¼ cup) water
- Zest of 1 organic or unwaxed orange or lemon
- 1 tbsp honey (optional)

01 In a large bowl, combine the flour and salt, then add the cold butter and cut into small cubes. Work quickly with your fingertips to rub the butter into the flour, then gradually add the cold water. Form the mixture into a smooth ball without kneading too much. Wrap the dough in clingfilm and leave to rest for 30 minutes in the fridge.

02 Meanwhile, prepare the filling. Place the chopped dried figs, sugar, water and orange zest (or lemon zest, if you like) in a saucepan. Cook over a low heat for about 10 minutes, stirring occasionally, until thick and silky. For those with a sweet tooth, add 1 tablespoon of honey before setting aside at room temperature, you cheeky monkeys. Then leave to cool completely.

03 Preheat your oven to 180°C fan/200°C/400°F/GM 6, then get on with the shaping. Roll out the shortcrust pastry on a clean, lightly floured work surface (no more than 2mm thick). Using a glass or cookie cutter, cut out circles about 8cm (3in) in diameter. Place 1 teaspoon of filling in the centre, moisten the edges with a pastry brush (or your fingers) dampened with a little water, then close to form a nice, plump turnover. Then pinch the ends with your fingers to prevent the filling from escaping during cooking (horror of horrors).

04 Place the casoncelli on a baking tray lined with greaseproof paper and bake for 15–20 minutes, until the pastry is a lovely golden brown. Then leave them to cool, call the kids, neighbours or friends and enjoy them together for dessert or afternoon tea.

+ **On repeat in the kitchen:** While the casoncelli are baking, play 'Marmellata #25' by Cesare Cremonini, a ballad about the singer's break-up at the age of 25. With nostalgia and a great deal of self-deprecation, he recalls the memories left behind by his ex and the kilos of jam he devoured to fill the void.

MULLED WINE!
Chinulille Calabresi

FOR 4 FRIENDS

<u>For the dough</u>
- 500g (1lb 2oz) type 00 flour
- 80ml (generous ⅓ cup) extra virgin olive oil
- 160ml (⅔ cup) sweet wine, such as vermouth or Marsala
- Zest of 1 mandarin or 1 organic or unwaxed orange
- 1 vanilla pod (optional)
- A pinch of cinnamon (optional)

<u>For the filling</u>
- *Mostarda d'uva*, a sweet mustard made from black grape must
- A few walnuts
- A few raisins

<u>For frying and the finishing touch</u>
- Peanut oil
- A few spoonfuls of honey

01 Pour the oil, sweet wine and the zest of your chosen citrus into a saucepan. Add a touch of vanilla and cinnamon for flavour and heat gently until the mixture reaches 40°C/104°F. If you don't have a thermometer, the rule is simple: it should be warm, not boiling.

02 In a large bowl, pour in the flour, then add your warm flavoured oil, stirring with a wooden spoon. When the dough begins to form, knead by hand until you obtain a soft, smooth ball. Leave to rest for 30 minutes at room temperature under a clean tea towel.

03 Once rested, roll the dough out thinly (2mm thick) on a work surface. Using a glass or cookie cutter, cut out circles 8–10cm (3–4in) in diameter, then fill the centre of each with 1 spoonful of *mostarda* and a few nuts and raisins. We trust you to manage this composition with a chef's touch: neither too much nor too little. The aim is to prevent the nuts and raisins from escaping during cooking: more in the pan than on the plate never satisfies anyone. Then moisten the edges with a pastry brush and water, fold each disc into a half-moon shape and seal the edges well with your fingers.

04 When it comes to cooking, there are two schools of thought. For the frying team: heat the oil to 170°C/375°F and fry your turnovers in it in small batches. If you still don't have a thermometer at home, follow Chef Flavia's advice and drop a small piece of dough in to test: you should immediately see lots of bubbles appear. Brown the chinulille on both sides, then drain them on kitchen paper. For the oven team: preheat the oven to 180°C fan/200°C/400°F/GM 6, place your chinulille on a baking tray lined with greaseproof paper and bake for 15–20 minutes, until they turn a nice golden colour. In both cases, after cooking, coat them with honey for an even more indulgent treat.

05 Then there's just one rule: enjoy them warm, not piping hot. Hang in there, the wait is part of the fun.

+ **On repeat in the kitchen:** Ligabue's gold disc and iconic summer 2006 hit, 'Happy Hour', is a rock anthem that perfectly accompanies these little sweet wine chinulille. Because it's bound to be snack o'clock somewhere.

TORTELLI DOLCI DI CARNEVALE

Filled with pastry cream

FOR 4 FRIENDS

For the dough

- 250g (8¾oz) plain flour
- 1 egg
- 1 small glass of liqueur (your choice: Marsala, anisette, limoncello, etc.)
- Juice of ½ organic or unwaxed orange
- 15g (1 tbsp) butter
- 75g (2½oz) caster sugar

For the crème pâtissière

- 250ml (1 cup) milk
- 1 whole egg + 1 egg yolk
- Zest of ½ organic or unwaxed lemon
- 25g (generous ¾oz) plain flour
- 75g (2½oz) caster sugar

For frying and the finishing touch

- Peanut oil
- Icing sugar

01 For this recipe, we opted for crème pâtissière, but you are free to choose the filling of your choice, or even leave your tortelli unfilled (these are called *tortelli vuoti*, i.e. empty tortelli, and can be served with chocolate sauce or jam on the side). In a saucepan, heat the milk with some lemon zest (without bringing it to the boil). Meanwhile, in a bowl, whisk the whole egg, egg yolk and sugar until the mixture turns pale. Stir in the sifted flour, then add the hot milk in a thin stream, stirring constantly. Pour everything back into the saucepan and thicken over a low heat, stirring constantly and keeping a close eye on it. Once the crème pâtissière is smooth and creamy, remove from the heat, remove the lemon zest with a sieve, cover the saucepan with clingfilm and leave to cool.

02 While the crème pâtissière is cooling, prepare the dough. In a large bowl, place the egg, flour, sugar and orange juice. Mix, then add the liqueur and softened butter. Knead until you have a smooth, even dough. Too sticky? Add a little more flour. Shape into a ball, wrap in clingfilm and leave to rest for 30 minutes in the fridge.

03 Once the dough has rested, it's time to shape it. On a clean, floured work surface, roll out the dough with a rolling pin or pasta machine (if you have one at home), then cut into squares of about 7cm (3in). Place 1 spoonful of crème pâtissière in the centre of each square. Moisten the edges with a pastry brush and a little water, fold into a triangle and seal the edges. Then fold the two corners of the base towards each other and press lightly to form a plump tortello. Repeat the process as many times as your quantity of dough allows.

04 Heat the oil in a large saucepan to approximately 170°C/375°F. If you do not have a thermometer at home and don't fancy knocking on your neighbour's door, here is a little tip: drop a small piece of dough in to test; if there are lots of bubbles, it is ready. Fry the tortelli in small batches and let them brown gently until they are a nice, even colour. Drain them with a slotted spoon and place them on kitchen paper (away from the hands of any lurking kiddos; be careful, they're quick!).

05 Sprinkle with icing sugar just before serving. Enjoy warm or at room temperature during carnival season . . . and the rest of the year.

\+ **On repeat in the kitchen:** We board a gondola and glide between the masked silhouettes of the Venice carnival to the sound of 'Serenissima' by Rondò Veneziano, an orchestra inspired by baroque music to produce modern sounds, somewhere between court music and 1980s pop. A treat for the ears as you savour your little delicacies.

TAGLIATELLE DOLCI

Fritti sensation

FOR 4 FRIENDS

For the tagliatelle

- 200g (7oz) plain flour
- 2 eggs
- 1 tsp sugar
- 50g (1¾oz) caster sugar (to sprinkle on the dough)
- Grated zest of 1 organic or unwaxed lemon or orange

For frying and the finishing touch

- Peanut oil
- Icing sugar

01 On a clean work surface, pour the flour into a mound and make a well in the centre. Add the eggs and 1 teaspoon of sugar. Knead until you have a smooth, even dough. Cover and leave to rest for 30 minutes at room temperature.

02 Once ready, roll out the dough thinly (about 2mm). Sprinkle with 50g (1¾oz) of sugar and the grated lemon or orange zest.

03 Roll the dough into a long log shape, like a Yule log, and cut it into slices about 2cm (¾in) thick. In Emilia-Romagna, this dessert is traditionally eaten during carnival season and looks just like a plate of tagliatelle. The more skilfully you shape it, the more perfect the trompe l'oeil will be.

04 Heat the oil to 170°C/375°F and drop in your slices. If you don't have a thermometer at home, here's a little tip: test with a small piece of dough; if there are lots of bubbles when you drop it into the oil, it's ready. Let them simmer gently until they are golden brown and crispy, then drain them on kitchen paper.

05 Place your 'fake' tagliatelle in a dish, sprinkle generously with icing sugar and, most importantly, don't say anything when you serve them. Watch the intrigued looks around the table then reveal the secret behind this success.

+ **On repeat in the kitchen:** Play Gazzelle's 'Zucchero filato' (candy floss), which, like these fried tagliatelle, instantly transports us to a fairground or carnival atmosphere. Can you smell the sweet aromas, the coconut shies and the confetti flying everywhere?

STRUFFOLI
Christmas pops

Struffoli are small balls of fried dough coated in honey. A favourite Christmas dessert in Naples, they are traditionally prepared for the festive season, but if we knew how to live properly, we would eat them all year round.

FOR 4 FRIENDS

<u>For the dough</u>
- 400g (14oz) plain flour
- 3 eggs
- 40g (1½oz) caster sugar
- 80g (2¾oz) butter (or 60g/2oz lard, as tradition dictates)
- 2 tbsp liqueur (your choice: Marsala, anisette, limoncello, etc.)
- Grated zest of 1 lemon and 1 orange, organic or unwaxed
- 1 tsp baking powder
- A pinch of salt

<u>For frying and the finishing touch</u>
- Peanut oil (for frying)
- 300g (10½oz) honey
- 1 tsp caster sugar

<u>For decoration</u>
- Coloured sprinkles or candied fruit (optional, but it looks nice, and it's better when it looks nice)

01 Start by preparing the dough. On a clean, floured work surface, put the flour and baking powder, make a small well in the centre and add the eggs. Mix with a fork, then add the sugar, softened butter cut into pieces, liqueur, salt and citrus zest. Knead by hand until you have a smooth, even dough. Shape into a ball, cover with clingfilm and leave to rest for 30 minutes at room temperature.

02 Once the dough has rested, take fist-sized pieces and roll them into long strips about 1cm (½in) thick. Cut them into small 2cm (¾in) pieces, then roll them into balls between your palms. Get the whole family to help you and repeat the process until all the dough is used up. Then place the *struffoli* on a lightly floured work surface.

03 Heat the oil to 170°C/375°F. If you don't have a thermometer at home, follow Chef Flavia's advice and drop a small piece of dough in to test the temperature: both the oil and pastry should immediately bubble. Then fry your loot in small batches so that the balls brown evenly. Drain them on kitchen paper and keep them safe from hungry mouths lurking in the kitchen.

04 In a large saucepan, heat the honey with 2 tablespoons of water and 1 teaspoon of sugar over a very low heat until the mixture becomes fully liquid. Then pour in the *struffoli* and mix gently so that they are completely coated with this golden syrup.

05 Now it's time to plate up. Pour your honey-coated fried balls onto a dish and form a crown or pyramid, as is traditional in Naples. Call the little ones and the big ones over and sprinkle everything with *diavulilli* (your little multicoloured sprinkles) and a few candied fruits. Isn't it pretty?

+ **On repeat in the kitchen:** '24,000 Baci' (24,000 kisses) by Adriano Celentano, because with all these sweet balls, all we want is love.

PIGNOLATA MESSINESE

The ultimate ball game

FOR 4 FRIENDS

<u>For the dough</u>

- 260g (9oz) type 00 flour
- 2 eggs
- 50g (1¾oz) melted and cooled butter (or lard, for a traditional recipe)
- 30g (1oz) sugar
- 2–3 tbsp grappa
- Grated zest of 1 organic or unwaxed lemon
- A pinch of salt

<u>For frying</u>

- Approximately 600ml (2½ cups) peanut oil (or lard)

<u>White icing for the *pignolata*</u>

- 150–200g (5¼–7oz) icing sugar
- A few spoonfuls of egg white
- 1 tsp lemon juice

<u>Black icing for the *pignolata*</u>

- 200g (7oz) dark chocolate
- 2 tbsp melted butter
- Hot water

01 Prepare your dough. On a work surface, pour the flour, sugar and a pinch of salt. Form a volcano shape. Add the eggs to the hollow and begin to mix gently with a fork. Add the melted butter (or lard). Be careful, it must be completely cold so as not to heat the dough. Add the grated lemon zest, a dash of grappa (wait until the end of the recipe for the chef's shot), then knead by hand until you obtain a soft but not sticky ball (if it is still sticky, add a little more flour). Cover with clingfilm and leave to rest for about 30 minutes at room temperature.

02 Once ready, divide the dough into equal fist-sized pieces. Roll each piece into a long roll and cut into small pieces about 1cm (½in) long.

03 Time to fry. Heat the oil (or lard) in a deep saucepan (to around 170°C/375°F). If you don't have a thermometer at home, follow Chef Flavia's advice and drop a small piece of dough in to test: there should be lots of bubbles straight away. Fry several pieces of dough at a time until they are lightly golden. Drain them with a slotted spoon and place them on kitchen paper to remove excess oil. Leave to cool, keeping an eye on little thieving hands lurking in the kitchen – they're quick!

04 The distinctive feature of this Sicilian dessert, which comes straight from Messina, is its two-tone icing. So, roll up your sleeves and get started. Light side: in a bowl, mix the icing sugar with a little egg white and a few drops of lemon juice until you obtain a white, smooth cream that is not too runny (if necessary, add a little more icing sugar to thicken it). Dark side: gently melt the dark chocolate in a bain-marie, add the melted butter and a little hot water to obtain a smooth cream.

05 Now it's time to separate the doughnuts. Divide your fried dough balls evenly between two bowls. In one bowl, coat them with white icing and mix well. In the other bowl, dip them in melted chocolate and mix gently.

06 Next, it's time to plate up: in the dish of your choice, form two small mountains side by side – on one side, the white sugar balls; on the other, the black chocolate doughnuts. Leave both teams to rest for 1–2 hours (until the icing hardens) and then begin your ascent of bliss by tackling the side of your choice.

+ **On repeat in the kitchen:** With her song 'Rossetto e cioccolato', Ornella Vanoni celebrates the sweet pleasures of life, just like this *pignolata*, which are tender, melt-in-the-mouth and deliciously retro.

MERINGUES

As you may have noticed from our recipes, making fresh pasta requires a certain number of egg yolks. Because there's no question of wasting anything and it's always a good time to think about the next snack of the day, here's something that combines business with pleasure: a meringue recipe that will use up your egg whites and delight all your guests at home.

For 4 friends:

- 150g (5¼oz) white caster sugar
- 150g (5¼oz) icing sugar
- 3 egg whites
- 60g (2oz) grated coconut

---

1 Preheat the oven to 90°C fan/110°C/230°F/GM ¼. In a mixing bowl, beat the egg whites until stiff using a whisk or electric mixer. As soon as they start to foam, gradually add the caster sugar until you obtain a firm, shiny texture. Sift the icing sugar and gently fold it in with a spatula. Put the meringue mix into a piping bag and pipe onto a baking tray lined with baking paper, then sprinkle with grated coconut.

2 Bake the meringues for about 3 hours. They should remain white while becoming perfectly crisp.

3 Finally, serve these little clouds for dessert or store them in an airtight container to enjoy throughout the week. A lovely treat to look forward to.

Melenzane sott'olio
Panettone (Lillina)
di zucchero
Torta Di Mele
Coniglio alla cacciatora
500 farina
300 zucchero
3 uova intere
olio arachide

TENNERATA DEL CILENTO

Easter cake

Here we offer you a cake that is both a pasta dish and an Easter cake. This rustic dessert from the countryside of Cilento is traditionally prepared during Easter week, but there's no reason why you can't make it at other times of the year. You don't just make pancakes on Pancake Day, do you?

FOR 4 FRIENDS

- 200g (7oz) candele (or ziti, or rigatoni, as long as it's tube-shaped pasta)
- 400g (14oz) cow's milk ricotta
- 200g (7oz) caster sugar
- 4 eggs
- 400ml (1⅔ cups) milk
- ½ glass of Strega liqueur (made from no fewer than 70 herbs and spices from around the world)
- 1 tbsp ground cinnamon
- A little butter (for the mould)
- A pinch of salt

01 Break the candele (or ziti, or rigatoni) into pieces. Cook them in a large saucepan of salted boiling water, but drain them 3 minutes before the end of cooking (they will finish cooking in the oven). Then arrange them, well spaced, on a clean tea towel and leave them to cool.

02 Meanwhile, in a bowl, mix the ricotta with the sugar. Gradually add the eggs, milk, Strega liqueur and cinnamon. If you're not a fan of cinnamon (some people aren't), bear in mind that it's an essential ingredient: it's what gives *tennerata* its traditional flavour. That said, it's up to you whether you add it or not. Then stir gently with a fork until you have a smooth cream.

03 Dip the candele into the ricotta mixture and stir gently so that they are generously coated with this fragrant cream.

04 Butter a fairly deep mould (the *tennerata* will rise during baking) and pour in the mixture. A little tip from our pastry chef Flavia: arrange the candele horizontally in the mould so that they are well filled with cream during baking.

05 Bake in a preheated oven at 180°C fan/200°C/400°F/GM 6 for about 1 hour.

06 Leave to cool, carefully remove from the tin, then serve in slices on small dessert plates.

\+ **On repeat in the kitchen:** Dessert is served, the Moka coffee pot is singing and 'Rossetto e caffè' by Sal Da Vinci plays in the background. A ballad that evokes a love story summed up in a single image: a trace of lipstick on a coffee cup.

CJARSONS FRIULANI

Amaretti or not, here it comes

Cultural note: Friuli-Venezia Giulia, an Italian region bordering Slovenia, is renowned for its cjarsons: small sweet and savoury ravioli that are as delicate as they are surprising.

FOR 4 FRIENDS

For the dough
- 250g (8¾oz) type 00 flour
- 1 tbsp extra virgin olive oil
- ½ glass of lukewarm water

For the filling
- 200g (7oz) potatoes
- 200g (7oz) fresh Swiss chard
- 50g (1¾oz) amaretti
- A pinch of cinnamon
- A pinch of grated nutmeg
- 1 tsp bitter cocoa powder
- A pinch of salt

For the sauce
- 35g (generous 1oz) butter
- 1 tbsp cornflour

For the finishing touch
- A few amaretti biscuits
- A dusting of bitter cocoa powder
- Smoked ricotta or grated Parmigiano Reggiano DOP

01 Pour the flour onto a work surface and form a small crater in the centre. Pour in the olive oil, then the lukewarm water. Knead by hand, adding a little more water if necessary, until you obtain a soft dough. Form a ball, cover with clingfilm and leave to rest for 30 minutes at room temperature.

02 Start on the filling. Place the peeled potatoes in a saucepan of cold salted water. Bring to a boil and cook for about 30 minutes until tender. Mash them with a fork or potato masher in a bowl (do not use a blender).

03 Now for the Swiss chard: wash it, chop it coarsely and cook it for a few minutes in a saucepan of salted boiling water. Drain and squeeze it with your hands to remove all the water. The less water there is, the better your stuffing will be, so put your heart and soul into this step. Then chop it finely and add it to the potatoes.

04 Crumble the amaretti biscuits into the same bowl, then add the cinnamon, nutmeg, bitter cocoa powder and a pinch of salt. Mix until you have a smooth filling.

05 Take your dough and roll it out thinly (2mm maximum) on a floured work surface. Using a glass or cookie cutter, cut out circles about 7–8cm (2¾–3in) in diameter, then place 1 teaspoon of filling in the centre of each circle. Moisten the edges with a pastry brush and water, then fold to form a half-moon shape and seal the edges with your fingers.

06 In a small saucepan, toast the cornflour to thicken it slightly and add a toasted flavour to the sauce, then melt 35g of butter.

07 Bring a large saucepan of salted water to the boil. Add the *cjarsons* in small batches: when they rise to the surface, they are ready. Drain them using a slotted spoon.

08 When serving, place your *cjarsons* in the centre of a small plate, coat them with butter sauce and, if you like, grated smoked ricotta or Parmigiano. If you're feeling adventurous, add a few crumbs of amaretti and a sprinkling of bitter cocoa powder for a sweet and savoury twist.

+ **On repeat in the kitchen:** It's hard to resist these little gems of *cjarsons*. We could sum up how much we love them with a little shower of heart emojis. So we're launching 'Cuoricini' (little hearts) by Coma Cose, a melody as addictive as these beauties from Friuli.

THE CHERRY ON THE TORTELLO

Tortelli di ciliegia

FOR 4 FRIENDS

For the dough

- 250g (8¾oz) type 00 flour
- 50g (1¾oz) *semola rimacinata* (remilled durum wheat semolina)
- 1 egg
- 2 tbsp cooked beetroot
- A pinch of salt

For the filling

- 250g (8¾oz) De.C.O. Ceresara cherries, a variety of very sweet cherries native to Lombardy (if you can't find them, use ripe, sweet cherries)
- 250g (8¾oz) cow's milk ricotta, well drained
- 50g (1¾oz) breadcrumbs (ideally made from day-old bread, lightly toasted)
- 50g (1¾oz) grated Parmigiano Reggiano DOP
- 30g (1oz) candied fruit mostarda of your choice (a typical Italian mustard, don't use Dijon mustard here)
- Spices: cinnamon, pepper, nutmeg, ginger . . . whatever you like, as long as it comes from the spice rack
- Salt QB

For the sauce

- Fresh butter QB
- A few fresh cherries

01 Start with the cherries: wash and stone them, then blend them coarsely. Set aside 200g (7oz) for the filling and use the remaining 50g (1¾oz) to make a coloured juice in a blender to incorporate into the dough. Strain through a sieve if necessary, as we want it to be very liquid.

02 Then move on to the pasta dough. On a clean, lightly floured work surface, mix the flour, semolina and a pinch of salt. Make a well in the centre and add the egg and blended beetroot, then gradually pour in the cherry juice, mixing with a fork. When the dough begins to form, knead it for a good 10 minutes until it becomes soft. Cover with clingfilm and leave to rest for 15–20 minutes at room temperature.

03 Prepare the filling: in a bowl, mix the ricotta with the reserved cherries, finely chopped mostarda, Parmigiano, breadcrumbs, a pinch of salt and your spices. Taste and adjust seasoning.

04 Roll out the dough thinly (2mm maximum) on a floured surface. Cut out circles about 6–7cm (2⅓–2¾in) in diameter. Lightly moisten the edges, place 1 spoonful of filling in the centre, fold into a half-moon shape and seal well with your fingers.

05 Bring a large pot of salted water to the boil, add the tortelli and cook for 2–3 minutes. Tip: when they rise to to the surface, they are ready. Drain them.

06 Melt the butter in a large frying pan. Pour the tortelli into the sauce and toss gently.

07 Serve immediately with a few fresh cherries on top. The result: a beautiful one-colour dish that will make you blush with pleasure.

\+ **On repeat in the kitchen:** Naturally, play Lucio Battisti's 'La collina dei ciliegi', a classic song in which the singer invites his beloved to find the sun hidden behind the hill of cherry trees, a metaphor for a bright and unhindered future. Just like your meal.

TORTELLI CREMASCHI

Sweet and savoury bombs

Emblematic of the city of Crema in Lombardy, this ancestral recipe turns heads with its savoury, lemony, spicy and slightly sweet filling. A killer dish that will have people asking for more.

FOR 4 FRIENDS

For the tortelli

- 300g (10½oz) plain flour
- 1 whole egg + 1 egg yolk
- 1 tbsp extra virgin olive oil
- A pinch of salt

For the filling

- 100g (3½oz) amaretti biscuits, crushed into powder
- 50g (1¾oz) finely crumbled *mostaccini.* These are spiced biscuits typical of the town of Crema – bring them back in your suitcase after a short trip or have them brought back for you, or replace them with a mixture of speculoos and gingerbread
- 50g (1¾oz) raisins, soaked for 15 minutes in lukewarm water, then drained
- 10g (2 tsp) fruit jam (ideally prune or quince)
- 10g (2 tsp) very finely chopped candied organic or unwaxed lemon peel
- 5g (1 tsp) bitter cocoa powder
- 1 tsp cinnamon
- 1 dash of liqueur (maraschino or rum)
- 50g (1¾oz) grated Grana Padano DOP
- 50g (1¾oz) candied pears or candied citron (optional, but very tasty)
- Salt and pepper QB

To serve

- 100g (3½oz) unsalted butter
- A little grated Grana Padano DOP (optional)
- A few more amaretti biscuits

01 Start with the base: the tortelli. Pour the flour onto a work surface, form a small well and add the eggs, oil and a pinch of salt. Knead until you have a smooth, supple dough, cover and leave to rest for 30 minutes at room temperature.

02 Meanwhile, prepare the filling by mixing all the ingredients in a large bowl by hand, with love and clean fingers (a blender? Taboo! Tradition forbids it). The texture should be grainy but malleable, so feel free to adjust the consistency by adding a little liqueur or jam if necessary.

03 Next, it's time to shape the tortelli, see page 392 for instructions.

04 Then plunge your tortelli into a pan of simmering salted water for 3–4 minutes, until they rise to the surface.

05 Meanwhile, melt a generous knob of butter in a large frying pan. Drain the tortelli gently and toss them in the melted butter.

06 Serve hot, sprinkled with grated Grana Padano cheese or a few pieces of amaretti biscuit to echo the filling, if you like. And yes,, we can hear the question coming: 'But is this a dessert or a *primo piatto*?' The answer is somewhere inbetween: it's a dessert with savoury accents. So you're free to serve it as a starter or a dolce. One thing is certain: it will receive a standing ovation either way.

+ **On repeat in the kitchen:** Sweet and savoury pasta, what a concept! Let's kick off with the Italian funk standard 'Ma quale idea', in which singer Pino d'Angiò recounts his slightly naughty stories of flirting.

CHAPTER 8

PASTA SHAPES

WITHOUT THESE, NO PASTA

The 9 utensils to keep close at hand when you want to start making pasta like the pros.

1 THE SIEVE

The *setaccio* is your sieve for life. Thanks to this superhero, say ciao to lumps and hello to light and airy pasta.

2 & 4 CORZETTI STAMPS

These little stamps, which make you want to get out your fancy drawing paper, are actually used to print decorative patterns (flowers, geometric designs, etc.) on corzetti, the fresh pasta medallions typical of Liguria. Originally, families had their coat of arms or initials engraved on them, the height of Italian chic.

3 & 10 ROUND COOKIE CUTTERS

Did you think a small glass from a certain Swedish brand would do the trick? Wait until you come across these cutters, they are the best friends of your mezzelune and other small stuffed pasta shapes. They cut them into perfect discs, ready to be filled and folded like no other, without ever holding your dough hostage. Available in several diameters, with smooth or serrated edges for a stylish effect.

5 THE PASTRY BRUSH

When preparing ravioli, a little stroke of a brush can make all the difference. Just a little water on the edges is enough to seal the two layers together and prevent the filling from leaking out during cooking. Of course, you can also do the job with your fingers, but it's way less effective.

6 THE GNOCCHI BOARD

The *rigagnocchi* is the wooden board that gives gnocchi their attractive ridges. It's the essential tool for rolling the dough with your thumb to form small balls that hold sauce well. The mini stick that comes with it? It is used to replace your fingers and shape certain pasta shapes with a more precise movement.

7 THE ANOLINI STAMP

This stamp is used to cut and seal the small stuffed pasta shapes from Emilia-Romagna known as 'anolini'. It is clean, precise and guarantees no leaks during cooking. Some stamps are even engraved with elegant patterns (such as rosettes or flowers) and are passed down like family heirlooms.

8 THE CHITARRA

The *chitarra* (guitar) is a wooden frame strung with steel wires reminiscent of the strings of the musical instrument. And although it is very tempting to use it to compose a little melody in the kitchen, it is (only) used to shape square-edged spaghetti by placing a sheet of fresh pasta on it and pressing it with a rolling pin. And you'll see, it's just as enjoyable as great music.

9 THE ROLLING PIN

If you could only keep one utensil, it would be this: *il mattarello*, the rolling pin. Essential for rolling out dough by hand, the basis of all homemade pasta. Traditionally made of beechwood, it can measure from 30cm (12in) to over 1 metre (40in) depending on the region. Choose the one that suits you best, it will become your ally for life.

11 THE PASTA WHEEL CUTTER

Smooth, serrated, zigzag or wavy . . . the pasta cutter cuts and seals the dough in a single stroke. Depending on your mood, you can give free rein to your desires and, above all, help you make pasta worthy of the greatest chefs in one go. Few utensils will win you over so quickly.

1
2
3
4
5
6
7
9
10
11

PASTA SHAPES

Aka the little tutorial for making your most beautiful creations

A ravioli that makes you want to say, 'Wait before you eat that, I'm going to take a photo' or *zebra lasagne* that will spark conversations like 'how did you make such a masterpiece?' It all comes down to folding, cutting, or even a little collage, skilfully done according to the rules of the art.

We'll teach you all the most typical and effective techniques to turn you into an expert pasta-maker. Thanks to them, you'll soon discover that it's harder to pronounce *culurgiones* correctly than it is to make beautiful ones. So, get out your rolling pins and pasta machines and, *andiamo*!

Sfoglia lasagna

1 Roll out the dough very thinly with a rolling pin or pasta machine until it is as thin as possible (ideally 1mm, max 2mm), almost translucent.

2 Form a pile of dough with wavy folds, ribbon-style, sprinkling with semolina to prevent it from sticking.

3 Unroll your dough and cut your lasagne sheets (approximately 10 x 20cm/4 x 8in) using a thin, sharp knife.

Tonnarelli

1 Once your dough is rolled out thinly, cut strips measuring approximately 20 x 60cm (8 x 24in), then fold each strip in half, making regular folds 5cm (2in) wide, making sure to align the edges with each fold.

2 Cut your tonnarelli into strips approximately 2mm wide with the chitarra (if you have one) or with a sharp knife.

3 Carefully separate the tonnarelli by hand and sprinkle with semolina to prevent them from sticking together.

Tajarin

1 Once your dough is rolled out thinly, cut strips measuring approximately 20 x 60cm (8 x 24in), roll each sheet up lengthways, sprinkling with semolina to prevent it from sticking.

2 Cut your tagliolini to a width of approximately 1mm using a thin, sharp knife.

3 Gather the tagliolini and shape into small, separate nests. Sprinkle with semolina to prevent them from sticking together.

Maltagliati

1 Once your dough is rolled out thinly, cut strips measuring approximately 20 x 60cm (8 x 24in) and stack them on top of each other, sprinkling them with semolina to prevent them sticking together.

2 Cut the stack of strips into squares or diamonds (the pasta is literally called 'maltaillées', i.e. badly cut, so no stress) using a smooth pasta wheel.

3 Gather your maltagliati, sprinkle them with semolina to prevent them from sticking together and removing any excess with a sieve if necessary.

Corzetti

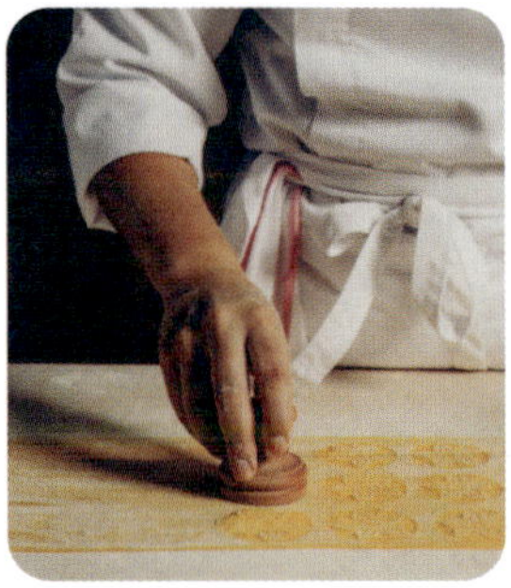

1 Once your dough is rolled out thinly, cut into strips approximately 20 x 60cm (8 x 24in) then press the corzetti stamp firmly on each strip to make several impressions and mark the patterns clearly.

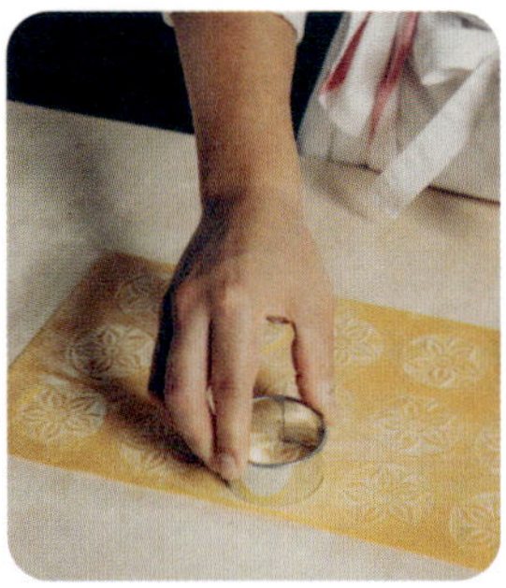

2 Use a round cookie cutter the same size as your stamp to shape your corzetti. Press firmly to make a clean, precise cut.

3 Remove the excess dough and repeat the process. Sprinkle with semolina to prevent the corzetti from sticking together.

Fettuccine

1 Once your dough is rolled out thinly, cut strips of approximately 20 x 60cm (8 x 24in) and roll each end towards the centre of the strip until the two rolls meet and are joined together.

2 Cut the fettuccine (approximately 8mm/⅓in wide) using a thin, sharp knife. Sprinkle with semolina to prevent them from sticking together.

3 Keeping the knife blade flat, slide it under the cut pasta then gently lift it between the two rolls. Moving slightly, let the ribbons unroll: they will fall on either side of the blade.

Pappardelle

1 Once your dough is rolled out thinly, cut strips approximately 20 x 60cm (8 x 24in) and stack them on top of each other, sprinkling semolina between each layer to prevent them from sticking together. Roll the stack into a log shape.

2 Cut the pappardelle into strips approximately 2cm (¾in) wide using a sharp knife.

3 Gently separate the pappardelle by hand and sprinkle with semolina to prevent them from sticking together.

Quadrucci

1 Once your dough is rolled out thinly, cut strips measuring approximately 30 x 50cm (12 x 20in) and stack them, sprinkling them with semolina to prevent them from sticking together.

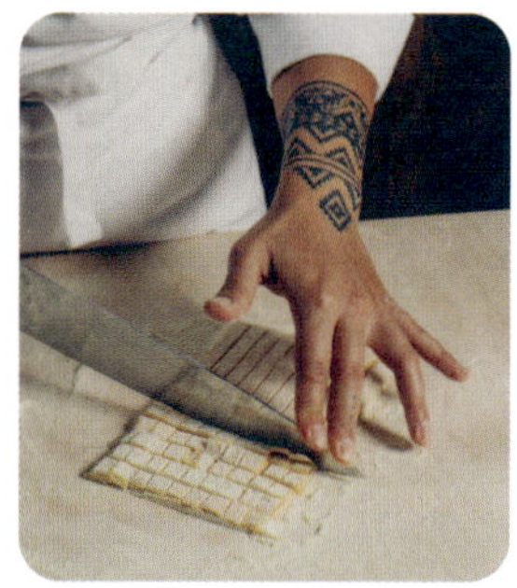

2 Using a sharp knife, cut horizontal then vertical strips no more than 1 or 2cm (½–¾in) wide: we want small squares.

3 Gently lift the quadrucci with your fingers, sprinkle them with semolina to prevent them from sticking together and remove any excess semolina with a sieve if necessary.

Mantovano

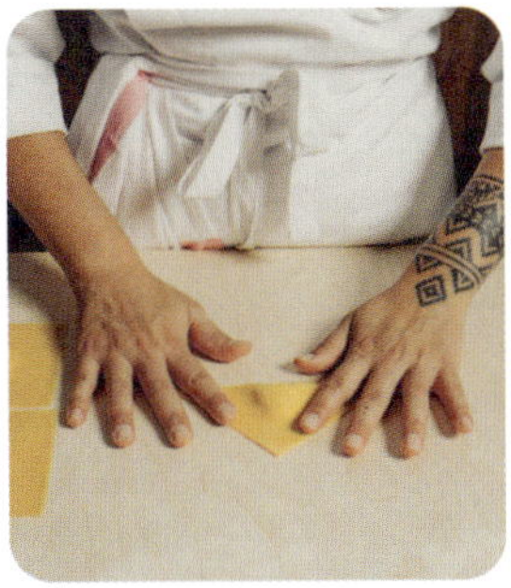

1 Once your dough is rolled out thinly, cut into 7 x 7cm squares. Use a piping bag to put the filling in the centre. Moisten the edges and fold into triangles, pressing firmly around the filling to remove any air.

2 Cut the edges of your stuffed triangles with a serrated pasta wheel.

3 Fold the base of the triangle (where the filling is) over itself and press firmly with your fingers to seal and remove any air.

Cappellacci

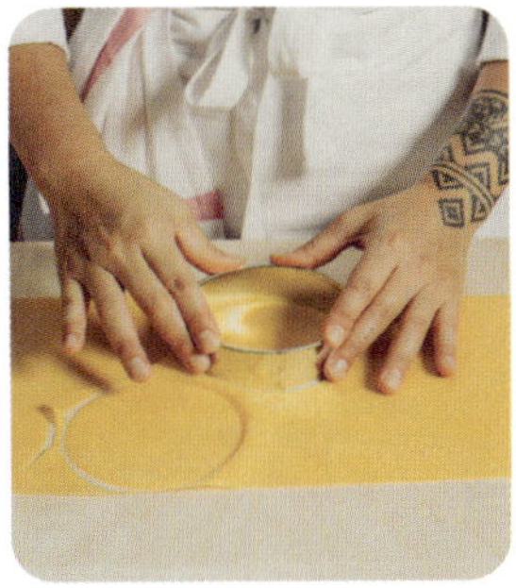

1 Once your dough is rolled out thinly, cut out discs with a cookie cutter about 7cm (2¾in) in diameter. Use a piping bag to put the filling in the centre. Moisten the edges with a pastry brush dipped in water.

2 Close them into a half-moon shape, pressing firmly around the filling to remove any air.

3 Fold the edges towards you until they meet, then seal them securely by pressing firmly.

Cappellacci XXL

1 Once your dough is rolled out thinly, cut out 15cm (6in) squares. Use a piping bag to put the filling in the centre. Moisten the edges and fold into triangles, pressing firmly around the stuffing to remove air.

2 Cut the edges of your stuffed triangles with a serrated pasta wheel.

3 Fold the edges towards you until they meet, then overlap them. Press firmly to seal.

Pansoti XXL

1 Once your dough is rolled out thinly, cut out 15cm (6in) squares. Use a piping bag to put the filling in the centre of each square.

2 Moisten the edges with a pastry brush dipped in water, then close them, forming a rectangle and pressing firmly around the filling to remove any air.

3 Bring the two points at the base of your rectangle towards you until they meet. They surround the characteristic plump belly of the pansoto. Press them firmly to seal them.

Fazzoletti XXL

1 Once your dough is rolled out thinly, cut out 15cm (6in) squares. Use a piping bag to put the filling in the centre of each square.

2 Moisten the edges with a pastry brush dipped in water, then fold into triangles, point to point, pressing firmly around the filling to remove any air.

3 Cut the edges with a smooth pasta wheel, then sprinkle with semolina to prevent them from sticking together.

Piramidi

1 Roll your dough out thinly, cut out 10cm (4in) squares and use a piping bag to pipe the filling into the centre. Moisten the edges with water using a pastry brush and fold each square into a rectangle without sealing it.

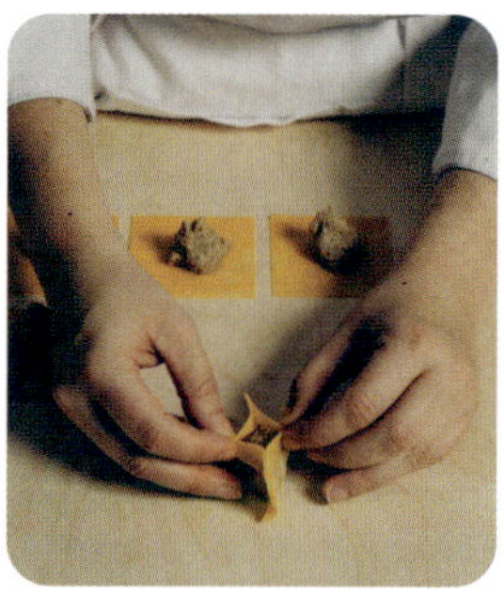

2 Keeping the open part of the ravioli facing upwards, gently pull the side edges apart, then pinch them together above the filling to form a diamond shape.

3 Pinch the 4 points of the pyramid to seal the dough without letting any air escape. Lightly moisten the edges with a little water if the dough is too dry.

Tortellini

1 Roll your dough out thinly, cut into 10cm (4in) squares, place a small ball of filling in the centre of each square and moisten the edges with a pastry brush dipped in water.

2 Close the pastry into a triangle point to point, pressing firmly around the filling to remove any air.

3 Wrap the small triangle around your index finger and bring the two ends together. Press firmly to seal.

Tortelli Cremaschi or chinulille

1 Roll your dough out thinly, cut out circles about 10cm in diameter with a cookie cutter. Using a piping bag, place the filling in the centre.

2 Moisten the edges with a pastry brush using water and fold into a half-moon shape, pressing firmly around the filling to remove any air.

3 Crimp the edges of the tortello by pinching the dough together all the way round.

Bottoni

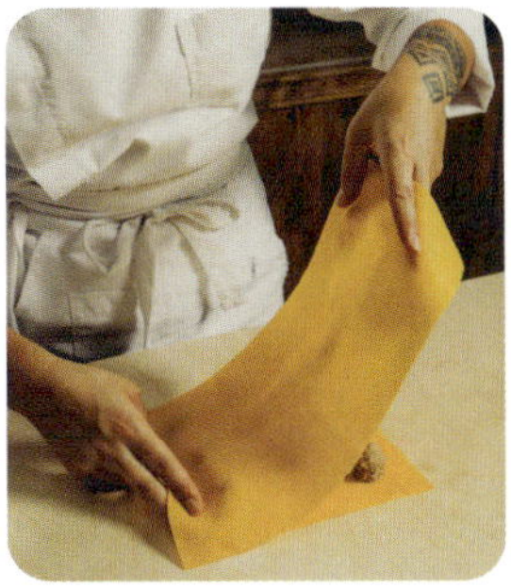

1 Roll your dough out thinly, cut 2 strips into 20 x 20cm squares and moisten the edges with a pastry brush and water. Place 9 small piles of filling on the first strip, then cover with the second strip.

2 Mark the round shape of the filling using a small cookie cutter, but without pressing down: the aim is not to cut, but to create a nice rounded shape.

3 Cut with a round cutter that fits the shape of the filling perfectly (you want very little dough between the filling and the edge). Remove the excess dough and repeat the process.

Casoncelli

1 Roll your dough out thinly, Cut out two strips (20 x 60cm). Moisten the edges. Place small piles of filling every 8cm (3in) and fold the dough in half lengthwise. Cut into half-moon shapes using a round cookie cutter.

2 Pinch the ends to seal them, while gently tilting the plump belly of the casoncello forward.

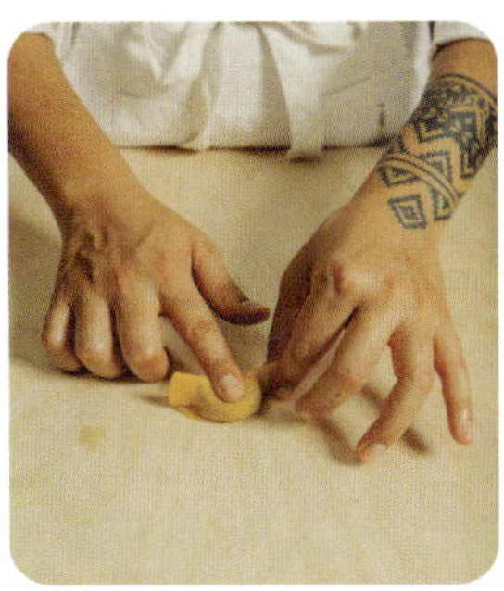

3 Using your index finger, press gently on its belly to give it its characteristic sweet shape.

Anolini

1 Roll your dough out thinly, cut 2 strips measuring 20 x 60cm (8 x 24in). Moisten the edges with a pastry brush and water and place 12 small piles of filling on the first strip.

2 Cover your anolini with your second strip of dough, pressing out any air with your hands.

3 Use a cookie cutter or anolini stamp to cut out ravioli in the shape of little suns. Remove the excess dough and repeat the process.

Mezzelune

1 Once your dough is rolled out thinly, cut out circles with a cookie cutter approximately 10cm (4in) in diameter. Use a piping bag to place the filling in the centre.

2 Moisten the edges using a pastry brush dipped in water and fold into a half-moon shape, pressing firmly around the filling to remove any air.

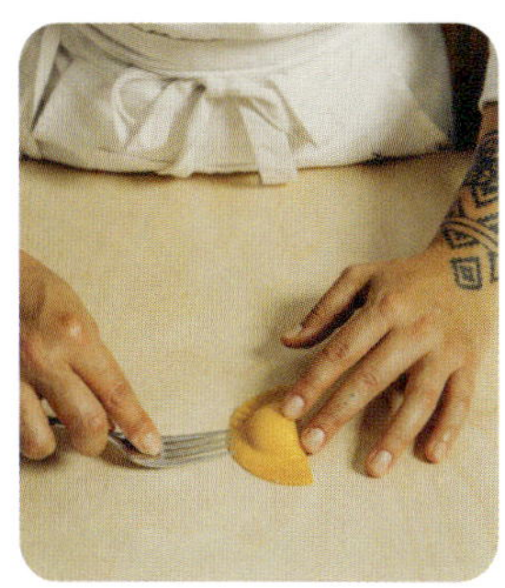

3 Seal the edges by pressing down with the tines of a fork to create a small, ridged turnover.

Fazzoletti

1 Roll out your dough thinly, then cut into 15cm (6in) squares and, using a piping bag, place the filling in the centre of each square.

2 Using a pastry brush dipped in water, moisten the edges then fold each square into a triangle, point to point, pressing firmly around the filling to remove any air.

3 Cut the edges with a serrated pasta wheel, then sprinkle with semolina to prevent them from sticking together.

Agnolotti del plin

1 Roll out your dough thinly, cut strips (20 x 60cm/8 x 24in) and place a small sausage of filling along the length of each strip. Moisten the edges and fold the dough over, pressing down every 5cm (2in) with your fingers to remove any air.

2 Cut off the edge of the sausage shape with a serrated pasta wheel.

3 Cut each raviolo with the serrated pasta wheel, accompanying the movement with a slight forward rolling motion. You should end up with small, well-sealed envelopes, like little pillows.

Girella

1 Roll out your dough thinly, cut strips (20 x 60cm/8 x 24in) and place a small strip of filling along the length of each one. Moisten the edges and fold the dough over, pressing out any air with your fingers.

2 Seal the edge and cut with a serrated pasta wheel.

3 Roll the girella up like a snail. Wet your fingers and press the end to seal it (this will help it keep its shape during cooking and on the plate).

Ravioli con tuorlo

1 Roll out your dough thinly, and cut out two 15cm (6in) squares. Place the filling on the first square, make a small well in it and place 1 raw egg yolk in the centre.

2 Moisten the edges with a pastry brush dipped in water, gently close with the second strip of dough, taking care not to break the yolk, and form a slight dome using a cookie cutter.

3 Using the cookie cutter a similar size to the dome, remove the excess dough around the edge and press down with your fingers to seal it well. We don't want the egg to escape during cooking.

Two-coloured cappellacci

1 Roll your dough out thinly, then cut out discs 7cm (2¾in) in diameter with a cookie cutter. Place the filling in the centre of each disc with a piping bag and moisten the edges with a pastry brush dipped in water.

2 Close in a half-moon shape, pressing firmly around the filling to remove any air.

3 Fold the edges towards you until they meet, then seal them well by pressing down firmly.

Culurgiones

1 Roll your dough out thinly, then cut out discs about 7cm (2¾in) in diameter with a cookie cutter. Place the filling in the centre of each disc with a piping bag and moisten the edges of each one. Pinch one end of the disc.

2 Seal the end of one disc and braid your culurgiones by pinching the seal all the way along your raviolo to the other end.

3 Once your wheat ear is complete, remove any excess filling and seal the second end by pressing firmly to remove any air.

Tagliatelle paglia & fieno

1 Roll out your green and yellow dough, then cut strips (20 x 60cm/8 x 24in), then fold each strip in half, making regular folds 5cm (2in) wide. Place them side by side and cut into strips approximately 6mm (¼in) wide.

2 Carefully separate the tagliatelle by hand and sprinkle with semolina to prevent them from sticking together.

3 Form small nests of two-coloured pasta that you will put straight into the pan to cook.

Two-coloured & stuffed ravioli

1 Roll your dough out thinly, one green and one yellow, cut strips (20 x 60cm/8 x 24in). Press them together side by side using a rolling pin or pasta machine. Moisten the edges, then place a small strip of different filling on the edge of each strip.

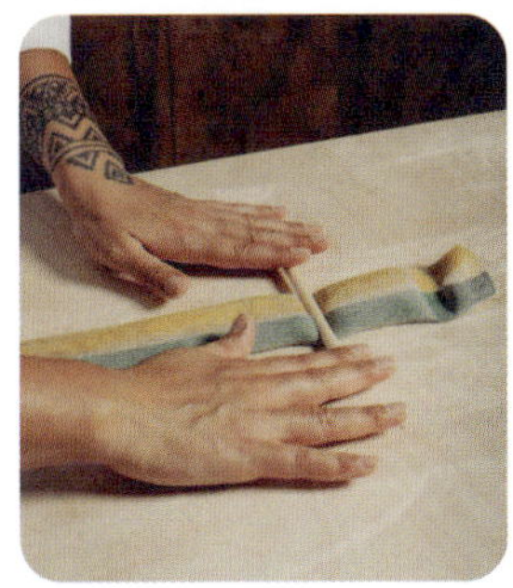

2 Roll the dough on each side towards the centre to form two tubes side by side. Press gently with a small stick from the [illegible] (or use your finger) and seal the raviolo well.

3 Cut approximately every 10cm (4in) with a serrated pasta wheel.

Ravioli sheet

1 Roll your dough out thinly, cut 2 strips approximately 20 x 60cm (8 x 24in). Place the first one on a ravioli tray, then fill each pocket with the stuffing. Cover with the second strip.

2 Roll the rolling pin over the top to seal the ravioli and cut off the excess dough on the sides with a thin, sharp knife.

3 Turn the tray over with a firm motion, remove it carefully, and voilà! There's no need to separate the ravioli: the whole tray will go into the boiling water.

Tagliolini (black)

1 Once your dough is rolled out thinly, cut strips of approximately 20 x 60cm (8 x 24in), then roll each long side towards the centre of the strip until the two rolls meet and are joined together.

2 Cut the tagliolini into strips about 3mm wide using a sharp knife.

3 Slide the blade under the cut pasta and gently lift it between the two rolls. Move it slightly to allow the ribbons to unroll: they will fall on either side of the blade.

Lasagna zebra

1 Arrange your tagliolini nero like intertwining threads on your lasagne sheet.

2 Use a rolling pin to press the lasagne sheet and tagliolini together.

3 Pass everything through the pasta machine to seal the two layers together properly. Your dough should be thin, almost translucent (aim for 1mm).

Agnolotti

1 Roll your dough out thinly, then cut strips measuring 20 x 60cm (8 x 24in). Place a strip of filling along the edge of each strip. Use a pastry brush to moisten the edges with water, then roll the dough over to form a tightly sealed tube.

2 Using the small stick from a gnocchi board (or a straw or your finger), press down every 5cm (2in) to form your agnolotti.

3 Cut each raviolo with a serrated pasta wheel to seal your agnolotti.

Orecchiette

1 Roll your dough by hand into a thin sausage about 1cm (½in) in diameter, then cut into small 2cm (¾in) pieces.

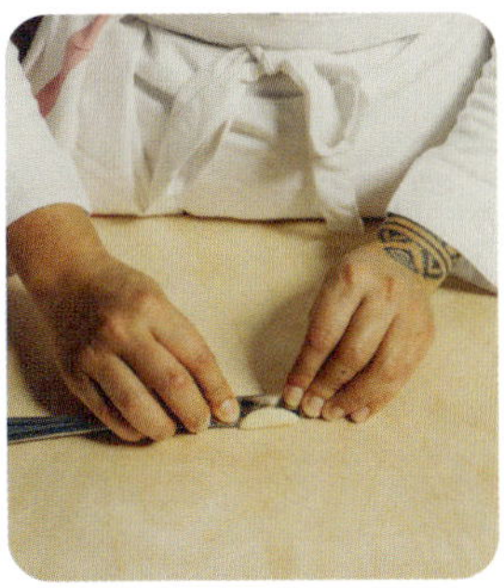

2 Put a piece of dough on the work surface, then put the blade of a knife flat on top of it and pull it towards you, applying slight pressure. The dough will stretch and roll up on itself, as if by magic.

3 Place the orecchietta on the tip of your finger, like a little hat, and press gently to give it its cup shape. The aim is to create slightly raised edges to catch the sauce.

Foglie

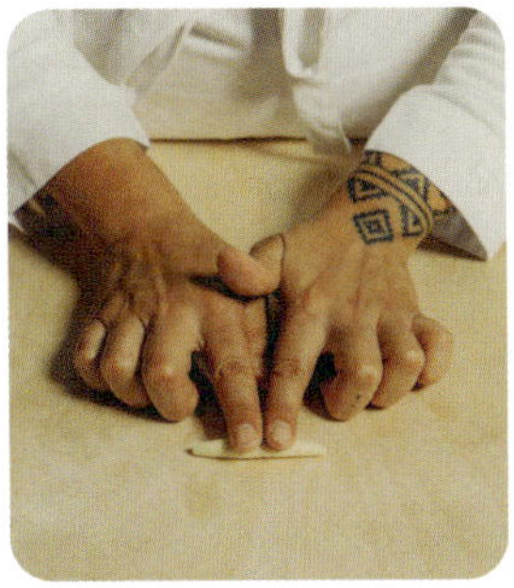

1 Roll your dough by hand into a thin sausage about 1cm (½in) in diameter, then cut into 5cm (2in) pieces. Shape each piece by rolling it lightly under your index fingers.

2 Place the blade of a knife flat on each piece of dough and pull it towards you, applying slight pressure. The dough will stretch and form a leaf shape.

3 Take the leaf in your hand, gently stretch it lengthwise, slightly hollow out the centre with your fingers, then pinch the ends to form a boat shape.

Cavatelli

1 Roll your dough by hand into a thin sausage about 1cm (½in) in diameter, then cut into 4cm (1½in)pieces.

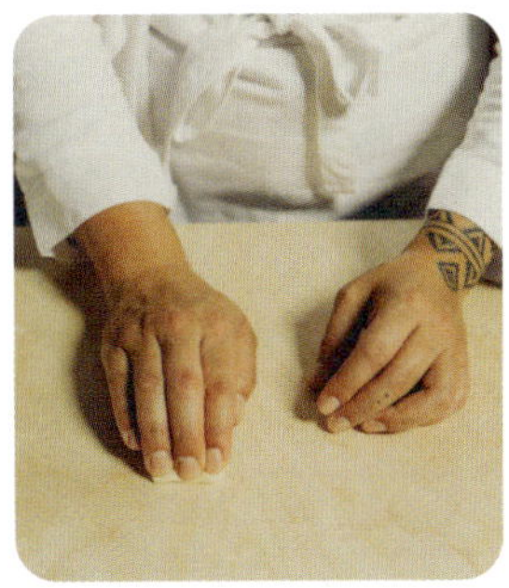

2 Place your three fingers (index, middle and ring fingers) on your piece of dough and pull it towards you, applying light pressure.

3 The dough rolls naturally forming a sort of central cavity. Your cavatelli are ready.

Trofie

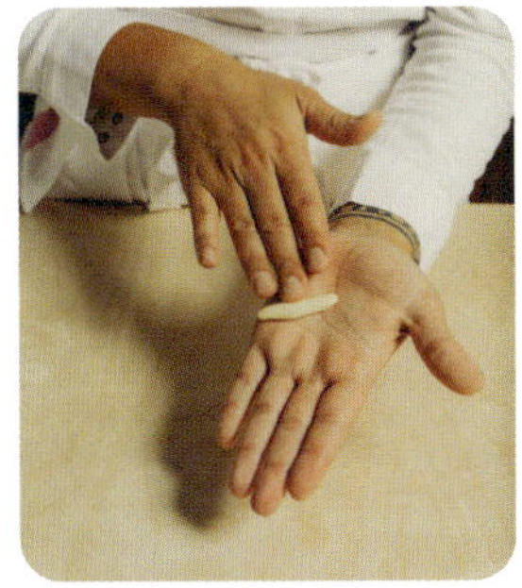

1 Roll your dough by hand into a thin sausage about 1cm (½in) in diameter, then cut into into 5cm (2in) pieces. Shape each piece by rolling it lightly between your palms.

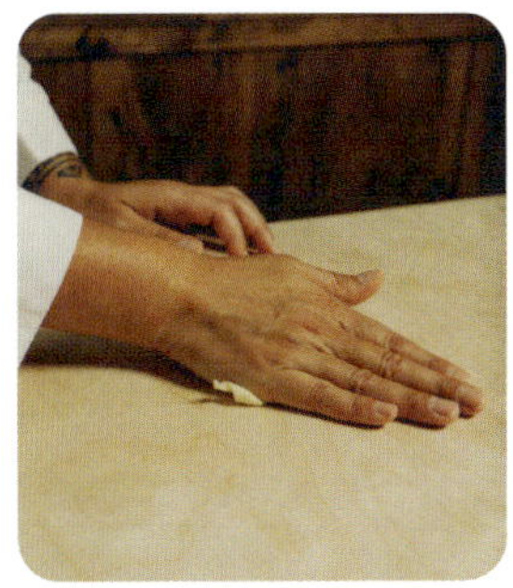

2 Place the dough on the work surface. Using the edge of your hand – your palm still in contact with the roll – roll each trofia diagonally towards you applying light pressure.

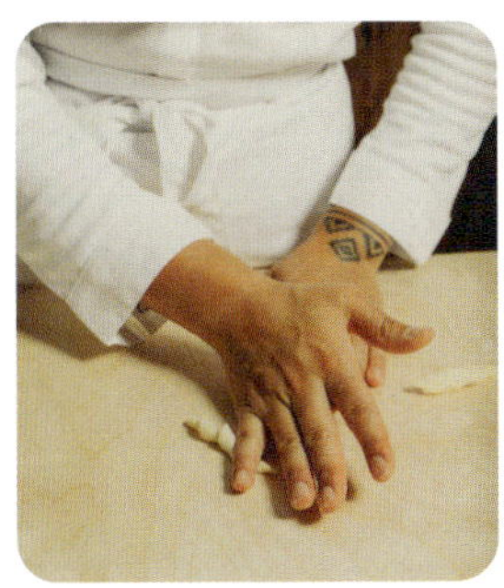

3 It's the pressure of the movement which gives it its shape, but you mustn't press too hard, otherwise the dough will stick. The dough will naturally form a kind of spiral.

Pici or bigoli

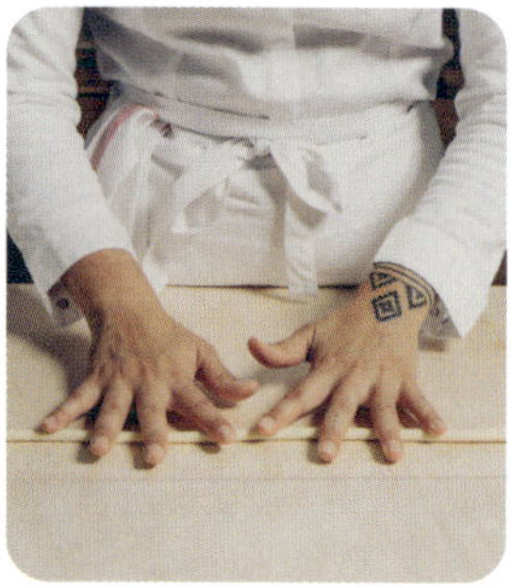

1 Roll out a small sausage of dough by hand . . .

2 until it is thin . . .

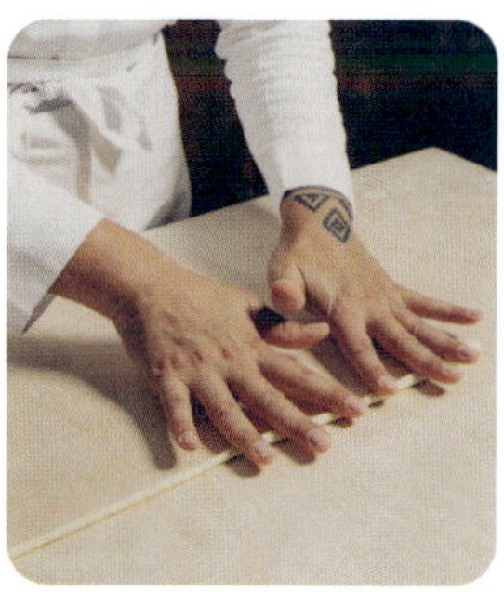

3 or very thin: 2mm in diameter.

Lorighittas

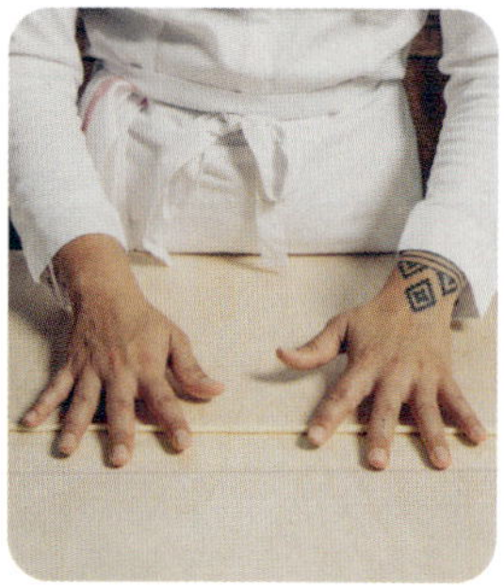

1 Roll out a very thin sausage of dough, about 3mm in diameter, by hand.

2 Take your thread in your hand and wrap it twice around your thumb and index finger. Cut off the excess dough and seal it well by pressing firmly with your fingers.

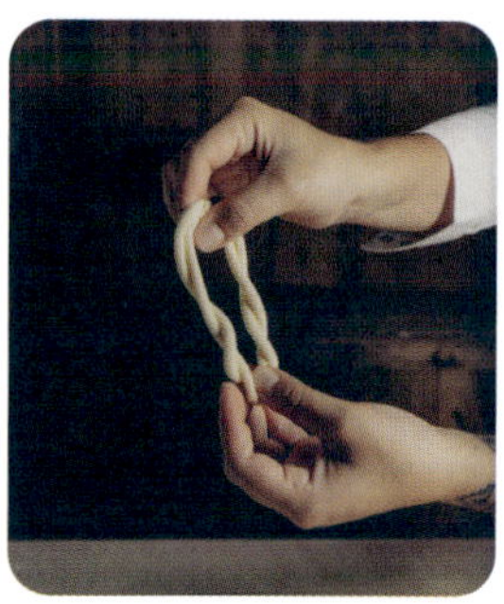

3 Twist the two strands together, as if you were making a braid.

Busiate

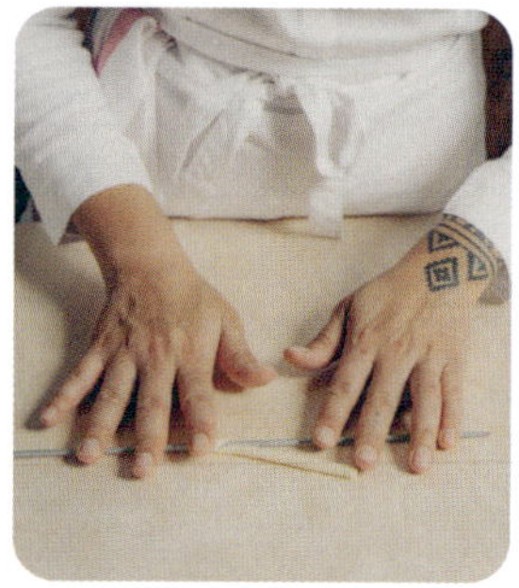

1 Roll out a very thin sausage of dough, about 3mm in diameter, by hand. Cut out mini sausages approximately 10cm (4in) long. Place a skewer (or knitting needle) at the end of your strip, squashing the dough slightly.

2 Roll the skewer around the dough so that the pasta wraps around it like a spiral.

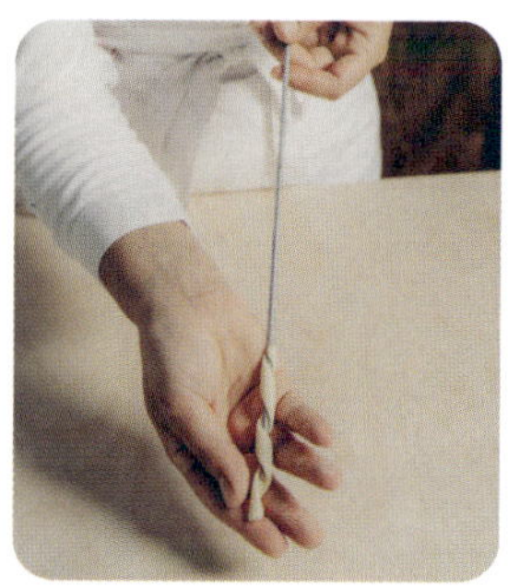

3 Carefully remove the skewer. taking care to preserve the shape of the busiate. The tighter the spiral, the better the result.

Scialatielli

1 Once your dough is rolled out thinly, cut strips measuring 20 x 60cm (8 x 24in) and fold each strip over itself, making regular folds 5cm (2in) wide, taking care to align the edges with each fold.

2 Cut your scialatielli about 3cm (1¼in) wide with a thin, sharp knife.

3 Sprinkle with semolina, slide the blade of your knife under the pasta and lift it up so that the scialatielli unravel gently.

Chicche

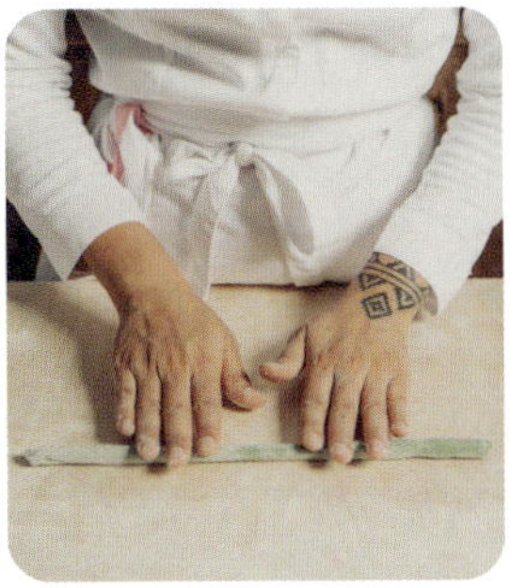

1 Roll out small sausages about 1cm (½in) in diameter and place them side by side.

2 Cut small pieces approximately 2cm (¾in) wide.

3 Form small balls by rolling them in the palm of your hands (yes, they look like peas).

Pizzoccheri

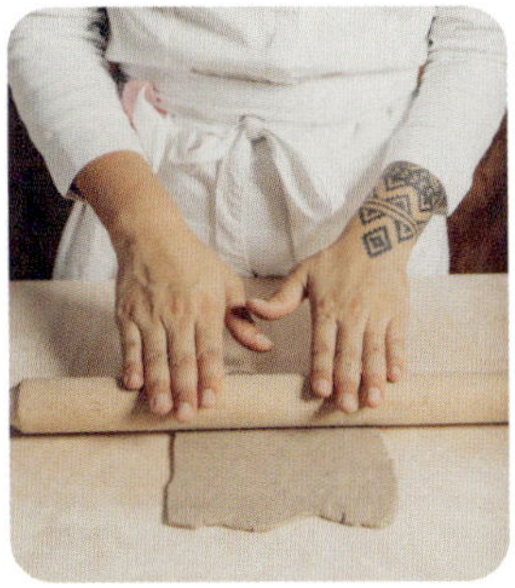

1 Sprinkle your work surface with semolina and gently roll out your buckwheat dough with a rolling pin.

2 Cut strips about 2cm (¾in) wide using a thin, sharp knife.

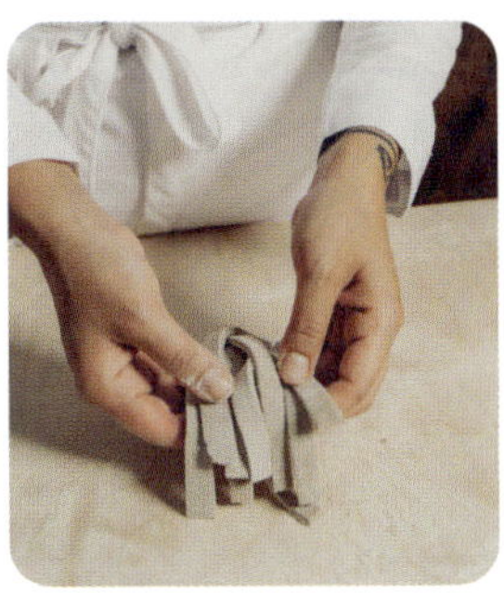

3 Slowly separate the strips with your fingers. They are very fragile, so we trust you to handle them gently.

Passatelli

1 Place your ball of dough into a potato ricer.

2 Close the potato ricer and press down to make your passatelli. Don't be afraid to press firmly, after that, we promise, the hard work is done

3 Cut your passatelli from the ricer using a thin knife and gather them on the work surface.

Gnocchi

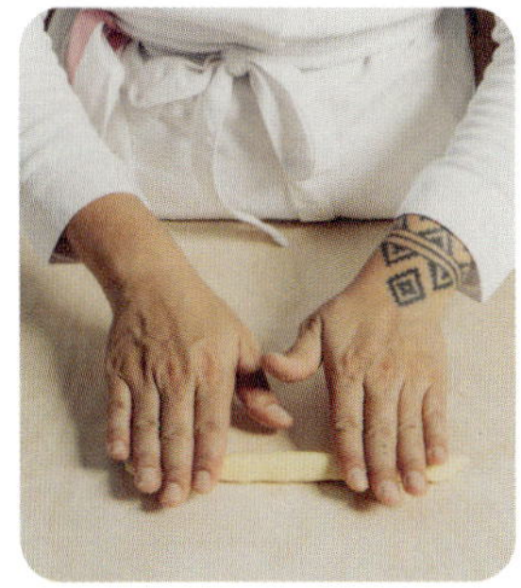

1 Roll out strips of dough approximately 4cm (1½in)in diameter and place side by side.

2 Cut into small pieces. about 5cm (2in) long. Sprinkle with semolina.

3 Place the piece on a gnocchi board, press down with your index and middle fingers, and roll it gently towards you.

APPENDICES

TABLE OF RECIPES

CHAPTER 1

Essential pasta dishes

CHAPTER 2

Stuffed pasta

CHAPTER 3
5-star pasta

CHAPTER 4
Pasta bakes

CHAPTER 5
Alternative pasta dishes

CHAPTER 6
Pasta salads

CHAPTER 7
Desserts

INDEX BY TYPE OF PASTA

INDEX BY INGREDIENTS

P

R

S

Grazie

A huge thank you, from the bottom of our hearts, to all our chefs who bring these recipes to life every day. Special thanks to Virginia Baldeschi, Alberto Suardi, Pietro Zamuner, Dario Tosto, Michela Madeo, Stefania Armante, Elisa Consolo, Michele Di Bella, Flavia Di Fusco, Chiara Mariani, Lorenzo Giardino, Eric Azoug, Luigi Gallo, Michelangelo Graziano, Giuseppe Morciano, Salvatore Taurisano and all the other *maestri della cucina* behind the dishes and memorable moments in this book. To Alberto Sinibaldi and Marica Tonucci for sharing their expert advice and insider secrets with us.

Big shout-out to all our favourite producers and their wonderful products, who have been with us since the very beginning. We love you.

This book is all about Italian families, recipes that are passed down and shared from generation to generation. A million thanks to our chefs Luigi Venturo, Nino Ciufo, Manuel Prota, Flavia Di Fusco and their wonderful families who welcomed us into their homes with open arms and loads of pasta in Minturno, Giugliano, Formia and Baia, to immortalise an unforgettable moment in cooking. You turn the word family into something real.

Finally, a (very) big thank you to each and every member of our incredible team, who make the Big Mamma adventure such a crazy story that we continue to write every day. To Clara Barbry, Sarah Jobert and Isaure Berger, whose joie de vivre and boundless talent make every day a celebration, to Laura Maniscalco with Chefs Gennaro Vattucci and Filippo La Gattuta for their devoted attention and care, to Justine Pinaud and her writing skills, to Evie Horsell, Francesca Weblin, Ilaria Cirigliano and Bronia Moszynska for their careful translations and joyful puns, to Valentin Pons, Chloé Douris and Emmeline Lescure, for their porcelain treasures and other tableware that only antique dealers know how to find. To Clémentine Philippon, Charlotte Martinez, Peppe Cacciapuoti, Nicolas Heintz, Victor Lugger and Tigrane Seydoux and the entire Quarto team who brought this book to life.

This edition first published in 2026 by White Lion Publishing,
an imprint of The Quarto Group.
One Triptych Place, London, SE1 9SH,
United Kingdom
T (0)20 7700 9000
www.Quarto.com

EEA Representation, WTS Tax d.o.o., Žanova ulica 3, 4000 Kranj, Slovenia
www.wts-tax.si

A catalogue record for this book is available from the British Library.

ISBN 978-1-80570-527-7
Ebook ISBN 978-1-80570-528-4

10 9 8 7 6 5 4 3 2 1

Recipe photography: Lucile Casanova
Photographs of chefs: Sam Alexander Gregg
Cover and chapter illustrations: Hannah Bonn
Graphic design: Mathilde Selli & Mathilde Vogt from the Big Mamma creative studio
Layout: Nicolas Galy and Laura Borée for NoOok

Printed in Guangdong, China TT062026

MIX
Paper | Supporting responsible forestry
FSC® C016973